The Politics of L(

Some cities manage to mobilize innovation potentials and respond to challenges, such as demographic change and immigration as well as economic restructuring, while others do not. This book solves this problem by answering the following question: what are the conditions for the development of local innovation?

In order to identify these conditions, the book explores case study cities which are perceived as success cases of local innovation by the respective local community, and sometimes also nationally or internationally. The conditions for local innovations are not sought primarily in economic, social, or institutional circumstances. Instead, this book focuses on the communicative interactions by which local actors develop locally embedded knowledge or a specific social imaginary about those circumstances, as well as the constraints and opportunities deriving from them. The authors focus on a comparative case study of ten cities—Bensheim, Frankfurt, Kassel, Leipzig, and Offenbach in Germany, and Athens, Chania, Elefsina, Kalamata, and Thessaloniki in Greece. The book is based on content analysis of policy documents and local newspapers as well as in-depth interviews with key local actors.

This book will be of interest to scholars and students of political science and policy analysis, as well as sociology, geography, urban studies, and planning. It will also interest local politicians and bureaucrats concerned with achieving innovation in cities.

Hubert Heinelt is Professor in the Institute of Political Science at Technische Universität Darmstadt, Germany, and Advisory Professor at Tongji University in Shanghai, China.

Björn Egner is Adjunct Professor in the Institute of Political Science at Technische Universität Darmstadt, Germany.

Nikolaos-Komninos Hlepas is Professor in the Faculty of Political Science and Public Administration at the National and Kapodistrian University of Athens, Greece.

Routledge Studies in Governance and Public Policy

For more information about this series, please visit: https://www.routledge.com

The Politics of Local Innovation

Conditions for the Development of
Innovations

**Edited by
Hubert Heinelt, Björn Egner
and Nikolaos-Komninos Hlepas**

LONDON AND NEW YORK

First published 2022
by Routledge
2 Park Square, Milton Park, Abingdon, Oxon OX14 4RN

and by Routledge
605 Third Avenue, New York, NY 10158

Routledge is an imprint of the Taylor & Francis Group, an informa business

British Library Cataloguing-in-Publication Data
A catalogue record for this book is available from the British Library

Library of Congress Cataloging-in-Publication Data
A catalog record has been requested for this book

ISBN: 978-0-367-53408-0 (hbk)
ISBN: 978-0-367-53988-7 (pbk)
ISBN: 978-1-003-08400-6 (ebk)

DOI: 10.4324/9781003084006

Typeset in Times New Roman
by codeMantra

Contents

Illustrations

Figures

Tables

Acknowledgment

The editors and authors are grateful to the funding institutions of the joint research project, namely the German Federal Ministry of Education and Research (grant no. 01UI1801) and the Greek Ministry of Development and Investment (grant no. T2DGE-0584) as well as the European Union.

Notes on contributors

Björn Egner is Adjunct Professor in the Institute of Political Science at Technische Universität Darmstadt, Germany. He chairs the research group "Methodology and Philosophy of Science" at the institute.

Hubert Heinelt is Professor in the Institute of Political Science at Technische Universität Darmstadt, Germany (retired since April 2018), and Advisory Professor at Tongji University in Shanghai, China. From 1997 to 2018 he chaired the research group of Public Policy, Public Administration and Urban Research at the institute. Between 2010 and 2013 he was the President of the European Urban Research Association (EURA).

Nikolaos-Komninos Hlepas is Professor in the Faculty of Political Science and Public Administration at the National and Kapodistrian University of Athens, Greece. He has worked for many years on local government studies. He is an ordinary member of the Group of Independent Experts of the Congress of Local and Regional Authorities at the Council of Europe. Furthermore, he was the President of the National Centre for Public Administration and Local Government (EKDDA) in Greece.

Max A. Kayser works as a Consultant for the international advisory and advocacy communications consultancy APCO Worldwide. Previously, he was a researcher in the Institute of Political Science at Technische Universität Darmstadt, Germany, and worked in the research group "Methodology and Philosophy of Science."

Panos Koliastasis works as a postdoctoral researcher at the University of Athens, Greece, and is a teaching fellow at the Hellenic Open University, Greece. In parallel, he acts as Country Team Leader for Greece in the international program Executive Approval Project.

Melina Lehning is a researcher in the Institute of Political Science at Technische Universität Darmstadt, Germany. She works in the research group "Methodology and Philosophy of Science" and in the research group "Transnational Governance" at the institute.

Georgios Terizakis is Professor of Political Science at the Hessische Hochschule für Polizei und Verwaltung, Germany. He is working on the research project "Police, Politics, Polis—On dealing with fugitives in the city."

Alexia Timotheou is a researcher at the National and Kapodistrian University of Athens, Greece. Since 2008, she has been working as a freelancer for private enterprises and public institutions on studies and projects in the fields of good governance, local government, regional policies, and environmental policy.

1 Introduction
About the origin of local innovations

Hubert Heinelt, Björn Egner and
Nikolaos-Komninos Hlepas

Some cities manage to mobilize innovation potentials and respond effectively to challenges such as demographic change and immigration as well as economic restructuring, while others do not. This book will address the problem of failure to innovate by asking the following question: *what are the basic conditions for the development of local innovation?* We do not locate these conditions primarily in economic, social, or institutional circumstances, but focus instead on the communicative interactions by means of which local actors develop a locally embedded understanding or knowledge of these conditions as well as the constraints and opportunities deriving from them. It is assumed that this knowledge or "imaginary" (as it is called by Sum and Jessop 2015) "provides entry-points and standpoints for their [those of the actors] social practices and projects" (Sum and Jessop 2015: 130).

1.1 An interpretive approach as a starting point for studying innovations

The focus on the communicative interactions through which local actors develop a locally embedded understanding of constraints and opportunities for innovation is inspired by a socio-constructivist or, more precisely, an interpretative approach. This approach mirrors the new trend toward post-positivist social sciences in general and discursive institutionalism (Schmidt 2008; 2010) in particular. Discursive institutionalism

> acknowledges the importance of ideational structures for constraining which ideas are considered politically viable (or even mentionable), it conceptualizes actors as sentient and critical actors able to critically engage with the ideas they hold (Carstensen 2011 [...]), as well as to think, speak and act collectively to (re)construct the structures by which they may be constrained or appear to be determined.
>
> (Carstensen and Schmidt 2016: 320)

DOI: 10.4324/9781003084006-1

Such an approach implies a certain understanding of actors and their relationship to structures (and thus agency)—which Bevir and Phillips (2017: 695) aptly summarized as follows:

> Social facts cannot explain political activity because humans are agents that act on beliefs and desires that are their own. Because humans are agents, social facts do not contain a social logic that explains some outcome. Rather, it is actors' ideas that do the explanatory work, including beliefs about interdependence.

Furthermore, interpretive approaches are characterized by a radical departure from variable-based positivism. Interpretive studies are "framed against the positivist presupposition that straightforward, matter-of-fact observation would provide ready access to an objective world where meaning was not a problem" (Yanow 1995: 111). In addition, meanings are not seen as variables "that are subject to experimental manipulation" (Yanow 1995: 112). Furthermore, it is emphasized that "social construction [cannot] be 'eliminated' from policy processes" (ibid.) as it can be seen that they are an integral part of them. This does not mean that the existence of certain events is negated, but what is important is their interpretation or meaning. Or in the words of Laclau and Mouffe (1985: 108):

> An earthquake or the falling of a brick is an event that certainly exists, in the sense that it occurs here and now, independently of my will. But whether their specificity as objects is constructed in terms of "natural phenomena" or "expressions of the wrath of God" depends upon the structuring of a discursive field.

By focusing on discourses[1] about innovations in cities, we contextualize the definition of innovation by taking into account that innovation could be defined very differently by actors, according to the local context (see Section 1.2).

Taking the actors' meaning of innovation seriously is crucial for an interpretative approach[2] characterized by an understanding of explanations, which is called "interpretivism." To avoid going into this approach more deeply (see Heinelt 2019) while still clarifying our understanding of it, we refer to Fay and Wagenaar, who define "interpretivism" in the following way:

> This approach to explanation in the social sciences, in which we explain social phenomena through uncovering the intentions of the actors involved, is called *interpretivism*. Interpretivism "may be defined as the view that comprehending human behavior, products and relationships consists [sic] solely in reconstructing the self-understandings of those engaged in creating or performing them" (Fay 1996: 113). This is a broad definition. It states that interpretative explanations must "capture the conceptual distinctions and intentions of the agents involved (Fay 1996: 114)."
>
> (Wagenaar 2011: 16)

In this book we argue for a perspective that takes local actors seriously and focuses on their views of local challenges and innovations that have been introduced (see below).

However, it is not just a matter of explaining social phenomena in terms of the intentions of the actors involved in the interactions that gave rise to the phenomena to be explained. The socially constructed meaning from which the intentions of the actors emerge and are to be fathomed is also involved. As Wagenaar states, "this is what we mean when we speak of actions having meaning. This is also the bare-bones formulation of how we understand meaningful action; how we acquire valid knowledge of it through intentional explanation" (Wagenaar 2011: 16). Thus, innovation, like any other political change, is understood "as an 'action' that is defined and structured by intentions, rather than as an abstract behavioral phenomenon" (Serrano-Velarde 2015: 52).

1.2 How should innovation be defined?

There are numerous publications on innovation in cities, and although these many publications are accompanied by a multitude of concepts with overlapping meanings, innovations are widely seen as attempts to solve urban challenges or to improve policy interventions. In this sense, the more narrow definition seems to center on policy innovations (see, for instance, Bartlett 2017; Arundel et al. 2019) and public service innovation (see, for instance, Bianchi et al. 2018; Chen et al. 2019). Whereas research on policy innovation is primarily concerned with the reorganization of decision-making and implementation processes (*process innovation*), work on public service innovation usually focuses on changes in policy content or measures/instruments and thus on improvements in services (*product innovation*). In addition to publications on process and product innovations, there are others which deal with a third subject—namely, *innovation policy*. This is a policy field that aims at creating favorable conditions for the development of innovations (Edler and Fagerberg 2017).

The debate about innovation policy is actor-centered insofar as attention is paid to the collaboration between various public and private actors which jointly create conditions favorable to the development of innovation. However, the debate about innovation policy can refer to urban innovation (Hall 1998; Dente and Coletti 2011) and urban innovation systems (van Winden et al. 2014; Putra and van der Knaap 2018), but is also related to national innovation systems (Freeman 1987) or regional innovation systems (Cooke 1992; 2001; Norck 2014; for an overview of the debate on regional innovation systems see Asheim et al. 2019). Studies on regional and urban innovation systems have highlighted several conditions that are conducive to their development, such as proximity, favorable infrastructural conditions, networks and trust between partners, and complementary or shared knowledge.

The achievement of product and process innovations through urban innovation systems was also a key issue in the debate on urban regimes (see, for example, Elkin 1987; Stone 1989; 2004a; 2004b; and for critical comments see also Davies 2002; 2003; 2004; Imbroscio 2003; 2004; Pierre 2005), although the terms themselves were usually not used in this debate. Its focus was more on cooperation among particular public and private actors and how these actors were able to dominate local politics—not only through institutional and economic power but above all through hegemonic domination of the local public discourse. The hegemonic dominance of local public discourse was, of course, an issue relevant to the research on which this book is based.

The debate on national and regional innovation systems reveals a particular understanding of innovation that is limited to promoting economic growth and competitiveness. Although such an understanding of innovation can also be found in the literature on urban innovation systems, it is not a central theme in this literature. For scholars and practitioners interested in urban innovation systems, it is not just a question of how to create "urban growth machines" (Molotch 1976; Logan and Molotch 1987). Instead, interest can also be focused on innovations leading to achieving and sustaining an "inclusive city."[3]

This applies especially to research on social innovation focused on how to achieve (better) social inclusion (see, for example, Moulaert et al. 2005). This research approach is normative in that it is focused on "first and foremost *innovation in social relations* based on values of solidarity, reciprocity, and association" (Moulaert and MacCallum 2019: 1; emphasis in the original). Furthermore, it is fundamental to this approach that it

> recognises the limitations (or even the impotence) of existing capitalist relations to deliver well-being and justice for all and [...] therefore looks to alternative kinds of social, economic and political arrangements which may complement, defy, resist and/or reconfigure the social order.
> (Moulaert and MacCallum 2019: 3–4)

This book does not share this view of innovation. However, as with advocates of this approach, the research on which this book is based paid "attention to the historical, spatial, political, economic, social and ecological particularities of the sites in which [innovation] is realized" (Moulaert and MacCallum 2019: 4). Moreover, the notion of innovation shared by the people who live at a particular site was given serious consideration by the authors of this book (as will be explained later).

Efforts to achieve and secure an inclusive city are often connected to interest in a particular aspect of process innovation—namely, *democratic innovations* (Smith 2009; Newton and Geissel 2012; Escobar and Elstub 2019). These innovations are intended to broaden and deepen the process of public participation, thus improving the quality of democracy (Geissel 2009) in general and the inclusiveness and responsiveness of policy making in particular.

The debate on urban innovation systems is closely aligned with the conceptual ideas underlying this book because discourse focuses on innovation processes and the contextual conditions favorable to them. However, it has one crucial shortcoming. Although it accentuates the processes through which innovations are brought about, not enough thought has been given to what it is that lies at the core of these processes—namely, communicative interactions between the actors involved and the mechanisms at work in these interactions. In addition, as mentioned above, either contextual conditions are confined to proximity, favorable infrastructural conditions, networks, and trust between partners or they are only sketched out in terms of complementary or shared knowledge and not elaborated further. But how is this knowledge brought about and reproduced? Communicative processes again play a role here, not only in terms of what we understand by communicative mechanisms (see Chapter 2) but also in terms of the narrative patterns that dominate in a particular spatial context, in other words, a city.

In this book, the main focus is not on specific process or product innovations or the content of innovations (as is the case, for instance, in debates on democratic innovations, "urban growth machines," the "inclusive city," or social innovations). Instead, the notion (meaning) of innovation which developed in the context of a given case, that is the city being studied, was taken seriously, because such a perspective is essential for an interpretive approach (as already briefly mentioned above). Thus, we start with a simple definition of innovation—namely, the view that innovations are "new ideas that work" (Mulgan et al. 2007: 8), and we specify innovations in terms of the "material or social artifacts which are perceived by observers as both *a novelty and an improvement*" (Braun-Thürmann 2005: 6; emphasis in the quote by the authors). Furthermore, innovations are understood (by referring to Geissel 2009: 53; see also Sorensen and Torfing 2011: 849–850) as "consciously and purposefully introduced with the aim of [an improvement] within one [city], irrespective of whether the innovation in question has already been tried out in another [city]." This specification is important, for it makes it possible to take serious account of different perceptions of actors in particular cities, such as why they have "consciously and purposefully introduced [one thing] with the aim of improving" something—whether or not this is something new for other cities too. This applies, for example, to some innovations in the provision of social services by civil society groups that have emerged since the outbreak of the financial and economic crisis in Greece at the end of the 2000s. Such activities have been common in German cities for decades.

1.3 How to identify conditions of innovation in cities using case studies?

To identify the discursive conditions of innovation and how these conditions have evolved, the book will present case studies of cities and draw lessons from them. The selected cities were chosen because they are perceived as cases of successful local innovation by the respective local community as well as in the national debate in their countries or even from an international perspective. Furthermore, it was considered important that smaller and bigger cities should be included in the studies.

The cities chosen are Bensheim, Frankfurt/Main, Kassel, Leipzig, and Offenbach/Main in Germany and Athens, Chania, Elefsina, Kalamata, and Thessaloniki in Greece. These cities were analyzed in a research project on "Conditions for Institutional and Cultural Innovation in German and Greek cities" (CICI) jointly funded by the German and Greek government.[4] The authors of the chapters of this book were directly involved in this project as researchers.

The selection of the cases requires an explanation or even a justification in at least two respects.

First, it must be explained why a comparative case study of ten German and Greek cities is sufficient to answer the research question. It could be asked why we did not include more cities (perhaps within the framework of a large-*N* analysis) and also refrained from selecting cities from third countries. The reason for this is simply that our research started at a point where we were able to speculate about the conditions in which local innovation occurred, but did not know exactly which *communication mechanisms* (see Chapter 2) were applied in which city and how they brought about innovation. Thus, any city could have been the starting point for our exploratory study, because all should reveal the same abstract *generalized* interdependencies ("verallgemeinerte Wirkungszusammenhänge"; Mayntz 2002: 25) or *communicative interaction effects*. As the empirical analysis has shown, this is indeed the case. The same is true for the *narrative pattern* (also presented in Chapter 2). We also argue that a comparison of German and Greek cities is of interest because local actors face very different circumstances, not only regarding the overall political and socio-economic conditions but especially in connection with the autonomy of local government in general (Stolzenberg et al. 2016: 18; Ladner et al. 2019) and vertical and horizontal power relations in particular (Heinelt et al. 2018).

It could also be asked why only innovative cities were selected as cases—and, as a consequence, if non-innovative cities could have contributed to the analysis as "negative cases" where the absence of a vital condition led to "no innovation." It is true that cities were indeed selected in which local actors themselves and external observers assume that innovations were achieved. In some of our case studies, however, we observed that not everything that was conceived as an innovation in the past has been continued—as in Thessaloniki. It also happened in some of the cases selected that innovations in policy areas were not achieved, although they were also considered necessary. Housing policy in Frankfurt is an example in this regard. Moreover, previous innovations may have been so successful that they led to urban growth. From the perspective of local actors, this may have led to calls for new innovations, which have not (yet) been agreed upon. Leipzig is an example of such a case. Finally, some of the cities selected were characterized by a lack of innovation in the past, but have recently been able to implement remarkable innovations. This applies to Athens, Thessaloniki, Kassel, and Offenbach. Thus, we did not confine our study exclusively to success stories, but also included failures, which is even better from a case selection perspective: we thus have intra-case variance, which enables us not only to compare degrees of innovation among cities, but also to study changes in conditions and different degrees of innovativeness within cities.

1.4 How the comparative study was conducted

The study of local discourses on innovations in the ten selected cities, the implementation of these locally perceived "novelties and improvements," and their possible changes is based on an empirical analysis of various sources.

For the analysis of the German cities, *local newspapers* were an essential source because they depicted local debates. Local newspapers could not be used as an important source for the analysis of all Greek cities, as in the smaller ones e-media report local debates. Where possible, more than one local newspaper was consulted.[5] The newspapers—but also the documents mentioned in the following section—were accessed with the help of a list of common keywords that form a word field around the concept of innovation.[6] In addition, city-specific search terms were used, which, based on the work on the case study descriptions (Chapters 3–12), were expected to lead to further references to local innovations.[7]

Local newspapers were complemented as sources for the analysis of *minutes of meetings of the municipal councils*, *policy documents* (particularly master plans, urban development plans, and strategy papers), *programs of local parties*, and *statements published* by various local actors involved in the innovations studied, because they also involved local debates.[8] All these documents were collected for the period from April 2016 to the end of December 2019. Additional documents created before this period were used in some cities if the innovations in question were developed considerably earlier. For those cities where debates on innovations considered necessary were still ongoing at the time (such as in Bensheim, Elefsina, Frankfurt, Leipzig, and Thessaloniki), the collection of the above-mentioned documents continued until the end of April 2021. In concrete terms, this means that more than 80% of the documents collected for the cities in Germany and Greece stem from the period between April 2016 and December 2019. The chronological sequence of the documents was taken into account in their analysis and is reflected in the presentation of the results of the analysis (in Chapter 13).

Finally, *interviews* with local politicians, (high-ranking) employees of the municipal administration, representatives of local interest groups and associations, as well as local journalists played a crucial role in the analysis of the ten selected cities. On average, 20 interviews were conducted per city

Table 1.1 Number of documents in cities and document types

City	Actors' positions	Concept papers	Council minutes	Media	Interviews	Total
Athens	92	10	20	210	19	351
Bensheim	103	12	0	286	17	418
Chania	24	6	19	89	21	159
Elefsina	19	11	13	96	24	163
Frankfurt	160	26	38	230	22	476
Kalamata	8	11	5	79	11	114
Kassel	134	14	0	367	14	529
Leipzig	158	10	52	202	13	435
Offenbach	89	17	0	37	11	154
Thessaloniki	26	16	39	161	21	263
Total	813	133	186	1,757	173	3,062

(see the anonymized list of interviewees in the appendix of the book). The interviews conducted in the German and Greek cities were based on a topic guide developed jointly by the German and Greek project partners. The interviews were particularly important for reconstructing earlier debates on innovation because, as just mentioned, most of the documents related to the 2016–2019 period.

The documents mentioned above and the transcripts of the interviews were collated and transformed into a dataset that could be processed with the qualitative analysis software MAXQDA. This software was used especially for the comparative analysis of the cases, the results of which are presented in the last chapter of the book. To ensure inter-case and inter-coder reliability for the comparative analysis, the German and Greek project partners jointly developed a codebook for the corpus analysis using MAXQDA.

Table 1.1 depicts the number of documents integrated into the corpora.[9] It should be noted that the number of documents collected is a little larger than the number of documents subsequently integrated into the corpus analysis. A total of 457 documents (286 from Germany and 171 from Greece) had to be left out, mainly for these reasons:

- the documents did not involve a connection with the cities or the innovations analyzed but were harvested by accident (e.g., private advertisements in newspapers concerning cars, where one car type is named "Innovation");
- the documents were exact copies of other documents already acquired (e.g., speeches from local councilors held in the municipal council and subsequently posted on the party's website);
- the documents consisted largely of other documents and did not contain new arguments or information (e.g., a summary report of a council meeting in a newspaper article consisting mainly of quotes from

politicians as well as a list of decisions made and a preview of the up-coming meeting, newspaper articles that reproduced press releases from political parties word for word, etc.).

The corpora differ from one another in several ways:

- In some cities, access to local media was difficult, which is reflected in a significantly lower number of usable media reports. This is particularly the case in three out of five Greek cities where there are only smaller newspapers and electronic archives do not exist or are not easily accessible. The same is true for Offenbach, where the *Offenbach Post* as the only local newspaper has no usable electronic archive from which articles can be retrieved. Consequently, in the case of Offenbach the two daily newspapers published in Frankfurt (searches of the *Frankfurter Rundschau* and *Frankfurter Allgemeine Zeitung* archives were carried out for articles about Offenbach).
- In two of the German cities under investigation (Frankfurt and Leip-zig), the proceedings in the respective city councils are documented by stenographic minutes. In the other German cities, minutes do not reflect the content of debates, but only the results of the proceedings, such as changes made to the agenda, the resolutions taken, and the number of votes cast. As a result, the spoken word dominates strongly in the cor-pora of Frankfurt and Leipzig, and in these two cities this form of doc-ument makes up a larger share of the overall corpus than in other cities. In the Greek cities, negotiations in city councils are documented in the minutes, but it must be noted that their quality varies: while in Athens and Thessaloniki, protocols follow "quasi-parliamentary" standards, this is not the case in the smaller cities except for Chania—city council negotiations there are publicized on YouTube.
- The number of documents written by political actors also varies greatly among the cities. On the one hand, the number of documents depends on how many parties and voter groups are active locally and how strongly they are active—particularly regarding the innovations con-sidered. On the other hand, in cities where there are no verbatim records in the council, the documents written by actors partly compensate for this gap. For example, in the corpus for Bensheim, the speeches of the city councilors are not included in the council documents (because no verbatim records are kept), but the speeches of the councilors appear at least occasionally as documents published by political actors. The reason for this is that some speeches of city councilors are published by the party to which they belong in the context of a press release aimed at "gleaning" the city council meeting. This is of course not true for every speech, but it is reasonable to assume that a party reveals its priorities on a topic by publishing speeches deemed useful in expressing the par-ty's point of view.

- In some cases, however, different publication practices have led to "duplication" of texts across genres. For example, some parties in Frankfurt publish excerpts from speeches by their city councilors which are already part of the corpus because they are in the minutes of the council meeting. In addition, newspaper articles about meetings of the municipal representative bodies are delighted to repeat particularly concise quotations or statements made by municipal politicians during council meetings, thus creating a further instance of such quotations within the corpus. The same thing happens in the Greek cities, especially in Athens and Thessaloniki. Where such multiple annotations were unmistakably attributable to one source, only the original source was used and the replications were not counted—as already mentioned above. This led to a significantly different amount of text in the "actors' position" category across cities.
- Concerning the number of interviews, it should be noted that not all interviews were integrated into the corpus of documents, especially since the interviews that were conducted for exploratory purposes at the beginning of the research were not recorded, so that no transcripts were available for analysis.

Overall, the different numbers of documents per document group, as well as variations in the kinds of document, also result in significant structural differences between the corpora for each city (see Table 1.2).

It should also be noted that the documents vary greatly in length, so that the simple number of documents does not allow any conclusion to be drawn about the actual amount of text represented by the number of individual document types and thus text categories. Table 1.2 provides an overview of the mean document lengths.

The numbers reveal similarities, but also variations in the dataset which partly result from the document acquisition processes:

Table 1.2 Average number of words by document type and city

City	Actors' positions	Concept papers	Council minutes	Media	Interviews
Athens	3,696	41,481	4,762	820	6,610
Bensheim	424	10,261	–	432	7,378
Chania	3,608	35,028	3,536	316	4,071
Elefsina	4,772	10,220	8,444	1,442	4,501
Frankfurt	1,230	9,726	56,140	519	8,122
Kalamata	1,271	36,218	32,489	760	5,592
Kassel	959	23,742	–	1,374	6,953
Leipzig	1,645	24,500	36,817	480	5,804
Offenbach	1,152	8,697	–	396	6,773
Thessaloniki	4,820	14,706	3,900	858	5,973

- There are striking similarities concerning the length of the interviews. Since they were conducted using the same topic guide, the length is typically negotiated between the interviewer and the person being interviewed beforehand (approximately 60–90 minutes). As a result, the number of words per interview is roughly the same for the five German and the five Greek cities, while also taking the differences between the two languages into consideration.

- In the case of the actors' position papers, there seems to be a difference between Bensheim and the other four German cities, with the papers from Bensheim being significantly shorter. This may be attributed to the fact that Bensheim is by far the smallest city selected in Germany. This may lead to shorter position papers by the actors, such as shorter press releases by council groups that are often focused on a single issue. In the bigger cities, actors' position papers often combine a certain proposal with a broader political approach, or link topics to other current topics—and are thus longer. In Greece, actors' position papers are longer than the German ones and this is obviously due to the fact that in Greece parties are not allowed to run in municipal elections. Municipal lists are usually short-lived (usually one to two terms) and they are obliged to present their positions and programs without (explicitly or implicitly) referring to party programs.

- Concerning concepts, it is striking that there are two cities with comparably extensive concept papers (Kassel and Leipzig), which are nearly two times longer than their counterparts in the other German cities. This is mainly an effect of the organization of papers within the city: some cities have an integrated concept, but the concept is technically split up among one central document and several attachments (e.g., plans, lists of measures, supporting evidence, databases, etc.). Other cities merge all documents into one, which may result in a concept with around 200 pages. Among the Greek cities, Athens published the longest concept papers, while in other cities these papers are considerably shorter, with the exception of Chania. The small size (in relation to the city's size) of concept papers in Thessaloniki results from the fact that the city developed a considerable number of specialized concepts (leading to the highest number of concept papers among the Greek cities).

- Regarding council meetings, there are—as already mentioned—only two German cities where word-by-word minutes are taken. The minutes are significantly longer in Frankfurt than in Leipzig, but the fact that the council in Leipzig meets more frequently due to an agreement that limits council meetings to seven hours (usually from 2 p.m. to 9 p.m.) must be taken into account. This also causes speakers to limit themselves to short speeches. By contrast, the council of Frankfurt may meet until late in the evening, sometimes ending the meeting well after midnight. The number of council members in Frankfurt (93) is greater than in Leipzig (70), and thus proceedings of the council take longer in

Frankfurt, despite the coalition ruling. In Greece, council minutes are shorter even in big cities like Athens and Thessaloniki. This is because minutes are strictly divided according to the issue being discussed. Furthermore, the agenda of municipal councils in Greece is usually overloaded with many different items. As a result, time pressure is a constant problem, and even when important issues are being discussed the time limits are extremely strict. By comparison, council minutes are relatively long in Elefsina, the city with the smallest population and the smallest number of councilors among the Greek cases.

• The length of media reports is very similar across four of the five cities selected in Germany, resembling the typical length of a local news article: a few introductory sentences, some reporting on something going on, some original citation of somebody involved, a member of the council, a full-time politician, a representative of a political group, etc., some sentences which refer to the future. The only exception is Kassel, where on average media releases are about four times longer. This is a direct effect of the document acquisition process: in Kassel, media reports were not available as single articles, but as full newspaper pages only. This means that the average word count in Kassel displays the number of words for the whole newspaper page the article was printed on. Given that there are about three to four articles per page—depending on the issue—the actual length of the pertinent article corresponds well with press releases in the other cities. In Greece, the length of media reports is similar to that in Germany, with the exception of Elefsina, where a phenomenon similar to Kassel can be observed.

However, despite their different structures, the corpora for the ten cities are similar enough to be analyzed comparatively. It should be noted, however, that the different lengths and weightings of the individual text categories in the various cities can lead to shifts in emphasis in the quantitative analysis. This had to be taken into account in the interpretation of the results of the analysis (presented particularly in Chapter 13).

To stress the comparability of the corpora and to ensure reliability of the coding work, we counted the actual codings against a standardized number of words per document (see Table 1.3). As the table depicts, there is common ground between the cities and the countries insofar as there is a typical number of codings per standardized quantity of text. Although there is variation in some fields, this is explicable as a result of the document acquisition procedures and case-specific peculiarities, not of systematic bias and lack of objectivity on the part of the researchers.

For example, *actors' positions* have a similar standard number of codes—with the exception of Offenbach, where one single document which was especially rich in codings resulted in a high overall number. Concerning *concepts*, Elefsina can be mentioned as an outlier because one of the documents included more than 100 pages, since it was the city's final application

Table 1.3 Average number of codings per 10,000 words

City	Actors' positions	Concept papers	Council minutes	Media	Interviews
Athens	2.4	1.0	18.9	6.1	17.0
Bensheim	3.9	1.3		3.2	8.6
Chania	2.8	1.1	5.7	32.1	26.8
Elefsina	3.9	6.5	3.5	12.9	28.9
Frankfurt	5.9	1,3	3.3	16.6	5.8
Kalamata	18.7	0.5	1.2	18.0	32.0
Kassel	4.0	0.6		1.8	9.7
Leipzig	3.4	1.4	1.0	7.7	13.9
Offenbach	13.7	3.1		13.7	13.4
Thessaloniki	2.6	2.5	14.9	7.3	15.5

for the role of European Capital of Culture for 2021. Concerning *council meetings*, the high density of codings in Athens and Thessaloniki can be explained by the document acquisition process: in both cities, only those parts of the council minutes were analyzed in which local innovations were addressed, whereas in the other cities complete minutes were used which also covered other topics and even formal procedures such as openings, debates about changes to the agenda, elections of executive managers, budget proceedings, etc. Regarding *media reports*, there is also an explanation for the variations among the cities: in Chania and Elefsina, the articles in local papers are significantly more focused on the innovations being analyzed, whereas in the other Greek cities the innovations may be only one topic within a long article. The same is true for Frankfurt and Offenbach, where short articles about innovations dominate over the lengthy multi-topic articles seen in the other cities. In addition, the very low number of codings in Kassel is explicable by the same technical issue referred to above: because we had to acquire complete newspaper pages instead of single articles, the number of codings per 10,000 words is low. Concerning the *interviews*, it can be noted that the interviews conducted in Greek cities are often more fruitful in terms of codings. This may be because most of the interviews were conducted during the COVID pandemic and thus had to be conducted by telephone or by video conference, which led to a more focused interaction between the researcher and the person being interviewed. Furthermore, interviews with actors from small cities in general seem to be focused more on the innovation at hand than on general politics or other topics. For two German cities, it should be noted that interviews connected with two already completed research projects were also used to complete the corpus. Since both former projects were not specifically related to local innovations, only parts of the interviews were usable and this reduced the proportion of codings and keywords. As a result, the corpus exhibits some variation in the richness of codings, but the variety is not a result of different persons carrying out the coding but of different cases and different circumstances in the process of the corpus creation.

1.5 Structure of the book

The approach on which the book is based is explained in Chapter 2 (by Hubert Heinelt and Georgios Terizakis). It is an interpretive approach (presented in detail in Heinelt 2019) which argues that constraints (such as deficiencies in different kinds of infrastructure) and opportunities (such as those made possible by institutions of higher education and research centers) are not in themselves crucial "external" factors. Instead, knowledge of the constraints and opportunities is of central importance. In other words, actors have to know what constrains them and have to develop an understanding of what they can achieve, how, and with whom. According to the interpretive approach, it is thus not the "external" factors themselves that are explanatory variables, but rather the knowledge about these factors that actors possess. With regard to the question addressed by this book, this means that actors need to develop their understanding of the conditions for innovations in their city. This understanding—expressed in a particular narrative—gives meaning to action, and has to be developed through communicative interaction. To take effect, that is, to make action meaningful, this understanding needs to be constantly reproduced or—into the context of innovation—it has to be transformed during communicative interactions. We will show what mechanisms are at work in such communicative interactions and how these mechanisms influence local narratives about the feasibility of innovations, but also need to be adapted to such particular local narratives. Furthermore, an attempt is made through the communicative mechanisms described to conceptually decode the intersubjective phenomena which the different concepts of learning try to grasp.[10] The study on which this book is based deliberately refrained from using these concepts to avoid transferring supposedly decoded everyday learning processes of individuals to intersubjective processes. Thus, "learning" is not used simply as a metaphor. All the same, "the learning metaphor with its rationalistic and affirmative undertones suggests a positive change in the direction of problem-solving" (Münch 2016: 31).

In the following ten chapters, the cities which were studied—or, more precisely, the innovations achieved in these cities and how they were achieved—are presented. All ten chapters have the same structure: after a brief description of the city (its location, historical development, and current challenges) what locals, as well as outside observers, perceive as innovations in the city are presented. This description is followed by a longer section on how these innovations have been achieved and how far and in what way specific local discourses structured the processes through which the innovations were made possible. Each of these ten chapters ends with a short section with "general observations." To avoid repetitions, these general observations are only included in the concluding section of each chapter for the case study cities that are not systematically reflected upon further in the book's concluding chapter (Chapter 13).

In the chapter on Athens (Chapter 3), Nikolaos Hlepas shows how it was possible to address some of the challenges that have arisen in this city due to the fiscal crisis in Greece since the end of the 2000s and to the influx of large numbers of refugees since 2015 through several new social initiatives and measures which offered remarkable new opportunities to Athenians as well as to migrants. These noteworthy innovations were made possible by actors who stimulated a public debate about the resilience of the city in general and "the right to the city," that is to say, inclusive action and social cohesion, in particular. A decisive factor in these innovations was the creation of a platform for citizen groups and initiatives, called *SynAthina,* which strengthened civic engagement and united the forces of a variety of actors. The name *SynAthina*—derived from the ancient Athenian saying ("ΣΥΝ ΑΘΗΝΑ ΚΑΙ ΧΕΙΡΑ ΚΙΝΕΙ") meaning that people should not simply wait for the help of the Goddess (and/or the city) Athena, but should act on their own initiative—expresses a new way of thinking which could hardly have been expected ten years earlier. This new way of thinking made innovation possible, and led to Athens receiving the "European Capital of Innovation" award from the European Commission in 2019.

The case of Bensheim is presented in Chapter 4 (by Hubert Heinelt). It is a town with about 40,000 inhabitants, in which local actors managed not only to locate sites for international high-tech companies but also to attract well-paid people who are working (earning their income) in the urban centers of the metropolitan Frankfurt/Rhine-Main and Rhine-Neckar regions (around Heidelberg, Mannheim, and Ludwigshafen). This has been made possible by the unquestioned acceptance of measures (social and cultural innovations) for remaining a city which is, on the one hand, a place with a flourishing economy but *not* based on "stinking factories" and, on the other hand, a place where people can wholeheartedly say (in the local dialect): "Hier bin ich dehaam!" ("Here I am at home!").

Chania, presented in Chapter 5 (by Hubert Heinelt and Panos Koliastasis), is a tourist center on the Greek island of Crete. What makes this case interesting is the fact that the local actors have managed to preserve the medieval town center and focus on visitors who like to stay in small "boutique hotels" or stay elsewhere on the island (not least in large hotel complexes) and come to the beautiful old town just for the day. This strategy has only been successful due to innovations in the fields of waste and traffic management admired by other Greek cities.

As Panos Koliastasis demonstrates in Chapter 6, local actors in the city of Elefsina have been able to turn the former main industrial center in the wider Attica region (around Athens), which suffered for years under deindustrialization, into a city that has been selected as the European Capital of Culture for 2021. For socially disadvantaged inhabitants, however, it is probably much more important that their living conditions have been improved through innovations in the social infrastructure based on activities of "third sector" organizations in collaboration with the municipality.

Frankfurt (Chapter 7 written by Hubert Heinelt and Max Kayser) has displayed the ability to perform as a front-running city of innovations in different policy fields for decades. Since the late 1980s, the municipality has developed the "Frankfurt way" in drug policy and set up at the same time the "Amt für multikulturelle Angelegenheiten" (AMKA) as one of the first municipal offices for multicultural affairs in Germany. In 1991 the "GrünGürtel" was established as the first legally protected urban green belt worldwide. Finally, it should be mentioned that in the early 1990s Frankfurt had already adopted an ambitious and—compared with other cities—successful local climate policy (see Heinelt and Lamping 2015a; Heinelt and Lamping 2015b). These achievements were made possible because local debates, as well as political practice in Frankfurt, are characterized by an attitude that all perceived challenges (drugs, a high percentage of migrants, climate change in general, and air pollution and overheating in the city in particular) are just (negative) side effects of being a boom town, for which the city—or better, local politicians and an active citizenry—should accept responsibility and act and not wait until others (upper levels of government) solve it (Barbehön et al. 2015: 68–97; Barbehön et al. 2016).

Kalamata (Chapter 8 written by Alexia Timotheou) is an interesting case of innovation because it was heavily damaged in 1986 by an earthquake. However, instead of adopting a fatalistic attitude, this dramatic event was taken by some local politicians (particularly the mayor) as an opportunity to rebuild the infrastructure in such a way that living conditions in the city center were improved and the space around the port and along the coastline was made attractive as a recreation area, for local people as well as for tourists. In addition, the city introduced a series of cultural innovations that aimed at broad participation of citizens in cultural activities.

Kassel is described (by Melina Lehning in Chapter 9) as a city that suffered from deindustrialization and a geographical location in "Hessian Siberia" (the northern part of the German state of Hesse). However, local actors took advantage of German reunification and European integration which placed the city at the center of the European Union (EU). Kassel changed not only economically from a city undergoing deindustrialization to a European logistics hub, but also from a poorhouse to a city of art and culture, by making use of the location of a university in the city and the city's cultural heritage as a *Residenzstadt* of one of the numerous German principalities until the 19th century. This is expressed by the "documenta," the world's most significant series of contemporary art exhibitions, and the naming of the city "documenta Stadt."

Leipzig (presented in Chapter 10 by Hubert Heinelt and Max Kayser) is one of the few places in Eastern Germany, that is, the territory of the former Socialist German Democratic Republic, which has succeeded in changing from a shrinking city (the population decreased from 713,000 in 1933 to 490,000 in 1999) to a center of growth in this part of Germany. This was not only a result of successful attempts to attract investors and companies to the city (e.g., BMW, Porsche, and Amazon) but, more importantly, it was intended to make the city attractive for young creative people by offering them vacant lots and fallow land by which the city was characterized (as a "perforierte Stadt"/"perforated city") until the end of the 2010s. However, Leipzig is also a good example of what can happen when innovations are successful, in other words, have resulted in the intended improvements. Since the late 2010s, there has been an obvious struggle over ideas of what should be done after the successful turnaround. This struggle over ideas has blocked the realization of (controversial) new ideas for years.

Offenbach (as presented in Chapter 11 by Max Kayser) was perceived by locals and external observers as the poor sister of Frankfurt. Indeed, Offenbach—located more or less in the shadow of the high-rise building of the European Central Bank—has in comparison with other cities in the prosperous Frankfurt/Rhine-Main region a relatively high unemployment rate, and its economy is dominated by a low-skilled service sector. Furthermore, the city has the highest proportion of inhabitants with a migration background in Germany. In total 61.6% of Offenbach's population migrated to Germany in the past or recently. Nevertheless, local actors have been able to reframe the negative image of the city positively and create a vision for the future by presenting Offenbach as an "arrival city." And indeed, the arrival city discourse in Offenbach is well-grounded, because the city has welcomed migrants looking for work and refugees looking for a place to live since the 17th century, when the first Huguenots settled in Offenbach and made the city a major location of the leather industry in Germany. This discourse has been successful in combination with the preparation of a master plan for urban development and attempts to improve the cultural infrastructure. As a result, in recent years Offenbach has acquired the image of being a vibrant place where young and creative people in particular can find a better place to live than in Frankfurt, where rents for housing and offices have skyrocketed in recent years.

Thessaloniki (presented in Chapter 12 by Nikos Hlepas) was a major center of Jewish life in Europe up to World War II. Being an attractive coastal city ("the nymph of the Thermaic Gulf") close to the tourist area of Chalkidiki, the second biggest city of Greece tried to revitalize its multicultural legacy immediately following the election of the non-partisan entrepreneur Boutaris as mayor in 2010. As a prominent active member of the Greek civil society, Boutaris adopted an open and innovative style of governance sharing, mirroring the approach taken by Athens in many ways. The municipality became the coordination hub for many formerly scattered activities of different actors, while several innovations in the business, social, and cultural sectors were introduced.

Chapter 13 (written by Björn Egner, Hubert Heinelt, Nikos Hlepas, Panos Koliastasis, Melina Lehning, and Alexia Timotheou) summarizes the results of a cross-case comparison in which the role of local narratives and their discursive patterns, as well as the relevance of communicative mechanisms in the emergence of certain local narrative patterns, were systematically investigated. This systematic comparison of case studies is based on an analysis of local discourses using the ten text corpora collected as described above (in Section 1.4). The chapter concludes with a summary of the results of the analysis, emphasizing that a crucial prerequisite for local innovation is to discursively identify the constraints and opportunities a city faces from the perspective of the local actors.

Notes

1   In debates among proponents of an interpretive approach, the notion of discourse is located (and moves) between two poles. For proponents of post-structuralism (following Foucault) the world is constituted through the discourse and the language by which it is created. This means that "meaning does not reside in the intentions of actors, but in the structural properties of the text" (Wagenaar 2011: 107) in which a specific kind of articulation (an "objective meaning"; Wagenaar 2011: 18–19) is expressed. In contrast, discourses are understood as communicative interactions in collective sense-making processes in which "the world is mediated by language" (Wagenaar 2011: 107) created by actors in their interaction. This leads to what can be called "subjective meaning" (Wagenaar 2011: 18–19). The authors of this book are clearly guided by an interpretive approach referring to "subjective meaning."

2   This applies at least to an interpretive approach, which does not follow a post-structuralist understanding of discourse structures (see note 1).

3   For an overview of the debate on the "inclusive city," see, for example, https://www.worldbank.org/en/topic/inclusive-cities.

4   The concept for this research project is based on previous work by Heinelt and Lamping (2015a and 2015b) and Barbehön et al. (2015 and 2016) synthesized by Heinelt (2019).

5   Searches for articles were done in the following newspapers: *Kathimerini*, *Avgi*, *Efsyn*, and *To Vima* for Athens, *Bergsträßer Anzeiger* for Bensheim, *Chaniotika News*, *Zarpanewws*, and *Flashnews* for Chania, *Epikairotita* and *Thriassio* for Elefsina, *Frankfurter Allgemeine Zeitung* and *Frankfurter Rundschau* for Frankfurt and Offenbach, *Kalamata Journal*, *Messinia Live*, Messinia Press, *Kalamata In*, and *Tharros News* for Kalamata, *Hessisch-Niedersächsische Allgemeine* for Kassel, *Leipziger Volkszeitung* for Leipzig; and *Makedonia*, and (in addition to the national newspapers already mentioned also used for Athens) *Typos Thessalonikis* for Thessaloniki.

6   The general search terms were *innovation, innovative, novelty, improvement, progress, smart, promotion, image, pioneer, city marketing, vision, reputation, urban development, district development, smart mobility, eMobility, e-government, digitization*, and *digital*.

7   The city-specific search terms were, for example, *Synathina, Atenistas, Culturenet, Open Schools, Kypseli Municipal Market, Polis2, InnovAthens, Resilient Athens, Athens Partnership, Athens Digital Council, Athens Digital Roadmap, Sculptures in Public Spaces, Right to the City* for Athens; *Haus am Markt, Marktplatz, MEGB, Innenstadtdialog, Bürgernetzwerk, Bensheim aktiv, Stubenwald* for Bensheim; *Traffic Management System, Recycling System, Smart City, Chania Citizen app, Social Grocery Store* for Chania; *Homeless Shelter, Shelter for*

Abused Women, Social Tutoring School, Social Grocery Store, Local Employment Service, Local Vegetable Garden, Center for Collection of Recyclable Materials, European Capital of Culture for Elefsins; *Frankfurt 2030+, Frankfurt Green City, Josefstadt, ABG, Grüngürtel, Frankfurter Weg, Drogen(-politik), Klimapolitik, Passivhäuser* for Frankfurt; *Dance Festival, Smart City, Digital Kalamata, City of Culture, European Capital of Culture, Cultural Decentralization, Master Plan, Reconstruction, Routes of the Olive Tree* for Kalamata; *Regionalmanagment, tiz, Kultur, Science Park, Kulturkonzeption, deNet* for Kassel; *Perforierte Stadt, Leipziger Freiheit, HausHalten, Wächterhäuser, Aufbauhäuser, Leipzig weiter denken, Leipziger Modell* for Leipzig; *Arrival City, Masterplan, DesignPort, HfG, Innovations Campus* for Offenbach; *Capital of Refugees, Technopolis Thessaloniki, THESSINTEC, OK!THES, Culture Society, Resilient Thessaloniki, Anti-Poverty Network* for Thessaloniki.

8 These documents were searched for in the information systems of municipal councils (where available) or via the websites of the municipalities and local actors involved in the innovations analyzed.

9 All quotations from these documents included in the following sections of this book had to be translated by the authors, as they were available in either German or Greek. The fact that this was the case will not be mentioned further in quotations from these documents. The same applied to internet sources and publications which—according to the websites listed in endnotes or the list of references—were available only in German or Greek.

10 Dunlop and Radaelli (2020) give a differentiated overview of the various concepts of learning and their basic assumptions and problems.

2 Why are some cities more innovative than others? An answer based on an interpretive concept

Hubert Heinelt and Georgios Terizakis

2.1 Innovation and communicative practice

The aim of this chapter is to introduce an analytical concept for explaining differences in innovations between cities. This will be done from an interpretive perspective. We will argue that a certain understanding of the conditions and possibilities as well as the desirability of particular changes is crucial for innovation in a city, and we will show that such an understanding can evolve through a set of *communicative mechanisms* (outlined in Section 2.2). Furthermore, we will show that these communicative mechanisms are related to particular local narratives about what innovations can and should achieve. Depending on a given local narrative, some statements are considered reasonable and others not—or even sheer nonsense or inappropriate. And more importantly, something that is perceived as an innovation in one city can be perceived as a quite long-established practice in another, or even as something which is done as a matter of course in another; one is thus not seen as innovative at all. Such a local narrative may serve as a hidden "map" for outsiders. However, it may guide local practice because it is an expression of a particular understanding of how the world is functioning and how it should be functioning and thus demonstrates why certain innovations can and should be achieved. Although these local narratives are or can be city-specific, *general discursive patterns* exist. Section 2.3 will show how a "storyline" can be established through these discursive patterns and make a narrative convincing—or at least plausible in a certain local context.

2.2 Different ways of explaining innovations

2.2.1 "Conventional" approaches to explaining innovations

There has been a great deal of debate about the conditions for innovation (see the reflection on this debate in the introductory chapter of this book and for an overview see Berry and Berry 2007). However, there is more or less substantial agreement that a basic distinction can be made between exogenous and endogenous conditions. Related to the question addressed

DOI: 10.4324/9781003084006-2

in this book, institutionally determined (a) local autonomy in general and in particular (b) fiscal capacities, as well as (c) organizational capacities/ competences of local government might be regarded as exogenous conditions for innovation in local government and local civil society. In respect to endogenous conditions, the following characteristics may be regarded as fundamental: (a) the particular structure of the local economy, (b) the specific financial situation of the municipality being analyzed, and (c) the social capital of the local community (i.e., social networks [including particular actor constellations], shared norms, and trust).

These conditions are captured by Ostrom (1999) as well as by Ostrom et al. (1994) in their Institutional Analysis and Development (IAD) Framework under the headings "attributes of the physical world," "attributes of the community," and "rules-in-use."

However, from our perspective, such a "conventional" (and usually positivist) approach in looking for conditions for innovation and for explaining differences in innovation among cities leaves two questions open: (a) how do these conditions (or [independent] variables) impact on interactions among actors when they have to make a decision about innovations? and—even more relevant to the question dealt with in this book—(b) how do actors recognize and use these conditions to implement not only innovations in general but the innovations they consider achievable and desirable under the circumstances?

For "conventional" approaches it seems to be clear that actors have to refer to "external" factors such as—in Ostrom's words—the "attributes of the physical world," the "attributes of the community," and the "rules-in-use," because these contextual circumstances affect their interactions. However, can such "external" factors simply be taken as constraints or opportunities which directly determine collective actions? From an interpretive perspective, it is of central importance that actors interpret collectively these constraints and opportunities that emerge from these "external" factors and develop an understanding of them jointly. In other words, actors have to know what constrains them and have to develop an understanding of what they can achieve, how, and with whom. From an interpretive approach, external factors are therefore not conceptualized as explanatory variables in themselves, but rather as knowledge held by actors about these factors. With respect to the question outlined at the beginning of this chapter, this means that actors have to develop an understanding of the conditions for innovation in their city. This understanding gives meaning to action, and it has to be developed through communicative interaction. To have an effect, i.e., to make action meaningful, this understanding needs to be constantly reproduced or—with respect to innovation—it has to be transformed during communicative interaction.

Whatever understanding of the conditions for innovation in a particular city may mean in terms of content, it should be noted that it does not necessarily mirror what is "objectively" possible. This understanding is merely an "image of objectivity" (Daston and Galison 1992) or "only accepted belief, not correct belief" (Haas 1992: 23) based on a "cognitively stylized expectation" (Luhmann 1992). It is therefore not to be understood as a representation of reality but as a social construction that may be based on accurate knowledge, but also on ignorance (Heinelt 2019: 37–42; Paul and Haddad 2019). However, every understanding of the conditions for innovation has to "pass the double test [...] of

- its *effectiveness* concerning the effects of actions based on specific causal assumptions; and
- its *legitimacy* in terms of achieving expected normative goals" (Heinelt 2019: 43).

This double test is an integral part of its development (including its possible changes) through communicative interaction among the actors in the particular (urban) context. In these communicative interactions, communicative mechanisms (see Section 2.2.2) and certain narrative patterns (see Section 2.2.3) come into play.

2.2.2 Explaining innovations through communicative mechanisms

To explain innovations we start from the ongoing debate in social sciences which emphasizes the role of causal and social mechanisms but goes a step further by focusing on the communicative mechanism, that is, mechanisms by means of which actors interpret and give meaning to their physical and social environment and develop a shared or even hegemonic understanding of what can and should be improved by an innovation and how this can be done.

This ongoing debate about causal and social mechanisms is grounded in an attempt to develop a "social theory" (see the subtitle of the volume edited by Hedström and Swedberg (1998)), which is *not* aimed at the identification of law-like principles. Rather, the existence of laws in the social sphere is questioned—and together with this a "variable-based approach" (Hedström and Swedberg 1998: 2), which aims at the verification and falsification of nomological hypotheses (for an overview see Hedström and Ylikoski 2010: 50, 54ff.). Instead, from a "mechanism perspective" attention is focused on interdependencies that can be identified in a variety of different interactions among actors, "which [...] produce the observed association in the variables" (Sorensen 1990: 308). Consequently, this debate is also of interest for an interpretive approach because the "quest for the reconstruction of the 'causal paths' is a step in the direction of the modification of our understanding of causality" (Nullmeier 2018: 75). Accordingly, mechanisms are defined as

> relatively abstract concepts or patterns of action that can travel from one specific instance, or "episode" (Tilly 2001: 26), of causation to

another, and that explain how a hypothesized cause creates a particular outcome in a given context.

(Falleti and Lynch 2009: 1145)

In other words, "mechanisms describe the action taking place in the process of causation" (Falleti and Lynch 2009: 1162). They can be characterized as abstract *generalized interdependencies* ("verallgemeinerte Wirkungszusammenhänge"; Mayntz 2002: 25). Furthermore, it is argued that reflections on independent and dependent variables lead only to "correlational arguments" (I → O; Falleti and Lynch 2009: 1144 ff.). Accordingly, statements on causation can only be made by including mechanisms that capture the processes mediating between input and output (I → M → O; Falleti and Lynch 2009: 1146). As emphasized by Peter A. Hall (2013: 22), as "a result of that debate, political scientists are much less likely to confuse correlation with causation than we were a few years ago," which reminds us that correlation is not the same as causality.

As already mentioned, the debate about a "mechanism-based explanation of complex phenomena" (Bennett 2013: 475) is about the development of a "social theory." Accordingly, it would be appropriate to speak of "social mechanisms" (see Banta 2012: 391) and, indeed, this is done (see Hedström and Swedberg (1998) and for an overview see Hedström and Ylikoski (2010: 55–58)). But especially in the Anglo-Saxon debate, the term "causal mechanisms" is used in a rather broad sense so that sometimes quite non-specific "physical, social, or psychological processes" (Bennett 2013: 466; see also George and Bennett 2005: 137) as well as biological and neurological processes (see Machamer et al. 2000 or Bunge 1997) are subsumed under it.

When it comes to the processes involved in developing a shared understanding of what can and should be improved by an innovation and how this should be done, such as shared understanding can only involve social mechanisms—namely, those mechanisms which operate in the communicative interactions among actors through which they collectively interpret their social environment regarding constraints and opportunities for improvement. Consequently, the discussion focuses on *generalized interdependencies in communicative interaction*, which are characterized not only generally as social, but more specifically as *communicative mechanisms*.

The examination of generalized interdependencies in communicative interaction implies an interpretive explanation insofar as an action (decision) can be interpreted as explained "if a reason is cited as a good reason, which, based on deliberations [in discursive interactions] has become the *reason that causes the action*" (Nullmeier 2012: 43; emphasis by Nullmeier). Accordingly, the following applies to an "interpretive explanation" (Nullmeier 2018: 72): "When the knowledge and interpretation of the actors are reconstructed, it becomes possible to explain political events as resulting from the interactions of the actors" (Nullmeier 2013: 24; translation by the authors; see also Nullmeier 2018).[1]

In the conceptual scholarly debate on mechanisms, they are rarely speci-
fied in a way that can be applied to empirical analysis, for example, to analyze the development of a locally shared or dominant understanding of how
and why certain innovations can and should be achieved. This deficiency
of the scholarly debate on mechanisms can be explained by the fact that—
as argued by van der Heijden et al. (2019) with reference to Hedström and
Ylikoski (2010)—"causal mechanisms need to be identified in the empirical
world in order to be an 'actual mechanism.'" This applies, for example, to
the study by Heinelt and Lamping (2015a, 2015b) on local climate policy.
They identified communicative mechanisms that are relevant for explaining differences in local climate policy. In our study, these mechanisms also
proved to be relevant for communicative processes that led to local innovations. Some of these mechanisms have already been mentioned in the
literature—also with reference to empirical studies.

This applies particularly to *observation of others and orientation toward
them* as a collective process involving the communication of those observing others. It can result either in imitation or in competition (outlined by
Benz and Dose 2010: 252 ff.), which is more or less the same as what Falleti
and Lynch (2009: 1150) called "adaptive expectations," meaning that "[p]
eople act in accordance with signals from others about the likely value or
necessity of an act." It has to be emphasized that what is called "observation
of others and orientation towards them" is *not* something that takes place
without communication (e.g., in the actors themselves). Rather, it is crucial
that in communicative interaction with others actors refer not only to what
they are observing but also to the reason why they think that their observation is relevant for them or their collective actions—being fully aware that
referring to the observation is relevant for the partners in this communicative interaction because they either identify with the observed third parties
or compete with them. In general, the mechanism of *observation of others
and orientation toward them* (or adaptive expectations) implies *justifying and
motivating one's own activities (e.g., in respect to innovation) by referring to
those of others.*

However, it is not enough to agree that something new has to be done
which will improve a given situation, because others may also wish to do
something which they see as an improvement. Obviously, observations usually differ among various people and groups and thus do not provide a clear
orientation for people's own activities. In addition, action orientations usually differ among actors who are looking around and seeking inspiration
from the actions of others. Thus, a common reference point for people's *own*
activities has to be agreed upon. This depends on patterns of communicative
interaction which represent a further mechanism—namely, the *discursive
development of reference points for further communication.* More precisely,
reference points for communicative interaction are developed through such
discursive processes. Reference points make argumentative communication

possible, because arguing[2] is characterized by a "triadic" structure of reasoning exchange (Saretzki 1996: 34–35), as participants refer to relatively well-defined, commonly shared, and accepted definitions of challenges and a basic understanding of how the challenges should be addressed. The discursive development of such reference points can be achieved by referring in communicative interactions to "epistemic authorities" (Zürn 2012). Such authorities can be found within the municipal administration. This was the case in Leipzig (see Chapter 10) where, in the early 2000s, the head of the municipal building department, Lütke Daldrup, played a crucial role in developing a reference point for innovative activities in using vacant buildings by delivering the diagnosis of Leipzig as a "perforated city" (and showing how to deal with this situation).[3] In addition, reference points for further communication can be developed through institutionalized as well as informal community involvement. In this way, actors from city hall together with actors from local civil society can define common challenges and measures seen as appropriate to meet them and refer to the results of such interaction with societal actors in future debates about innovations. Athens seems to be a good example in this respect (see Chapter 3 of this book). However, such a point of reference for argumentative exchange can also result from the fact that something is simply regarded as self-evident or associated with a tradition by emphasizing: "This has been known for a long time!" or "We have always done it this way!"

Another mechanism (already briefly mentioned by Falleti and Lynch (2009: 1150)) can be called *framing*—although the notions of framing and frames are used quite differently (see Braun 2015; Heinelt 2019: 19). The abstract generalizable causal relationship of interaction captured by this mechanism is that the *perception and assessment of the world is determined (i.e., framed) according to the pre-determined relevance of a particular policy choice which has set a specific frame*. This mechanism becomes manifest where an unquestioned orientation of actions (and decisions on which these actions are based) is implied by such a frame. Such behavior is complemented by an ongoing (self-)explanation and thus stabilization of a particular way of dealing with challenges as well as priorities regarding innovations. The latter is made clear in the unquestioned orientation of particular activities in Bensheim (see Chapter 4 of this book) with the reference to remaining a city that on the one hand is a place with a flourishing economy (but not based on "stinking factories") and, on the other hand, a place where people can say in a heartfelt way (in the local dialect): "Hier bin ich dehaam!" ("Here I am at home!"). The (self-)explanation and thus stabilization of a certain way of dealing with challenges arising from this particular mechanism is expressed above all in the fact that it is regarded as a *matter of course*.

A mechanism by which a particular local understanding of what can and should be done is protected against being questioned can be called *immunization*. Such immunization usually takes place by referring either to a self-commitment entered into earlier or to status as a role model for others (for other cities), claiming that this would come into question if the chosen path were left. Furthermore, reference to decisions made by other authorities, particularly upper levels of government, and the resulting restriction of local discretion, can have an immunizing effect. This applies in particular to decisions by other authorities on financial means, i.e., a distributive framework or grants, but also to the right of municipalities to raise taxes. They can have an immunizing effect in different ways—namely, by arguing either that former "investments" in innovations would be squandered by changing a given path or that new (other) innovations would require financial means which are not available.[4]

Finally, there is a mechanism which can be called *issue relabeling* (with reference to the debate on policy analysis going back to Lowi (1972) see Heinelt (2006: 110)). It implies an *upgrading of a measure (an innovation) by referring to its positive effects on other policy areas.* Cultural innovation linked to the improvement of the economic development of a city (from the establishment of enterprises to the attraction of tourists) can be cited as an example for this mechanism.[5] However, issue relabeling can also take place in another direction through the upgrading of measures in other policy fields by highlighting their contribution to the innovations pursued in the given context.

In addition to this outline of communicative mechanisms, the following should be emphasized. In the course of the formation, stabilization, and further development of a particular understanding of why innovations are feasible and desirable, the individual mechanisms play a specific role. Thus, the development of a reference point for communication is the basis for effective framing, and the mechanism of immunization has meaning only when a certain understanding of what can and should be done has been formed and needs to be protected against questioning (Table 2.1).

Coupled with their skepticism about the existence of law-like principles in the social sphere, representatives of the "mechanism perspective" emphasize that "mechanisms operate within specific contexts or causal fields, and their effects depend on interactions with the other mechanisms that constitute these contexts" (Bennett 2008: 213; see also Bunge (1997: 440, 447 and 449ff.)). This means that mechanisms that prove to be relevant within a "specific context or causal field" need not be a priori decisive for others. Or more precisely, the communicative mechanisms detected in the "causal field" of developing and implementing innovations might not be relevant in other fields.[6]

It seems to be self-evident that these communicative mechanisms have an effect only when they are used in communicative interaction among actors. However, what characterizes communicative interaction beyond these mechanisms? To answer this question, the issues discussed in the following subsection must be considered.

Table 2.1 Communicative mechanisms—their abstract generalizable effects and their materialization in particular contexts through practices or strategic adoptions

Mechanisms	Their abstract generalizable effects	Practices or strategies adopted
Observation of others and orientation to them	Justification and motivation of people's own activities by referring to those of others	• Comparison *and imitation* of activities of others • Comparison *and competition* with others • Comparison *and delineation* from others
Discursive development of reference points for triadic communication	Enabling of argumentative communication (of arguing)	Formation of as well as change to reference points for argumentative communication by referring to • something which is seen as self-evident • a tradition ("We have always done it this way!") • recognized expertise within the existing context • recognized external experts • results of public debates (with societal actors)
Framing	Perception and assessment of "reality" according to the pre-decided relevance of a particular policy choice	• ongoing orientation and justification of actions and decisions • (self-)explanation and stabilization of manners [ways] of dealing with problems • (self-)explanation and stabilization of priorities regarding particular measures
Immunization	Protection of a particular local understanding of what can and should be done from being questioned	Referring to • agreed (self-)commitments • status as a role model for others • financial means invested in innovations which would be lost through changing a given path or that are not available for new (other) innovations
Issue relabeling	Upgrading of a policy measure by referring to its positive effects on (solving problems of) other policy fields	Emphasizing the • contribution of the innovation concerned to achieving other policy objectives • contribution of other policies to achieving the innovation in question

Source: Authors' own elaboration based on Heinelt (2019: 66) and Heinelt and Lamping (2015c: 289).

2.2.3 Making use of communicative mechanisms by referring to dominant local narratives

To convince others, actors are not completely free to use the communicative mechanisms outlined above in their communicative interactions. The use of the mechanisms does not take place in a *"tabula rasa" situation*. Apparently, the mechanisms have to be adapted to a particular conversational context. In such contexts, individual communicative mechanisms can be used strategically if speakers are aware of their effects (this will be discussed further below with reference to Stone 1989). When the goal is to push through an innovation that is seen as something basically new, and it is also important to emphasize this novelty as a desirable, if not necessary, improvement, it is usually necessary to take into account not only a particular conversational setting but the existing narrative that is dominant in a particular (local) context. However, adapted to a given narrative, the mechanisms can be used to transform this narrative.

These "narratives [...] are essentially stories, either in oral or written form" (Fischer and Gottweis 2012: 12). From an interpretative perspective, narratives are based on "causal stories" (Stone 1989) "that indicate specific views of the world and of the relationship between cause and effect" (Barbehön et al. 2016: 241) because through "causal stories" different events, experiences, or observations are placed in relation to one another.

It is assumed that the narrative—like any use of language—does not depict the world neutrally, but rather constitutes it in a particular way, and thus creates possibilities for action and interpretation and, by doing this, for change (Schwartz-Shea and Yanow 2012: 52). Ultimately, what counts is a storyline which is convincing in a given local context as a result of being seen as causally correct and normatively appropriate. Moreover, storylines are the medium through which actors try to impose their view of reality on others, suggest certain social positions and practices, and criticize alternative social arrangements (Hajer 1993: 47).

These causal stories are sometimes conceived as conscious strategies. Deborah Stone (1989) in particular emphasizes these strategic aspects. In this respect, Stone leaves the narrower confines of social constructivism by focusing on "crafted arguments" (see also Fischer 2007: 225) and deliberately developed inventions (Münch 2016: 88). Thus, it should be emphasized that behind narratives there are people and interests who bring the narratives into the world. But these individuals give birth to narratives only within the limits of the available discursive possibilities (Fischer 2003: viii). We would also like to add that the communicative mechanisms outlined above are crucial when attempts are made to transform a narrative strategically.

Accordingly, and as already mentioned above, causal stories have nothing to do with objectivity. To be convincing in communicative interactions, however, they must have what can be called a coherent narrative pattern ("Erzählmuster") or "utterance order" (Barbehön et al. 2016). These are regularly recurrent patterns and forms, speech habitualities that emerge from a collectivity of factually uttered statements. From a purely linguistic point of view, these statements could have been made differently than they in fact were; and for this reason, it says a lot about the given propositional and epistemic context that it only works this way and not differently: that then or there one speaks this way and not in another way—and that one cannot speak successfully in any other way.

(Barbehön et al. 2016: 239)

This pattern is about "the construction of narratives to tell a plausible story about a problem, the development of coalitions of support and the deployment of institutional resources to ensure a response" (Jacobs et al. 2004: 5). Accordingly, a narrative pattern can be understood as a structured unity of certain "generalized narrative elements (forms) that can be applied across different policy contexts" (McBeth et al. 2014: 228). Through these narrative elements "objects are constituted as communicable entities in a given society" (Hajer 1995: 48).

Narrative patterns provide *"basic communicative infrastructures* that enable specific narratives or lines of argumentation in the sense of concrete articulations and make others appear inappropriate or implausible" (Barbehön et al. 2015: 41; translation by the authors). What is more, it is only through such structuredness that narratives convey the impression of clarity, stability, and order (Gottweis 2006: 468). The communicative construction of challenges or problems can thus be understood as a central component of any narrative pattern, as the construction of a problem also indicates the need for action—usually understood as an innovation—because to label something as a problem implies an expectation or demand for something new which will be better. Furthermore, consideration of appropriate problem-solving perspectives does not come without an interpretation of the causes of the problems.

Based on the study by Barbehön et al. (2015, 2016) it seems reasonable that narrative patterns are formed by the following elements[7]:

- To tell a plausible story about opportunities for innovation, the cause of the challenge that is to be addressed by the intended innovation has to be constructed. For instance, the case of Offenbach (see Chapter 11 of this book) shows that the former problem-centered issue of migration had become an issue requiring innovation. The hip label of an "arrival city" was crucial in addressing perceived challenges and bringing about change through innovations driven by a new image of the city shared by more and more people.
- A plausible story of innovation usually implies that past, present, and future (the challenge, the current activities addressing it by means of innovations, and the improvement envisaged) are convincingly related. The change in Offenbach was possible because past, present, and future

were related discursively in a particular way. It was argued that Offenbach has always been a city of migration since it opened up for Huguenot refugees in the 18th century. The image of being a "workers' city" continued in the 19th and 20th centuries, since most of the people who worked in Offenbach during this period came to the city from elsewhere, and its new role as an "arrival city" represented a positive approach to its acting as a gateway city for migration in the greater Frankfurt/Rhine-Main region.

- Knowing the cause of the challenge also means that either structural conditions or actors can be identified as the source of challenges or, to quote Stone (2012: 206), "we look for causes not only to understand how the world works but to assign responsibility for problems." At the same time, when responsibility for a problem and the resulting challenge have been identified, the capacity and willingness to address it have to be assessed. As far as local innovation is concerned, it is important that local actors believe that they have or can develop the capacity to successfully meet a challenge—even in the face of unfavorable structural conditions. This has become empirically manifest in all our case study cities.

- Attributing the responsibility for a challenge to certain actors and identifying the ability to meet the challenge through innovation may imply a distinction between "we" and "they" (the others)—or the opposite: "Let's stand together and work together!"

These four elements of narratives are mixed according to a particular context to yield a certain narrative pattern.

These elements are similar to the "generalized narrative elements" or "elements comprising the form of a narrative" elaborated by proponents of the *narrative policy framework* (see Jones et al. 2014b: 4–7; McBeth et al. 2014: 228; Jones and Radaelli 2015: 341; Shanahan et al. 2017: 175–176). This is not surprising, because we also assume that

> human beings are storytelling animals. [...] And if stories are important for us as individuals, then it also probably follows that stories must play an important role for groups and the collective action in which these groups engage, such as those present in the processes, outcomes, implementation, and design of public policy.
>
> (Jones et al. 2014b: 1)

Thus, it is also important for us to develop a "science of stories" (Jones et al. 2014a) in order to understand policy processes and their outcomes.[8]

A narrative will be plausible and effective in a particular local context if one or several of the above-mentioned communicative mechanisms are used in accordance with the locally prevailing features of the narrative pattern formed by a certain mixture of the "generalized narrative elements" just outlined. A "good story" is not sufficient on its own to change or maintain a local decision about innovation. Only if use is made by means of communicative mechanisms and the "good story" about innovation is related to a narrative pattern that prevails locally will a strategic and practical change become possible. When this is the case, local actors can be convinced to follow the new narrative about how to be innovative in a particular local context. Depending on how the communicative mechanisms are employed and their sequence, it is possible to explain from this perspective why cities differ in terms of innovation.

2.3 Conclusion: innovation from an interpretive perspective

As argued in the introductory chapter of this book, innovation implies an improvement in a given situation. As a result attention must be paid to the local narrative which justified the local way of achieving innovations. These narratives, we assume, guide local practices in a cognitive and normative sense, i.e., by a particular understanding of how the world is functioning and should function. Thus, to elaborate these narratives is to explain why, in a given local context, particular innovations have been possible. These narratives are shaped by communicative mechanisms that are embedded in a certain narrative pattern and act as a hidden structure underlying collective actions. This process can be analyzed in terms of the formation, stabilization, and change of a specific local understanding of why innovations are feasible and desirable. However, the actors involved—and not only outside observers—are able to detect how this "structuring" (Giddens 1984) of their actions is happening.

Considered in this way, communicative mechanisms in combination with local narratives develop explanatory potential. Moreover, by identifying general communicative mechanisms an analytical concept or even social theory can be developed, which can be used in case studies to explain persistence and change in different local practices "structured" (deliberatively) by context-specific narratives.

Notes

1 See also the comments on "interpretivism" in Chapter 1 of this book.
2 For the distinction between arguing and bargaining see Elster (1991: 3): "To argue is to engage in communication for the purpose of persuading an opponent, i.e. to make the other change beliefs about factual or normative matters. [...] To bargain is to engage in communication for the purpose of forcing or inducing the opponent to accept one's claim."
3 With reference to local climate policy, Heinelt and Lamping (2015b: 290) showed that not only the Intergovernmental Panel on Climate Change/IPCC, but also research institutes and studies commissioned by them play a major role in helping authorities to agree on a reference point for further argumentative communication.
4 Heinelt and Lamping (2015b: 291) showed that in local climate policy immunization also took place through references to (a) decisions of upper-level government

to stress that a chosen path is inevitable and (b) different (self-)commitments of cities on CO_2 reduction and other related measures agreed voluntarily at an international level.

5 Concerning local climate policy, Heinelt and Lamping (2015b: 291) drew attention to the example that energy-efficient retrofitting in social housing in the German cities they studied is linked to the issue of payment of housing costs, including heating, of needy people by the municipality. It is argued that expenditures incurred by city hall for these costs are decreased when energy-efficient retrofitting of social housing is financially supported by the municipality.

6 Nevertheless, the communicative mechanisms detected in the "causal field" of developing and implementing innovations are the same as the ones identified by Heinelt and Lamping (2015a; 2015b) in local climate policy—with two exceptions: First, according to the study by Heinelt and Lamping on local climate policy, observing others can lead to the point where what others do can become a reference point for the observer. This could not be detected empirically in the study on local innovations, although this might depend on the ten cases selected. Second, for local climate policy, Heinelt and Lamping found that framing results from a simultaneous interaction involving (a) orientation and justification of actions and decisions, a (self-)explanation and stabilization of (b) ways of dealing with problems, and (c) applying priorities regarding particular measures. By contrast, we found that these are three effects of framing that also act separately.

7 The reflections of Barbehön et al. are empirically inspired by the results of a research project on urban problem discourses or what was seen as the problems of the city in Frankfurt, Dortmund, Birmingham, and Glasgow. The analysis was based on articles in the local press, council minutes, and public statements of various local actors, as well as interviews and group discussions with local politicians, representatives of local interest groups and associations, and local journalists.

While the empirical appearance of individual communicative mechanisms depends on the causal field, the empirical occurrence of the elements or dimensions of narratives seems to depend on their focal points. Thus, in our study of local innovations, one of the elements or dimensions of narratives identified by Barbehön et al. could not be found—namely that local politicians, the municipal administration or the local community (civil society) are ascribed either the role of the main "drivers" or (usually) hesitant sceptics. This may be due to the fact that while responsibility for solving problems (a core topic of the study of Barbehön et al.) is attributed to certain actors or groups of actors, everyone wants to be responsible for the implementation and, above all, the success of innovations. However, as our case study on Leipzig shows (see Chapter 10), such attributions can shift over time and indicate changes in innovations.

8 However, in our study, we could not clearly empirically identify all of the "generalized narrative elements" that are central to the narrative policy framework. This applies first of all to "characters," i.e., individual humans (such as "heroes," "villains," or "victims"), but also to "anthropomorphized abstracts or broad categories" (Jones et al. 2014b: 6). Instead, the acting characters to be traced in detail were too disparate and diverse to be grouped into such abstractions or broad categories. Similarly, while plots of local narratives could be elaborated (see https://www.politikwissenschaft.tu-darmstadt.de/media/politikwissenschaft/ifp_dokumente/arbeitsbereiche_dokumente/methoden_files/cici/CICI_Practitioners_Handbook_20201103.pdf), they were not shared by all actors who otherwise supported the narrative being identified. Meanwhile, according to the narrative policy framework, what is called "setting" and "moral of the story"

corresponds to what we consider to be the most general elements of a narrative (see Section 13.4)—namely, problems or challenges that can and must be addressed and particular courses of action for achieving innovations.

But what distinguishes us most from proponents of narrative policy framework is that we do not share their assumption that generalized statements can also be made about the contents of narratives. We thus belong to those from whom proponents of the narrative policy framework distinguish themselves—namely the

> "brand of narrative scholarship—termed in the policy field 'post-positive'— [which] was [sic] primarily interpretative in the sense that it was [sic] highly descriptive, generally rejected scientific standards of hypothesis testing and falsifiability, and thus lacked the clarity to be replicated and allow for generalization."
>
> (Jones et al. 2014b: 3)

3 Athens

Nikolaos-Komninos Hlepas

3.1 Introduction

Within 100 years, modern Athens evolved from a small town of 7,500 souls into a metropolis which surpassed the one million population mark in 1937. Population growth and industrialization drastically accelerated after World War II. However, traffic and rapidly deteriorating environmental conditions triggered the exodus to the suburbs, while several enterprises moved to new business hubs.

In 2011, one year after the bailout agreement was signed by the Greek government and the Troika, 66,731 Athenians (20.38%) were unemployed. The percentage of people at risk of poverty and social exclusion risk had climbed from 19.3% in 2009 up to no less than 31.8% in 2013 (Petraki 2016: 302–303).

There is no doubt that Athens has been severely hit by the economic crisis and the austerity policies, particularly because it is a place that attracts shopping and entertainment activities from the wider metropolitan area. In 2015, an important part of the commercial and professional surface was standing empty, even though rents and real estate prices had fallen by more than 40%. Furthermore, the city was at the epicenter of an unprecedented refugee influx, since more than one million refugees spent some time in the city, mostly in public spaces.

The search for a new start in the city seems to be an overwhelming concern. Apart from its climate (the sunniest capital city of mainland Europe) and its strategic location, Athens has a considerable level of human capital: about one-third hold a university degree, while an important share have significant technical skills. Moreover, the city is the seat of several important knowledge institutions. Until the outbreak of the Corona pandemic, there were also some signs of economic recovery, especially through the considerable growth of tourism (five million tourists in 2017), while strategic Chinese investment in the Piraeus harbor (the biggest in the Mediterranean Sea, the fifth busiest container harbor in Europe) and a major urban regeneration project (the biggest in Europe)[1] in the former Hellinikon airport could boost growth in the wider metropolitan region.

DOI: 10.4324/9781003084006-3

In smaller cities, the lines of locally embedded politics and debates are visible, while Athens is a mosaic of social worlds (Maloutas 2018) with various debates and "trans-local" politics, where national politics intrude. Municipal elections are extremely party-politicized and some of the most prominent politicians of the country have spent a part of their career in the local political arena of Athens. Debates about major strategies and projects for the metropolitan area usually attract nationwide interest and even involvement.

In the municipality of Athens, it was right after the outbreak of the fiscal crisis, in 2010 that the long-lasting conservative dominance ended and the independent candidate G. Kaminis who was not a professional politician managed to win the election against the incumbent mayor, N. Kaklamanis, a veteran politician from the Nea Dimokratia. Kaminis was re-elected in 2014 and finally resigned in 2019 to move to the national political arena. He was thus following a career path that was similar to some of his predecessors.

3.2 Issues of Innovations

It became obvious during the crisis that neither fiscal consolidation per se nor the existing strategic plans would be sufficient to tackle upcoming challenges. The city had managed to survive, but it had to adapt further and transform into *"a more creative and collaborative city"* as part of Athens' resilience strategy for 2030, which followed a pattern adopted by the global network of "100 Resilient Cities."[2] Against this background, Athens elaborated a set of policy proposals under the title "Advancing Equity for Athens' Resilience" (open, green, proactive, vibrant city). The city followed, beyond legal requirements, a participatory approach that was calling on the insights of hundreds of stakeholders. In this way, Athens drafted its long-term resilience strategy. It includes a set of practicable actions that strengthen "what has made our city stronger: formal and informal networks and alliances."[3] Key instruments have been informal networking and "breaking down silos between administrative departments, different levels of governance, the public and private sectors, civil society and academic institutions" (A3), which were achieved by the innovations outlined in the following.

In July 2013, the municipality created *SynAthina* to strengthen civic engagement and function as a platform for several citizen groups and initiatives as well as regard the notion connected with its name as a reference point in public debates. The name *SynAthina* comes from an ancient Athenian saying meaning that one should not only wait for the help of the goddess Athena but also take their own initiative ("ΣΥΝ ΑΘΗΝΑ ΚΑΙ ΧΕΙΡΑ ΚΙΝΕΙ"). More than 400 different activities have been integrated into this platform, including mobile medical care, kitchens, and laundries for the homeless, low-cost playgrounds in free private or public space. Through this platform support is also offered for these activities, bypassing bureaucratic requirements that often block grassroots mobilization. *SynAthina* received a distinction among 155 initiatives competing for awards within the framework of the international competition "Mayors Challenge," organized by Bloomberg Philanthropies in 2014.[4]

According to assessments of interviewees (A3 and A6), the field of social policy is considered to be the one where the city, given the huge challenges, performed well. It created new infrastructure, like the homeless center, municipal kitchens, social groceries, pharmacies, and medical care centers, etc., most of which have been funded by the European Union (EU) and private donors.

The most remarkable achievement of the city, however, was the response to the refugee influx in 2015, "when the government practically did nothing, apart from encouraging people arriving in the islands from Turkey, to continue their travel right away to Athens" (A3). The city had to face the most disastrous situation for many years, with thousands sleeping in squares, public parks, and sports facilities. Assistance was provided in a chaotic way from NGOs, public services, citizen groups, and even from volunteers coming from Western Europe. Once more, coordination and networking were urgently needed to avoid overlapping activities and wasting of assets, donations, and services.

Therefore, the municipality created the *Athens Coordination Center for Migrant and Refugee Issues* (ACCMR), an e-bridge to cooperation and coordination which is a platform structured on the online city of Athens' digital platform SynAthina (see above). ACCMR was created with a special grant from the Stavros Niarchos Foundation under the "Migration and Refugees Coordination Center and Observatory" project, which is being implemented with the support of *Athens Partnership*, a special bureau launched by the municipality of Athens in 2015 to be a reference point and act as a kind of "innovation juncture" that brings together public services, private foundations, businesses, and NGOs and coordinates several innovative projects. ACCMR aims to support the effective mapping of services and activities concerning migrants and refugees and thus to facilitate the exchange of information and resources between the different stakeholder groups. The detailed mapping of services within the geographical boundaries of Athens offers immediate insight into possible gaps in service provision.

The year 2015 also marked the start of the *"Open Schools"* initiative. The municipality launched a program aiming to transform public schools into centers for sports, creative learning, language courses, and other activities for Athenians and refugees. Not only do these activities enhance language skills and cultural understanding of refugee children, but they also contribute to a direct exchange among newcomers and the resident population at all age levels. The program is also financed by the Stavros Niarchos Foundation and comprises 25 schools offering 170 courses to more than 10,000 participants.

An example of the different activities taking place in these "open schools" is the *"summer camps"* in the city, which are particularly important for lower-income and immigrant/refugee families. They also incorporate creative-educational activities in cooperation with theater groups, artists, and different sorts of volunteers. In 2018 2,400 children participated in this kind of "summer camps" (A6).

In the field of innovative entrepreneurship, a major actor is *"Innovathens,"*[5] the innovation and entrepreneurship hub belonging to the *"Technopolis"* development company of the municipality. Innovathens (IA) was founded in 2014, also taking advantage of a corresponding 15 million budget line in EU funding. IA is also sponsored by Samsung Electronics. IA initially cooperated with the *"Athens Start-Up Business Incubator"* (ΘΕΑ)[6] that had been founded by the Industrial and Commercial Chamber of Athens (EBEA) and is also collaborating, among others, with *Athens Synergies*, a network comprising six entrepreneurial associations listing more than 350 of the most innovative businesses. One key objective of IA is to attract new entrepreneurs and encourage joint projects promoting economic diversification. Meanwhile, IA has been established as an important center for tech transfer, where young entrepreneurs and creative people can effectively mingle with experienced businessmen, academics, and researchers, for the entrepreneurial ecosystem to flourish.

Quite important are also the educational activities of Innovathens and the organization of different events targeting education and training, networking, the exchange of good practices and ideas, and on-site development of innovative solutions.

In the field of digital strategy and policies, the municipality intensified its efforts in 2017 by creating a special post for the Chief Digital Officer (CDO) of the municipality (A5)[7] and renewing cooperation with Bloomberg Associates. Athens municipality was a bureaucratic, introverted organization that was not looking for synergies with other organizations like the universities or the regional level. Within the city administration, organizational fragmentation and bureaucratic silos prevailed, impeding coordination. The municipality created a strategic advisory body, the Athens Digital Council (ADC),[8] to attract capacities, engage relevant actors, mobilize knowledge into active use, and increase transparency (A5). Representatives of ten major companies (such as IBM, Nokia, Oracle, Microsoft, Accenture) and four renowned professors of informatics were selected as members of ADC. In this way, it was expected to receive valuable input both from the market and from knowledge institutions.[9] From this council, Athens' first Digital Roadmap (DR) emerged. The approach differed from many other cities in that the DR set targets for only a year ahead. This annual orientation should help to maintain focus on the plans, projects, and initiatives in the next 12 months.[10] This short-term approach is quite different from the long-term approach of the city's resilience strategy. Apart from the fact that the implementation of short-term targets is usually better in Greece, it is obvious that sustainability and resilience do need a long-term approach, while a digital strategy is also highly dependent on rapid and often unpredictable technological evolution.

The first (announced in 2018) *Digital Roadmap of Athens* focused on five key pillars: *infrastructure* such as networks and internet access for the municipality, public spaces, and residents; *government digital services*; *engagement with citizens*; and *innovation*. The fifth pillar was *digital skills*—particularly to help unemployed people and refugees, and to combat crime. As the CDO put it, this is not an overly ambitious roadmap with expensive projects,[11] but it includes very specific targets and, finally, these features delivered results. For instance, the city has delivered 10,000 opportunities for free digital skills training through schools, libraries, and local community centers, as well as a digital skills center funded by the Microsoft Foundation.[12]

One of the first initiatives provided by the digital strategy was the opening of the *Athens Digital Lab* (ADL)[13]—a research and development lab for smart city solutions. It was launched again with a grant from the S. Niarchos Foundation. Furthermore, it gets support from telecommunications companies. Another big area of work according to the 2018 DR was an investment in fiber optic wireless networks to make Athens a "gigabit society." A large ERP (Enterprise Resource Planning) project and a GIS (Geographic Information System) initiative are also under way. Other initiatives of the ADL included public Wi-Fi hotspots, e-government projects (including e-applications for childcare, which—according to interviewee A6—drastically increased transparency), electronic registration for sport and cultural events, etc. Athens is also in the process of rolling out participatory budgeting as part of the citizen engagement pillar of the DR and a corresponding new citizen app should be launched.

Participatory input from residents is part of another project called "*Interventions in the city*," which is offering financial and technical support to residents and businesses for implementing their own (submitted and approved) proposals for small-scale interventions in the public space of the city. This project is part of a wider program, called *POLIS*² (a pun for "city block"), which provides small financial grants and development support to residents, practitioners, and civil society groups to advance collaborative interventions in the city. POLIS² also includes the project "*Shop in the City Center*" that provides for the exploitation of abandoned shops and aims to give impetus to the degraded areas. The city offers partnerships to small private and social enterprises and organizes targeted interventions in specific areas, such as the "*Theater Square*" (Plateia Theatrou) near to the old City Hall, or the "*Passage of the Merchants*" (Stoa Emporon), one of the 40 historic commercial passages in the city center.[14] A similar approach prevailed in the Kypseli Market, a 90-year-old municipal market that was closed for many years and is a landmark of the formerly bourgeois but currently downgraded Kypseli neighborhood. Following an open deliberation procedure with the residents, this market was renovated and is now running as a joint project of the city and the *Impact Hub Athens* (IHA), which is part of the International Impact Hub Network.[15] IHA is now the manager of the market that is offering spaces to several social enterprises that seek to balance financial benefits with social and environmental goals.

Another innovation refers to the *protection of sculptures in public spaces* and the *active involvement of schools and pupils* therein. This was triggered by the phenomenon of vandalism that was growing since the youth riots of December 2008. Later on, some city officials and the "Technopolis" initiated a project for the protection of about 320 sculptures in public places, combined with the active participation of schools, teachers, and pupils. To this end, the city contacted the region and the Ministry of Education as well as school communities and parents' associations. The responses were positive, while the well-known civic group "Atenistas" also started a parallel initiative for these sculptures. Pertinent activities have been organized and coordinated by the "Technopolis" and an increasing number of schools have been organizing actions, events, and educational activities, while school classes have been "adopting" particular sculptures, taking care of them.

Against this background, it is not surprising that the city of Athens was given the award and the title of the "innovative capital of Europe" by the European Commission in 2018.

3.3 Actors, processes, and structuration through local discourses

The relation between the numerous civic networks and the extremely party-politicized municipality was characterized by mutual distrust. The turning point came in 2010 when Kaminis was elected as mayor, an independent personality who gathered support from PASOK (the governing socialist party), the "Democratic Left" party, the ecologists, and the liberals. This multi-party support meant that Kaminis could not rely on party-internal discipline. The municipal list headed by Kaminis occupied three-fifths of the council seats, but soon this heterogeneous coalition showed some first signs of disintegration. Kaminis had to foster issue-oriented and ad hoc alliances to pass his proposals in the municipal council.

The name of the municipal list headed by Kaminis—namely, "Dikaioma Stin Poli" which means "right to the city"—was inspired from the well-known slogan that was first proposed by Henri Lefebvre in his 1968 book *Le Droit à la ville,* implying that the municipality should open up to its citizens and their ideas.

But this opening could be silently undermined by the municipal civil service. Due to extreme party politicization and long-reaching clientelistic practices, most of the staff had not been selected on merit but according to party affiliation. Therefore, Kaminis could not rely on the loyalty and expertise of the staff. He was obliged to choose a small number of higher civil servants he could actively work with.

Apart from the civil service, there were several municipal entities and enterprises. Some played a crucial role in achieving political change and innovation, such as the municipal radio "9,84," which was important for public debate in and about the city, the "DAEM" development company, and the "Technopolis" (mentioned above). The mayor and the council majority could appoint their boards and CEOs. The city leaders selected some distinguished personalities from the business sector and from universities and some NGOs as managers. In this way, a tradition of exclusive spoils system was broken. The list "Right to the City" partly consisted of candidates coming from the greens, the liberals, and other small parties with close links to civil society; this made it possible for some civic activists and, generally speaking, some personalities who previously barely had any chance in candidate lists of major parties finally to be elected as Athenian councilors. Some of them even became vice mayors.[16] Furthermore, some of these people had an international biography and close ties to big cities in Europe and North America. These were the "cosmopolitans" of the council alongside with high-skilled advisors and collaborators, who served as targets of opposition populists and, at the same time, proved to be the key players for international networking.

The city urgently needed this new, extrovert orientation of its leaders who were searching for good practices and innovations in other countries. The brand name "Athens," the international interest in the Greek crisis and its consequences for the Greek people, networks of the Greek diaspora especially in the USA were some of the factors which facilitated contacts and involvement in several international networks of innovation. The city could take advantage of many new ideas and practices that had already been tested elsewhere and at the same time develop its innovations.

Important actors for innovations were also the universities and other knowledge institutions. In any case, they and their staff have been influential in putting issues on or out of the agenda. *Innova Athens* involved such institutions in innovative actions.

Local chambers also participated in several projects. The Industrial and Commercial Chamber of Athens (EBEA-ACCI), for instance, initiated one of the first business incubators (ΘEA) in cooperation with the municipality in 2014. Some other business unions of new industries and service providers, like the union of Information and Communication Businesses ("SEPE") and the Hellenic Association of Mobile Applications Companies (HAMAC), as well as single businesses, like Samsung, have been very active in several innovative projects.

Innovative actions could not be easily promoted through the civil service of the municipality that was subject to public law restrictions. Municipal enterprises and especially "Technopolis" were the organizational schemes that were far more adequate for flexible and responsive action since they were partially subject to private law. The municipality, however, used a plethora of schemes, such as special bureaus, non-profit companies, and contracting, to facilitate innovative actions. This flexible approach enabled external funding, donations, and several forms of volunteerism and mutual help (described in Section 3.2). Most of the innovations would have been impossible if the city had not bypassed the corridors of municipal bureaucracy. Nevertheless, city leaders have tried to modernize the municipal administration (where a new directory of strategic planning, resilience, innovation, and documentation was introduced), while many issues of innovation have been thoroughly discussed in the municipal council, as well as in committees.

Still, Kaminis was criticized for bypassing the council and the civil service. In reality, a big deal of this criticism simply expressed frustration about the new paths adopted beyond the traditional manner of local politics.

In fact, the city activated all participatory instruments that had been introduced by the Kallikratis Law in 2010 which implied a significant territorial and administrative reform (Tolika 2015). Athens was one of the first cities in Greece where a deliberation committee was constituted and an immigrant council was introduced. Kaminis paid specific attention to developing good ties with all immigrant communities and tried to facilitate the organization of their distinct cultural events. In public debate, he highlighted the legacy of a city that had managed to successfully integrate huge numbers of refugees of Greek origin from Anatolia and internal immigrants, as well as, more recently, big numbers of immigrants from the Balkans and Eastern Europe. From the outset, he strongly opposed the xenophobia of right-wing groups which had been emerging during the economic crisis and which propagated "solidarity with the Greek victims of the crisis" (A13). The city government demonstrated its openness to scrutiny by the wider public by publicizing, inter alia, in real time its financial data (A5). Moreover, Athens was one of the first Greek cities that introduced an independent municipal ombudsman, as provided by the Kallikratis Law.

After the outbreak of the fiscal crisis, relations with citizens became exceedingly difficult especially for the national government but also for lower tiers of government. The first few years were characterized by public rage against politicians, by mass and often violent protests that usually took place in the center of Athens. The city suffered a lot from a series of riots: shops were looted and destroyed, while some emblematic historic buildings were burned. Under these circumstances, new participatory initiatives of the city would face the risk of being transformed into new arenas of chaotic protest or even of fierce clashes with the radical right that had been "kissed back to life" by the crisis. Therefore, the city leadership rather avoided open forms of participation and turned to cooperation with NGOs and citizen groups, especially in social services, where the emerging needs were massive and available resources extremely limited due to unprecedented austerity policies. Since there was a lot of fragmented civic activity in the social sector, the municipality acquired the role of an urgently needed coordinator. The city had to gain the trust of active citizens and NGOs, of potential private donors and partners from the business sector. This was facilitated through transparency measures and through the fact that Kaminis was not seen as a professional politician and many of his collaborators were renowned personalities, contributing their human capital to networking efforts and innovative actions.

The city leadership was filling a policy vacuum that was obvious before it came to power: small-scale problems and challenges that had been left aside by previous city governments. This neglect mobilized a wide spectrum of citizen initiatives for coping with these problems (A10). Their activities were bypassing a municipal administration which ignored them in a relationship characterized by mutual distrust. Nevertheless, this civic or "alternative" mobilization seemed to revitalize public debate, which now focused on small-scale problems and practical solutions instead of the ambitious big-scale strategies which dominated the debate among the major parties before and right after the 2004 Summer Olympic Games (Getimis and Hlepas, 2005). Especially after the outbreak of the fiscal crisis, many citizens' groups began acting as solidarity networks at the neighborhood level. The city leadership focused on collaboration and bundling forces to face the emerging multi-faceted challenges. In fact, the multi-party list "right to the city" had announced from the very beginning that it aimed at overcoming the long-established bureaucratization of the city administration and its alienation from citizens and their actions. Municipal leaders focused on the social cohesion of an increasingly multi-cultural and at the same time impoverished city. New polarizations and new social cleavages were threatening urban coexistence.

Visible implications of the crisis triggered the mobilization of wealthy foundations in the city. This applies not only to Greek foundations, such as the Alexandros Onassis Foundation and the Stavros Niarchos Foundation but also to some major international foundations (Bloomberg, Rockefeller, Microsoft, Open Society), which have increased their activities in Athens. Several other less-known foundations[17] have also offered support to different social projects of the city. It was not only the municipality that took advantage of this support. A big number of NGOs and different local initiatives also benefited from such sponsorships that were urgently needed, since the government froze all state funds earmarked for NGOs in the summer of 2012 (Sotiropoulos and Bourikos 2014: 40). This was the critical moment when some foundations drastically increased their assistance to NGOs, most of which coexisted with informal social networks and self-help groups (Sotiropoulos 2004). Therefore, a revival or vitalization of civil society was, on the one hand, stimulated through the pressure of the fiscal crisis. On the other hand, this was practically made possible by the financial support of the donors mentioned before. Through this self-confident civil society new ideas evolved (like those behind the metaphor "SynAthina") which worked (as shown in Section 3.2).

In the wake of the fiscal crisis, the number of informal groups and networks increased from 81 to 444 between 2012 and 2016 (Sotiropoulos 2017). Informal organizations can easily adapt to changing needs and priorities.

Moreover, they are open to the active participation of their beneficiaries. On the other hand, informal organizations often lack the skills to plan their activities ahead and they are not easy to coordinate. It is quite common that their activities overlap in some areas while they are completely absent elsewhere (Sotiropoulos and Bourikos 2014: 48–49).

For all these reasons, it was necessary and important that the municipality coordinated these groups and actions. To this end, it was necessary to proceed in innovative ways (e.g., through the SynAthina platform) to avoid bureaucratic blockades and, above all, gain trust and attract a plethora of dynamic but often wasted efforts "to do something."

Decision-making power remained to a great extent in the hands of state, state-owned, and local government entities and bodies. However, it is obvious that considerable parts of *non-decision-making power*—particularly regarding agenda setting through public debates—shifted to private foundations, private enterprises, NGOs, and citizen networks. Furthermore, politicians, parties, public bodies, knowledge institutions, and the "traditional" media may still dominate in the field of *ideological power* in the sense of "shaping [...] *perceptions*, conceptions and preferences *in* such a way that [people] accept their role *in* the existing order of things" (Lukes 2005: 25; emphasis in the original text). However, a significant share of this power has shifted to social media, with civil society becoming, therefore, more pluralistic (A8). Ongoing mobility and international experience of many Athenians increased the awareness for international discourse at the local level, and the city too joined a series of innovative networks (resilient cities, mayors for inclusive growth, etc.). The reference to resilience and the "right to the city" are examples of this interpretation of ideas in local discourses.

That the city survived a series of crises, proving its resilience through various kinds of challenges and pressures, despite growing concerns about security in some downtown areas, is obvious from the current public discourse. It is quite characteristic that candidate mayors for elections in May 2019 promised to keep and further develop successful innovations, such as the SynAthina network, while some of the key initiators of innovations were included in candidate lists for the council. Candidates seemed to be eager to prove their openness toward citizens ("right to the city") and implicitly (or explicitly) distance themselves from patronage and party-politicized administrations of the past.

3.4 Key findings

Greece has been experiencing an unprecedented crisis that has persisted for several years. Municipalities in big cities had to respond to rapidly growing needs for assistance with rapidly diminishing resources. Athens was one of the most heavily affected cities, while it was also the main reception gate during the refugee influx of 2015. In November 2018, the European Commission awarded Athens with the European Capital of Innovation title. Reactions in the city were mixed since the feeling of urban decline and social alienation still seemed to prevail. However, a wide spectrum of different citizen groups could identify themselves with some of the actions that were the reasons for this Innovation Award.

The starting point for the development of many innovative actions was in 2010 when the old municipal establishment was swept out of power, while the new leadership avoided party politicization and clientelistic practices and was inspired by Lefevre's book *Right to the City* signaling the willingness to offer all inhabitants the right to participate and cooperate within a new scheme of open urban governance. This approach was a challenge to the mindset guiding the actors of previous municipal governments (A 13): according to their perceptions, Athens would be a "hopeless case" and the municipality would not be "the master of its own city" since central governments would take the most important decisions for the capital and control the resources. The only realistic way to gain legitimacy and support would be political patronage. A high level of social cohesion would not be feasible in a big city that is increasingly becoming multi-cultural, especially since the newcomers are not willing to integrate and consider Athens to be just an intermediary, uncomfortable station on their way to Northern Europe (A13).

As opposed to this approach, the new municipal governance since 2010 mobilized open-minded personalities that increased awareness at the local level for international discourses: the city joined a series of innovative networks (resilient cities, mayors for inclusive growth, etc.) and implemented good practices. The reference to resilience and the "Right to the City" are examples of this interpretation of ideas in local discourses. Besides, the "SynAthina" metaphor (the label of a platform that integrated more than 400 grassroots activities) expresses a new approach to local politics through the discursive development of reference points for (further) innovative practices, just as it happened with the e-bridge for migrants and refugees (AC-CMR) and the POLIS initiative. The communicative mechanism of "issue relabeling" promoted "open schools" and the protection of sculptures because these ideas, existing in the past, were linked to the new ideas which work and are seen as an improvement. *Innovathens* and the city's new digital strategy are the result of framing insofar as they have been guided by the new approach of how things should be done in Athens.

Summing up, it seems that current public discourse in Athens is gradually recognizing that the city survived various kinds of challenges and pressures due to the ability of actors to develop a new understanding of how things can be improved even under quite bad conditions (Vamvakas 2019).

Traditional self-understanding of Athens as a "capital city" and a "gate of innovations for a wider area," as well as the openness and resilience characterizing the city throughout its modern history, has certainly offered a favorable frame of mind, an already existing basis that served as a basis for a shift in public debate that facilitated innovations. Without the exceptional circumstances of the crisis, however, it is barely imaginable that this wider variety of different innovations would have been accepted and implemented.

It is an open question whether these innovations will prove to be sustainable when in the city the period of successive crises is definitively over and the pendulum swings back to "normality."

Notes

1 https://thehellinikon.com/en/ (last checked October 20, 2020).
2 https://resilientathens.wordpress.com/ (last checked October 20, 2020).
3 https://resilientathens.files.wordpress.com/2017/07/athens_resilience_strategy_-_reduced_pdf-compressed.pdf (last checked October 27, 2020).
4 See https://www.bloomberg.org/program/government-innovation/mayors-challenge/ (last checked October 27, 2020)
5 https://www.innovathens.gr/innovathens-en-2/ (last checked October 20, 2020) and interview with A2.
6 http://www.theathensincube.gr/ (last checked October 20, 2020). ΘEA also organized the first and the second Innovation Festival in Athens in November 2017 and 2018, with the cooperation of the Attika Region and of the Attika Region Development Fund.
7 The first post for a Chief Digital Officer was created in New York by Mayor Michael Bloomberg in 2011.
8 The Athens Digital Council was one of the five main innovations that were given as reasons for the European Capital of Innovation Award 2018 that was bestowed on Athens (see below).
9 Interviewee A5 stated:

> I told these companies: "We are not here for a contract, we're not here to do business, we're here for strategy—to help each other." It wasn't something that was very easy to do because a lot of people had to change mentalities. We had to learn to talk with big companies. We didn't have that mentality inside the municipality. The businesses had to learn to talk with the local authorities without discussing contracts and sales. And the universities had to talk more [openly] about what they are doing.

10 Interviewee A5 stated: "It's very easy to have a strategy for 2030, and then you're doing nothing—waiting for 2029."
11 As emphasized by Interviewee A5: "We're not discussing hyperloops or drones or even electric cars, which are good for other cities but not for Athens. If you have a lot of unemployed people, hyperloop is not something that's going to solve their problems."
12 http://www.kathimerini.gr/956142/gallery/epikairothta/ellada/h-e3ypnh-oikia-ths-lelas-karagiannh (last checked October 20, 2020).
13 https://www.athensdigitallab.gr/en (last checked October 20, 2020).
14 https://www.athensvoice.gr/life/urban-culture/athens/445284_poli2-o-dimos-athinaion-anoigei-tin-poli-stoys-katoikoys-tis (last checked October 27, 2020).
15 https://impacthub.net/; https://athens.impacthub.net/en/our-partners/ (both last checked October 27, 2020).
16 In the new posts, the following were nominated: as Vice-Mayor for Refugees and Immigrants the well-known activist Lefteris Papagiannakis; as Vice-Mayor for Children the renowned child psychologist Maria Iliopoulou; as Vice-Mayor for Urban Green and Urban Resilience the green activist Prof. Eleni Myrivili; as Vice-Mayor for Civil Society and Innovation the well-known activist Amalia Zeppou.
17 Such foundations are, for instance, the Laskarides Foundation, the Goulandris Foundation, the Theocharakis Foundation, and the Mpodosakis Foundation.

4 Bensheim

Hubert Heinelt

4.1 Introduction

Bensheim is a city with about 40,000 residents. The number of residents increased from 39,680 in 2006 to 42,999 in 2019, by about 8%, which underlines the dynamics of growth.[1] In the past, Bensheim was a place to which people moved because they liked to live there. This is evident from the number of manor houses of noble families from the surrounding rural area who built these houses centuries ago. Furthermore, at the beginning of the 20th century a number of Art Nouveau villas[2] were built in the city for rich people who wanted to enjoy the mild climate and beautiful landscape on the eastern edge of the Upper Rhine valley called the "Bergstraße."

The city is located in the south of the German federal state of Hesse where the metropolitan regions of Frankfurt/Rhine-Main and Rhine-Neckar (including the cities of Heidelberg, Mannheim, and Ludwigshafen) overlap.[3] It has good connections to two major motorways as well as to the German and trans-European railroad system. Furthermore, Frankfurt airport is only about 50 km away, which means that it can be reached by car within 30–45 minutes via the two motorways.

Between 2016 and 2019, the majority in the city council was formed by the Christian Democrats, the Greens, and a local voter association, called "Bürger für Bensheim" ("Citizens for Bensheim"). Between 2001 and 2016, the majority in the council had been formed by the Christian Democrats and the Greens only.[4] After the local elections in March 2021 a coalition was formed by the Christian Democrats, Social Democrats (SPD), and Liberals (FDP). It is unlikely that these new majorities in the council will bring about fundamental changes in the innovations described below.

4.2 Innovations issues

Bensheim appears to be a case where a number of "material or social artifacts [...] are perceived by [local] observers as both novel and an improvement" (Braun-Thürmann 2005: 6), but not as something which local actors

DOI: 10.4324/9781003084006-4

regard as intriguingly innovative. Instead, these changes and improvements are understood as something happening in Bensheim as a matter of course.

Recent innovations that are understood as something Bensheim is doing as a matter of course are, for instance, the development of a local climate policy by the "Masterplan 100% Klimaschutz" ("Masterplan for 100% climate protection").[5] Local climate policy in Bensheim refers to energy consulting, decentralized energy production and supply, subsidies for installing solar panels financed by the municipality in addition to the programs of upper-level government, and promotion of cycling through bicycle rental, e-bike sharing, and special lanes for bicycles (B12, B14, and B16).

The local energy supplier GGEW (Gruppen-Gas- und Elektrizitätswerk Bergstraße AG)[6] plays a crucial role in these and other activities in the field of climate policy. The GGEW is jointly owned by the municipality of Bensheim and eight neighboring municipalities. All members of the council and the municipal administration who were interviewed emphasized that it is crucial to be in a position to use the local energy supplier as an instrument for implementing innovations. This is relevant for local climate policy where the GGEW offers an infrastructure for fueling electric cars,[7] organizes vehicle sharing for electric cars as well as e-bike sharing, invests in renewable energy, and offers local homeowners a program for installing solar panels on the roofs of their homes and renting them. Furthermore, the GGEW is developing a high-speed internet for the city and beyond.[8] Finally, it runs both the outdoor and indoor public swimming pools and covers (at least partially) the costs of this public facility from its profits.

Another (innovative) instrument of the municipality for urban development is the "Marketing- und Entwicklungs-Gesellschaft Bensheim GmbH"/ MEGB (Marketing and Development Company Bensheim Ltd), an enterprise completely owned by the municipality.

> The core business of MEGB Ltd. is the marketing of commercial properties in Bensheim… Our strategic goal is the positioning of Bensheim as a leading business center in southern Hesse. We initiate cross-company projects and strengthen networks in Bensheim in order to support companies in the competition for customers and employees.[9]

Furthermore, MEGB manages municipal, private, and commercial buildings, including three parking garages. The profits from these activities and their sound financial basis make it possible for MEGB to buy, rebuild, and renovate houses, especially in the city center to make it more attractive. This is currently being undertaken in the case of a number of buildings which are important for making the market square more lively. "Access to real estate is considered critical to the strategic development of the inner city," as stated by a senior employee of the MEGB (in an interview carried out by the research team).

The crucial role of MEGB as an instrument of the municipality for reaching its political objectives and achieving innovations—particularly in respect to not only economic, but also urban development—is expressed in the close cooperation between MEGB and the municipality, particularly the (former) mayor and the planning department. For each project, there is clear responsibility on the part of one person, who acts as a contact person for the enterprise (interview partner B1; see also below). The use of MEGB as an instrument for making the city center more attractive is perceived as an innovation. However, according to most people interviewed, the major innovation achieved by MEGB is the development of the "Stubenwald," which is not merely a business park like those of many other cities. Since 2008, it has also been developed into a "campus" where the sites of companies have been deliberatively embedded in a particular infrastructure (B15) including a business hotel, sport facilities for (young) people employed there (a fitness studio, a bowling alley, and indoor climbing wall), as well as a kindergarten for their children. Furthermore, the campus concept of the business park strives to support "thinking that goes beyond one's own company at the location" (B15).[10]

For the municipality, it is clear (without much discussion) that it involves citizens in urban planning beyond the legal requirements. There have been a number of project-based forms of citizen participation in urban planning. This applies to individual development plans ("Bebauungspläne") for new construction areas and the development of the city center ("Innenstadtdialog 'Bensheim 2030'") or parts of the city (such as in Bensheim-Auerbach—as mentioned by B9) initiated by the municipality. In addition, a public dialogue about the future of the city is organized by an independent "Bürgernetzwerk" (citizens' network). The latter states in its website: "With the citizens' network, the voice of the citizens gains weight in [...] debates, because today without the wisdom of the many, no satisfactory answers can be found for the future."[11] Such forms of citizen participation would be seen in other contexts (other cities) as innovations. In Bensheim they are not perceived as a novelty, but as a matter of course, because it is taken for granted that they lead to better policy outcomes. Nevertheless, there have been calls in the citizenry in recent years, especially in connection with inner-city development, to expand citizen participation and to effectively take into account the positions thereby expressed in council decisions (see Section 4.4).

Although the Parktheater was built in 1968, this municipal theater and the events taking place there are still innovative in cultural terms. It is the only theater between Darmstadt and Heidelberg. It is operated by the municipal administration, or, more precisely, the "Eigenbetrieb Stadtkultur," the programming/repertoire of which is performed by touring theater groups, cabaret ensembles, musicians, etc.

The Parktheater is also a venue where two events of nationwide significance take place once a year (except for the current restrictions due to the Corona pandemic): the "Woche junger Schauspieler" ("Week of Young

Actors") organized since 1996 in cooperation with the Deutsche Akademie der Darstellenden Künste (German Academy of Performing Arts, which is based in Bensheim) and (since 1986) the Gertrud Eysoldt Ring Drama Arts Award presented annually in recognition of outstanding achievement in acting.

For many years, the municipality of Bensheim has been organizing exhibitions in its buildings where artists—mainly from Bensheim and the surrounding area—present their art.[12]

The creation of the "Eigenbetrieb Stadtkultur"—together with a similar Eigenbetrieb established as childcare facilities—can be considered an innovation in Bensheim (B15). Although Eigenbetriebe were already common in German public administration in the past,[13] their expansion in numbers since the 1990s is a particular form of implementing New Public Management ideas in Germany. Eigenbetriebe enable greater flexibility in terms of investment and staffing, facilitate swift decision-making, and allow performance control through special accounting mechanisms, while ensuring control by the municipal administration and council. The control is exercised by a "Betriebskommission," a special committee of the municipality.[14]

The Eigenbetriebe are organizationally separate from the municipal administration and can be seen as institutional innovations. This also applies to the MEGB (formally established in 1999/2000; B15) and the GGEW as municipal enterprises which are either owned only by the municipality of Bensheim or jointly owned by Bensheim and various neighboring municipalities.

An example of innovations in social services stemming from the local (civil) society is the "Hospiz-Verein Bergstraße," a legally registered hospice association founded by citizens of Bensheim. "Since 1994, founders and members, volunteers and full-time employees, friends and supporters have made extensive efforts to help the dying and their relatives in Bensheim and the surrounding area."[15] About 100 volunteers and 15 full-time employees work for this association.[16] The Hospice Bergstraße also belongs to this association. "The Hospice Bergstraße was opened in 2010. [It] provides a home for people in the final days of their lives, who are suffering from an advanced, incurable disease and cannot be cared for at home."[17]

Another innovative organization which has emerged from local (civil) society is the "Familienzentrum Bensheim" (Family Center Bensheim), established in 1996 by 13 women as a self-help organization. A core activity at the beginning was a "nanny exchange" and then the arrangement of childminders. Currently the association has 112 employees, runs kindergartens, and has expanded to two neighboring municipalities.[18]

Furthermore, there is the "Bürgerhilfe Bensheim" (what is called a "time bank" in Greece; see Section 12.2) which was established in the legal form of an association in 1997. Two years later it had 150 and currently 180 members.[19] Its aim is to organize self-help among its members by registering the time (hours) members invest in helping others which can in turn (as a kind of internal currency) be exchanged for help to be provided by other members.

The "Bensheimer Tafel" is also perceived by locals as an innovation. Its aim is to donate food to people who cannot secure for themselves the necessities for daily living due to low income or other debilitating circumstances. It is a legally registered association and currently has about 220 members, who are active in collecting food donations and distributing them to needy people.[20]

These organizations are only a part of local associations supporting the social and cultural cohesion of the town.

4.3 Actors, processes, and structuralization through local discourses

For the local business sector, the "Wirtschafts-Vereinigung Bensheim" (Bensheim Economic Association) is a relevant collective actor for interest intermediation. This association with about 300 members has been in existence for 70 years.[21] It "sees itself as a strong umbrella organization" representing the local economy "in constant dialogue with parliaments, authorities, political parties, the press, trade unions, business associations, chambers, churches, schools and universities." Furthermore, it considers itself an influential participant in local politics.[22] Indeed, the mayor and other members of the municipal executive board are not only actively involved in meetings of this organization; the municipality is a formal member of the organization. As emphasized by one of the interview partners (B3), the mayor and other members of the municipal executive board are willing to listen to representatives or even single members of the Bensheim Economic Association—particularly those from larger enterprises (as important employers and payers of local business tax; B3). The current chairman of this local business association is a manager of Dentsply Sirona and one of his deputies is a manager of the pharmaceutical company Reckeweg (for these two local companies, see below). The other deputy is the executive director of the GGEW (see above) and the treasurer is the executive director of the local savings bank (Sparkasse Bensheim).[23]

Another organization with strong links to the local business community is "Bensheim aktiv" (Bensheim active). Although local shop owners, owners of restaurants, and handicraft businesses in particular are members of Bensheim aktiv, this organization is open to all who are interested in enhancing the city's profile and its downtown area in particular.[24] Consequently, there are overlapping memberships with the Bensheim Economic Association. As a result, this organization functions as an intermediator of interests within a broad membership and between the membership and local government. It organizes the annual Christmas market as well as a number of other events.

There is also the "Verkehrsverein Bensheim." This organization has existed since 1879 and offers a platform for collaboration between the municipality (the mayor is the chairman of the association) and representatives of local retail, viticulture, and tourism as well as interested citizens. It organizes events (such as the "Bürgerfest" and the "Winzerfest"; see below), "all of which have one goal: to maintain the attractive quality of life in Bensheim and make the city even more attractive—to its citizens as well as to visitors."[25]

The close relations among these organizations and among their members as well as between them and local government have resulted in an informal "Allianz der Macher" ("alliance of doers"; B3) which facilitates swift decisions—ranging from the organization of different events (concerts, etc.) to exchanges or sale of land—for example, for the building of an urgently needed kindergarten. This kind of relationship among actors in Bensheim is characterized by a high level of reliability and trust (B15)—or as one interview partner (B3) phrased it: "you [...] know very quickly who is doing what and who is doing nothing."

However, this informal "alliance of doers" is complemented by a self-confident citizenry (B13), widespread civic engagement of the inhabitants (B10 and B11), and a high level of willingness of people to talk openly. This constellation ensures—as emphasized by a local member of an upper-level parliament (B4) in an interview—that there are only a few people who strongly disagree with the innovations mentioned above that have been achieved in the city. If criticism of the innovations mentioned is expressed, it concerns MEGB and the Eigenbetriebe, because these have a direct control of the council. Besides, the MEGB is criticized because its managing director is the brother of the mayor.[26]

However, as interview partners explain (e.g., B1, B5, and B12), decisions on the innovations described above have been more or less non-controversial. First, innovative organizations, such as the Bürgerhilfe Bensheim, the Hospice Bergstraße, and the Familienzentrum Bensheim, were initiated from "below," i.e., by active citizens. This means that they were established at the beginning without (financial) support from the municipality and without controversial public debate. Financial support from the municipality usually comes later when these initiatives receive backing by people locally—or the municipality supports initiatives more as a mediator than through financial means (B11). Second, and related to the first point, insofar as an innovation is perceived as *an improvement*, hardly anybody can be against it. Instead, when an innovation is perceived as an improvement, its benefits can easily be emphasized and possible (re-)distributing effects can be neglected. In cases in which (re-)distributing effects were highlighted in a controversial way, such as expenditures for cultural innovations or activities (the theater or the galleries, for example) or the foundation of the MEGB, their contributions to the achievement of what is broadly desired (see below) can and have often been highlighted.

Against this background, the innovations in Bensheim were brought about through processes which differ from "ordinary" local politics, which are centered in public perceptions on controversial debates and decisions of the municipal council about individual development plans or major investments (for instance, the renovation or pulling down and new construction of municipal buildings).

That the innovations mentioned in Section 4.2 were achieved may have depended on structural conditions outlined at the beginning of this chapter. However, these conditions were created or mobilized as potentials by local decisions. Such decisions are collective choices underpinned by particular interpretations of what could and what should be done or a widely shared understanding of what is desirable in a given context and what is also perceived as achievable (see Chapters 1 and 2).

In Bensheim a basic standard of appropriateness—which also expresses a particular normative orientation—is the widely shared image of being and remaining a city which is on the one hand a place with a flourishing economy but *not* based on "stinking factories" ("stinkende Fabriken"; statement of interview partner B2) and on the other hand a place where people can wholeheartedly say (in the local dialect): "Hier bin ich dehaam!" ("Here I am at home!").[27] This image has been stable for a long time. This is illustrated by the fact that there was strong resistance to the building of a factory by the Freudenberg Company in the early 20th century, resistance which was ultimately successful (B2). About 100 years later, there was again resistance in the city to the building of a logistics center by Tchibo, one of the biggest German companies in the consumer goods and retail business sector (particularly coffee). Such a large logistics center and the jobs it created would have attracted the interest of most other places. This was not the case in Bensheim, because the "aesthetic appearance" (B2) of such a center (in addition to noise and a great deal of heavy traffic) did not fit the image of the city where other companies had recently arrived. This applied particularly to the Stubenwald business park where the planned logistics center was to be located. Furthermore, it was emphasized (by B12) that the location of a logistics center was (and still is) not desirable because a "lot of land is consumed—without the creation of many jobs." This was underlined with numbers by a senior employee of the MEGB (B15): "We sell land for commercial use only when we get at least one new employee per 150 m^2." And another interview partner (B14) stated: "We are looking for clean and innovative enterprises that fit in with one another."

One of the two European headquarters of the Japanese car maker Suzuki has been located in this business park since the early 2000s. Suzuki moved to Bensheim from the neighboring city of Heppenheim because the municipality there was not able to provide assurances that the company could expand its site.

The same applied to a site of the TE Connectivity company now located in this business park. It moved from Langen (near Frankfurt) to Bensheim in 1979/1980 because the company could not expand, while the municipality of Bensheim was able to provide the required land. TE Connectivity was a part of Tyco International Ltd. and now has about 80,000 employees worldwide.[28] The TE Connectivity site in Bensheim is "the heart of the automobile industry end market" for TE Connectivity Ltd. where 500 electrical and mechanical engineers and precision mechanics work at the company's Technology and Development Center.[29] A total of 1,014 people were employed by TE Connectivity in Bensheim in 2017.[30] The company's employees are from 28 different countries with 20% of the workforce expatriates based at the TE Connectivity location in Bensheim (B11) for a limited period of time.

Furthermore, Dentsply Sirona has a strong link to Bensheim. This company, "the world's largest manufacturer of professional dental products and technologies," was established in 2016 through a merger between Dentsply International and Sirona Dental Systems. The latter traces its roots to Siemens Reiniger Werke AG, which in 1963 established "a production facility at Bensheim [...] which today remains a key production facility and includes the Sirona Dental Systems' Center of Innovation."[31] "In addition to manufacturing a large part of Dentsply Sirona's equipment portfolio, the core of its research and development team is located in Bensheim. Almost half of the company's 600 engineers and scientists worldwide work in Bensheim."[32] A total of 1,770 people were employed by Dentsply Sirona in Bensheim in 2017.[33] With approximately 15,000 employees and operations all across the globe, Dentsply Sirona, listed on the US NASDAQ technology stock exchange, achieved sales of around US$4 billion in 2015.[34]

Although it employs only 220 people, the Reckeweg pharmaceutical company is another global player based in Bensheim—namely, in homeopathic medicine. Of its products, 90% are exported.[35] However, unlike the sites of other global companies, Reckeweg can trace its roots locally.

The *Sanner* company, which manufactures plastic parts for the packaging of pharmaceutical products, also employs only 225 people in Bensheim, but around 500 worldwide—e.g., in the USA, China, India, and Indonesia.[36]

Another enterprise in the high-tech sector formerly located in Bensheim was SAP System Integration (SI). However, SAP decided to close this site in Bensheim in 2018 and concentrate activities in Eschborn near Frankfurt. This resulted in the loss of 600 jobs in the city.

The closure of the SAP site shows that even cities that flourish economically such as Bensheim may potentially lose jobs, even though their overall economic situation may appear to be good. The same applies to the decision by Suzuki in November 2018 to move half of its 360 employees in Bensheim to Esztergom, a Suzuki site in the north of Hungary.[37] At the same time, Dentsply Sirona announced job cuts at its sites around the globe to reduce costs. However, it remained unclear to what extent the site in Bensheim would be affected by this decision.[38] These decisions are the reverse side of the coin of having global players competing on world markets located in the city. These companies have to ensure they remain competitive globally by choosing locations for their business activities that offer the most benefits and are able (and willing) to move from one site to another within a relatively short period of time. Consequently, it is a permanent local challenge even for thriving cities to remain a "sticky place" (Markusen 1996) to which fluid global capital is attracted. The city of Bensheim has so far demonstrated its ability to succeed in this respect on the basis of institutional and cultural innovation developed through discourse about the current circumstances the city finds itself in and opportunities for its further development.

As previously mentioned, it is not just a widely shared perception Bensheim has of itself that it is and ought to remain a thriving city. This image, reproduced by a particular narrative or tale, also emphasizes the idea that the city is a place where people feel at home. This refers not only to the locals who have lived in the city for generations, but also to people who have moved to Bensheim.

This component of Bensheim's image or self-description is empirically underpinned by the fact that there are (as mentioned at the beginning of this chapter) a number of manor houses and Art Nouveau villas in the city. And today it is not only employees of the companies mentioned above who settle in Bensheim. The city is also attractive as a place to live for those working in the Frankfurt/Rhine-Main and Rhine-Neckar agglomeration. It is reasonable to argue that these people not only benefit from globalization economically, but a lot of them are also embedded in global networks in their professional (and private) lives. This is underpinned by the following statements by interview partners: "Bensheim is a livable town full of cosmopolitans" (B3) and "Bensheim has it [in respect to urban life], and it is a Lilliput Frankfurt" (B5).

However, Bensheim is an attractive place to live not only because of the mild climate, beautiful landscape, or good access by road or train. The city is also an attractive place, particularly for young families, because, over the years, the education infrastructure has been developed in a striking way. This applies to grammar schools (Bensheim has five of them) as well as to a large number of facilities for and different forms of childcare. The municipality spends 10% of its annual budget on the latter (B1), which demonstrates the high priority given to this kind of social infrastructure by the local government. Furthermore, the quality of life has been improved by local festivals as well as gastronomic events and small shops "which can also be found in Prenzlauer Berg" (i.e., a trendy district in Berlin), as emphasized in an article in a well-known German weekly newspaper.[39]

Furthermore, the whole area around Bensheim formed by the two metropolitan regions of Frankfurt/Rhine-Main and Rhine-Neckar makes the place attractive—particularly for expatriates and also "young urban professionals" employed by the global players located in Bensheim (B11)—because Frankfurt as well as the various medium-sized cities in these regions (e.g., Heidelberg, Mannheim, Mainz, and Wiesbaden) offer a great deal in terms of culture, dining, shopping, etc. As a manager of a global company with a site in Bensheim (B11) made clear: "When we want to hire such people we do not talk about Bensheim but Frankfurt and the surrounding area."

However, the social composition of the city seems to have been split in the past as well as in recent times. Nevertheless, the different components complement each other and have become more and more intermingled.

On the one hand, there have been the "locals" (as argued by interview partners B2 and B18). To come to be or to be recognized as a "local" (as stated by interview partner B2), people have to point to the fact that their family has been living in the city for two generations (Arche-). Typically, "locals" are Catholics, take part in the activities of the local Catholic-affiliated Kolpingfamilie,[40] and are members of the Bensheimer Karneval-Gesellschaft/BKG (Bensheim Carnival Society). The "locals" not only dominate these associations but are influential in other local associations as well. This applies only to some degree to the collective actors mentioned above (i.e., the Wirtschafts-Vereinigung Bensheim and Bensheim aktiv in particular). Nevertheless, a few "locals" from local retail, handicraft businesses, gastronomy, and tourism number among these collective actors.

On the other hand, there are those who have moved to the city. At the beginning of the 20th century, these were the people who built and resided in their Metzendorf villas. Even at that time, these people demanded development of the educational infrastructure[41] and engaged in cultural activities. They were followed in the period immediately after World War II by Germans who had to move from the former eastern parts of the German Reich to the West as refugees and (by chance) arrived in Bensheim. Finally, people who moved to Bensheim in recent decades due to the city's location, its educational infrastructure, and cultural events as well as the job opportunities both in the city and in the region are included in this category as well. However, most of the recent arrivals do not get "down to the nitty-gritty" ("Klein-Klein"; B18) of local politics, i.e., they do not engage in local politics mediated through party organizations and focus on debates and decision-making in the municipal council (as stated by most of the interview partners)—as has also been observed by studies in other places (for Barcelona, see Magre et al. 2016 as well as Vallbé and Magre 2017). Instead, the recent arrivals simply live in Bensheim and—if at all—become active according to their interest in particular local associations. These can be sports clubs, but also associations such as the Family Center Bensheim and the Hospiz-Verein Bergstraße. However, these associations are also places where the recent arrivals meet and interact with the "locals."

However, recent arrivals have also been involved with locals in referendums on controversial building projects—namely, the demolition and new construction or renovation of the "Bürgerhaus" (an event center) and the redesign of the marketplace.[42] Characteristic of this form of direct democracy, however, is that it does not require a long-term commitment to the "nitty-gritty" of local politics.

Nevertheless, the "locals" are able to strongly influence or even dominate local politics related to party organizations and are strongly focused on policy debates and decisions in the municipal council. However, similarly to the former "newcomers," the recent arrivals are those who are more open to innovation than the "locals" (B11) and introduce new ideas and the know-how to implement innovations effectively. Furthermore, they have a particular understanding of *how the world functions*, which can become meaningful in the local context and thus relevant to local decision-making—above all, regarding innovations. This applies particularly to senior staff of the "global players" who are usually members of the Wirtschafts-Vereinigung Bensheim and part of the so-called alliance of doers. In this capacity they are actively involved in local politics, although not so much in politics centered on the "nitty-gritty" of the work done within the municipal council. The "locals" are those in the city who strongly define local standards of appropriateness and uphold the normative dimensions of what innovation should look like—or *how the (local) world should function*. Both functions, namely,

- having and adapting a particular understanding of *how the world functions* to local conditions;
- upholding a local understanding of *how the (local) world should function* and readjusting it to changing circumstances

can be complementary because both contribute to the development of a common image and goal shared by the local society, namely, that Bensheim is and should remain an economically flourishing city where people feel at home.

4.4 Key findings

Without the shared understanding that Bensheim is and should be an economically flourishing city where people feel at home and like to live, the successful development of the innovative activities (outlined in Section 4.2) and the settlement and development of the local businesses described (in Section 4.3) would not be imaginable.

In developing this shared image and resulting goals and decisions, not only formal networks, such as the Wirtschafts-Vereinigung Bensheim, but informal ones, i.e., the "alliance of doers," are important. Events such as the Winzerfest in the first week of September,[43] the Bürgerfest (citizens festival) in June, and the Christmas market in December are important, but also particular locations, such as the "Kirchberghäuschen," a wine bar on top of a hill above the town, where large numbers of people gather together and have the opportunity to exchange views in a relaxed but serious way (as emphasized by B4, B5, B10, and B14). This applies even more to the "Gala" after the annual award of the Gertrud Eysoldt Ring (a dramatic arts award), where the number of people involved is far smaller (if not limited). Although this event is different in terms of its audience and appearance from those just mentioned, it offers particular opportunities for identifying people in interesting positions and with similar or even compatible worldviews and, as a result, for engaging in networking (B14). Reflecting on all these different events and locations as well as on their functions led one of the interview partners to argue: "Civil society works in Bensheim" (B5).

Nevertheless, a vibrant civil society exchanging ideas and working out reasons why they should be implemented at the events mentioned above and on a daily basis at particular locations does not ensure the ability to develop a common understanding in the local community of what should be done (and why) for the development of the city, because there is a high degree of fluctuation among the citizens involved. This also applies to the formal ways in which citizens take part (as argued by B15). This is different from collective actors such as Bensheim aktiv or the Bensheim Economic Association, which enable ongoing communicative interaction. This is similar to forms of citizen participation such as the Bürgernetzwerk. As argued by a member of it (B18), it is crucial that this initiative be, on the one hand, organized in groups working on a particular topic for a longer period of time (i.e., not just occasionally) and involve, on the other hand, individuals as well as collective actors—such as Bensheim aktiv or the Familienzentrum Bensheim—who are willing and able to take active part in the implementation of ideas developed by the network partners. Thus, an infrastructure or a "core of civil society" is necessary for developing a shared understanding of what can and should be done. Such a "core of civil society comprises a network of associations that institutionalizes problem-solving discourses on questions of general interest inside the framework of organized public spheres" (Habermas 1996: 367).

The existence of a commonly or at least widely shared image (that Bensheim is a city that is thriving economically where people feel at home and like to live) does not mean that there are no striking controversies or debates regarding problems faced by the city. Striking controversies emerged in Bensheim, particularly concerning decisions which implied obvious visual as well as financial effects—such as the decisions of the municipal council to renovate or pull down two important municipal buildings (the "Bürgerhaus" and "Haus am Markt"). However, these notable controversies were mainly set in motion by citizens who play a crucial role in decision-making processes neither in the municipal council nor in the politically influential local collective actors and informal "alliance of doers." Rather, these citizens criticized the informal influence of local collective actors (including the Bürgernetzwerk) as illegitimate and questioned their status as the "core of civil society." Nevertheless, this did not call into question the aforementioned image of Bensheim, but rather referred to core components of this image—for example, the "Schorschblick" (the preferably unobstructed view toward the entrance portal of St. George's Church), which, after the demolition of the "Haus am Markt" and a redesign of the marketplace, was to be preserved, because this would secure a central element of local identity.[44]

Finally, it is worth mentioning that there is a consensus in Bensheim about unsolved problems—namely, the shortage of housing and especially affordable housing or the increasing traffic load. However, these problems are perceived as side effects of Bensheim's success in being an economically prosperous city where people feel at home and like to live. (For a similar discursive pattern in Frankfurt, see Barbehön et al. 2016: 641–642.)

Notes

1 https://www.bensheim.de/wirtschaft/bensheim-in-zahlen#c302 (last check October 05, 2020).
2 These villas were mainly designed and constructed in a particular Art Nouveau style by the architect Heinrich Metzendorf (https://www.bensheim.de/fileadmin/media/bensheim/06-Tourismus/Metzendorfrundgang.pdf; last check October 05, 2020).
3 For further information about these two metropolitan regions see Heinelt et al. (2011: 79–137).
4 In the German federal state of Hesse local government is characterized by a *collective form*—according to the typology developed by Mouritzen and Svara which means "The decision center is one collegiate body, the executive committee that is responsible for all executive functions. The executive committee consists of locally elected politicians and the mayor, who presides" (Mouritzen and Svara 2002: 56).
5 https://www.bensheim.de/leben-in-bensheim/klima-umwelt-energie/klimaschutz.html (last check October 20, 2020).
6 The GGEW is not active as an energy supplier in the Bensheim area only. In total, it has about 140,000 customers (see https://www.ggew.de/unternehmen/; last check October 20, 2020).
7 GGEW provides 83 charging stations for electric vehicles. It owns 50 wind turbines and obtains two-thirds of the energy it sells from renewable sources (B16).
8 Currently, it operates its own fiber-optic network of about 350 km in total (B16).
9 http://www.megb.de/en/megb/ueber-uns/; translated by the authors (last check October 20, 2020).
10 A facility offering part-time care is planned at the "Stubenwald" business park for dependent relatives of persons employed by the companies located there (B15).
11 https://www.buergernetzwerk.de/de/wer-wir-sind.html (last check October 05, 2020).
12 https://www.stadtkultur-bensheim.de/galerien/artib/ (last check October 05, 2020).
13 *Eigenbetriebe* are an organizational form of municipal enterprise. They are a special public law form of enterprise without their own legal identity based on the municipality codes of the German federal states. They represent a special asset to be managed separately from the municipal budget.
14 The "Betriebskommission" of Bensheim's "Eigenbetrieb Stadtkultur" is composed of members of the executive board ("Magistrat"), the municipal council, the staff council (representative body of employees), and three residents well informed about cultural matters. The chairman is the mayor (http://www.stadtkultur-bensheim.de/stadtkultur-bensheim/wir-ueber-uns/; last check October 05, 2020).
15 https://www.hospiz-verein-bergstrasse.de/de/ (last check October 05, 2020).
16 See the article "Hospizarbeit ist künftig besser sichtbar" ("Hospice work will be more visible in the future") in the Bergsträßer Anzeiger, April 20, 2021.

17 https://www.hospiz-verein-bergstrasse.de/de/hospiz-bergstrasse/ (last check October 05, 2020).

18 https://familienzentrum-bensheim.de/ (last check October 05, 2020) and information provided by the chairwoman of this association by email on April 16, 2021.

19 http://buergerhilfe-bensheim.blogspot.com/p/aus-der-geschichte-der-burgerhilfe.html (last check October 05, 2020).

20 Cf. the article "Tafel versorgt mittlerweile 680 Haushalte" ("Tafel now supplies 680 households") in the Bergsträßer Anzeiger, August 21, 2019. See also https://www.tafel-bensheim.de/jahresbericht (last check October 05, 2020).

21 https://wv-bensheim.de/magazin/wvb-intern.html (last check October 23, 2020).

22 https://wv-bensheim.de (last check October 05, 2020).

23 https://wv-bensheim.de/kontakt/ansprechpartner/ (last check October 05, 2020).

24 The approximately 100 members of "Bensheim aktiv" are listed under https://www.bensheim-aktiv.de/ueber-uns/unsere-mitglieder/ (last check October 05, 2020).

25 http://www.verkehrsverein-bensheim.de/Der-Verkehrsverein/der-verkehrsverein.html (last check October 05, 2020).

26 See among others the article "'Mutbürger' fordern Richters Rücktritt" ("'Courageous citizens' demand Richter's resignation") in the Bergsträßer Anzeiger, August 06, 2019.

27 At the end of the interview, the people who had been interviewed were usually asked to describe their city metaphorically. One of the interview partners (B8) in Bensheim used the metaphor of a plush sofa, i.e., "a cozy, comfortable and quaint place." Another (B12) explicitly stated: "The city is my home!" ("Die Stadt ist mein Heim!").

28 https://www.te.com/usa-en/about-te/our-company.html (last check October 05, 2020).

29 Supplement of the Bergsträßer Anzeiger, October 21, 2016.

30 See the article "Hundert neue Arbeitsplätze in nur einem Jahr an der Bergstraße" ("One hundred new jobs at Bergstrasse in just one year") in the Bergsträßer Anzeiger, May 22, 2018.

31 https://corporate.dentsplysirona.com/en/about-dentsply-sirona/history.html (last check October 05, 2020).

32 Supplement of the Bergsträßer Anzeiger, November 10, 2017.

33 See the article "Hundert neue Arbeitsplätze in nur einem Jahr an der Bergstraße" ("One hundred new jobs at Bergstrasse in just one year") in the Bergsträßer Anzeiger, May 22, 2018.

34 Supplement of the Bergsträßer Anzeiger, October 21, 2016.

35 See the article "Reckeweg baut Fabrik und Logistiklager" ("Reckeweg builds factory and logistics warehouse") in Bergsträßer Anzeiger, December 08, 2018.

36 See the article "Sanner will im Stubenwald wachsen" ("Sanner wants to grow in the Stubenwald") in the Bersträßer Anzeiger, August 08, 2020.

37 See the article "Paukenschlag bei Suzuki nach der Mittagspause" ("Drumbeat at Suzuki after the lunch break") in the Bersträßer Anzeiger, October 30, 2018.

38 See the article "Dentsply Sirona baut Jobs [...] ab" ("Dentsply Sirona cuts jobs [...]") in the Bergsträßer Anzeiger, November 10, 2018.

39 http://www.zeit.de/2017/03/hessen-bensheim-sehenswuerdigkeiten-tipps (last check October 05, 2020).

40 The "Kolpingwerk" is a Catholic social association with about 260 local branches in Germany (http://www.kolpingsfamilie-bensheim.de/index.php/2014-02-19-09-59-08/geschichte; last check October 05, 2020).

41 The building of the "Alte Kurfürstliche Gymnasium" (AKG) was constructed in 1911 (see http://www.akg-bensheim.de/home/geschichte-des-akg; last check October 05, 2020).

42 See the article "Bürger sollen über Marktplatz abstimmen" ("Citizens should vote on marketplace") in the Bergsträßer Anzeiger, March 05, 2020 and https://www.bensheim.de/rathaus-politik/politik/wahlen/buergerentscheid (last check October 05, 2020).

43 A guest from the UK characterized the "Winzerfest" in Bensheim as "civilised public drinking."

44 See among others the articles "Testballoons für den Schorschblick" ("Testballoons for the Schorschblick") and "Am Schorschblick führt kein Weg vorbei" ("No way to pass the Schorschblick") in the Bersträßer Anzeiger, November 04, 2019, and December 20, 2019, respectively.

5   Chania

Hubert Heinelt and Panos Koliastasis

5.1 Introduction

In 2011, the year for which the latest census data is available, Chania had 108,642 inhabitants. The city is located in the north of the western part of Crete. As its Venetian harbor and the old city with a lot of buildings from the Venetian and Ottoman period remained, it has the image of resembling what is typical for a former East Mediterranean city. This image is perceived not only from the outside, but it is also emphasized by local people: "Chania was at a crossroads of cultures" (C2) and "this characteristic has to be preserved" (C2). It is widely perceived as an advantage that the old fortification of the city was only partly turned down. This preserved the old city—in contrast to Heraklion, the capital city of Crete(C1).

The city of Chania is considered as the main economic center in Western Crete. The tertiary sector represents the greatest part (82%) of the local economic sector. In this context, the tourism sector emerges as the backbone of Chania's economy as well as of Crete in general.[1] However, there are also several small enterprises for food and beverage.

In contrast to other cities (such as the Cretan city of Rethymno), there are no big hotels in the city. Hotels are small, ranging from nice but simple ones to expensive "boutique hotels" located in former palaces. Nevertheless, a lot of tourists stay in big hotel facilities outside the city.

Apart from tourism, there are attempts to modernize both the harbor and the airport of the city and in general to increase the importance of other services such as education and research. More specifically, there are two centers for research and development in the city—namely, the Mediterranean Agronomic Institute of Chania[2] and the Technical University of Crete.[3] In addition, the airport of Chania is connected to the international airport of Athens by three to four flights per day. Furthermore, it can be reached from several European cities, however, mainly by charter flights during the tourist session. In parallel, daily ferry boats connect the city (from the neighboring city of Souda) with Piraeus.

At this point it should be noted that although Chania benefits a lot from international tourism, the unemployment rate is high (17.7% at the end of

DOI: 10.4324/9781003084006-5

2017).[4] However, due to strong dependence on the tourist sector, unemployment in Chania is seasonal.

Chania is regarded as a former stronghold for liberals in the first half of the 20th century since it was home to the liberal statesman Eleftherios Venizelos. Since the restoration of the democratic regime in 1974 and particularly since the rise of the center-left PASOK (socialist party) in 1981, Chania has been a stronghold for PASOK, though the center-right New Democracy (ND) is in electoral terms stronger in the city than elsewhere in Crete. The main reason is that Chania is the homeland one of the most powerful center-right political dynasties in Greece, that of Konstantinos Mitsotakis whose son (Kyriakos Mitsotakis) is now leader of the ND and became prime minister of the country in 2019. From 2009 onwards and due to the impact of the economic crisis, the political landscape has changed. More specifically, the radical left SYRIZA has inherited the traditionally strong political position of PASOK that saw its vote share collapse. In parallel, it should be noted that as opposed to the Greek mainland, neo-fascist lists were not successful in Crete after the crisis.

Against this backdrop, it is no surprise that since 1975, three mayors were politically affiliated with PASOK, one was associated with SYRIZA, two were independents, and only one was associated with the ND party. The former mayor is considered as a left wing affiliated with SYRIZA, yet it should be noted that in the local elections in May 2019 he ranked in fifth position taking only 13.8% of the vote, while the newly elected mayor ran as an independent. Furthermore, it should be mentioned that the fragmentation of the national political system has been reflected in the local party system of Chania as well. In the local elections of May 2019, eight parties entered the city council, while nine parties were elected in the elections of 2014, seven in the elections of 2010, and only four in the 2006 elections.

5.2 Innovations

There are a number of material and social artifacts in Chania which are perceived by local and external observers as both a novelty and an improvement.

This refers, for instance, to a *traffic management system* which addresses the main challenge faced by the city (C10)—namely, a rising number of tourists staying either in the city or outside. As emphasized by a former local politician (C2) the number of tourists staying in the city has increased in recent years by 10% on an annual basis.

The problem is that a lot of tourists are coming to the city by rented cars or staying in the city with a rented car. In particular, traffic management in Chania is focused on the following measures:

- limiting or even prohibiting cars from entering the old city and its surrounding neighborhoods;
- creating car parks near the old city (mainly for the use of tourists and less for local residents);

- improving the network of public buses;
- building own lanes for bikes;
- taking strict action against illegally parked cars (by towing cars and imposing high penalties);
- extending public space by, among others, restricting its use, e.g., by restaurants or shops.

By these measures the living conditions for locals as well as for tourists should be improved, while at the same time, it should be ensured that Chania remains a "friendly city." However, it should be noted that many interviewees remain skeptical considering the implementation and the effectiveness of the local traffic management system (C4; C7; C8; C12).

Another innovation is the *recycling system* introduced in Chania in 2016 which is (according to interviewees) admired by people in other Greek cities. However, it was (critically) emphasized (C1) that it took more than two decades to realize the idea of recycling in practice since a local recycling company (named DEDISA) was already founded in 1993 by the municipality of Chania. Furthermore, all interviewees admit that the introduction of the recycling system in Chania was the result of strong pressure applied by the European Commission against Greece to shut down an illegal waste dump.[5] In addition, in 2013

> it was the first time that the program "door-to-door" for the collection and recycling of non-hazardous municipal waste and waste of electrical and electronic equipment was implemented initially in the old city of Chania, including the coastal front of the Venetian Port [...]. The later contributed also to the removing of big bins from the old city allowing space for the pedestrians.
>
> (C3)

A third innovation promoted by the municipality is to make Chania a *"smart city."* It received for activities in this field a *"smart city" award* within the framework of the Greek-Cypriot INTERREG 2014–2020 program.[6] So far, the municipality has created 20 online services. They include, among others, an electronic protocol containing 400,000 scanned documents,[7] online libraries,[8] e-service of the local construction unit, e-payment service, e-application for certificates, establishment of the *ChaniaTourGuide app*, online day care enrollment, e-application for the disabled (C10), and online registration for the "social grocery store," where needy people can get goods and other products for their daily needs (see below).

Furthermore, the *Chania Citizen app* was established in June 2017, according to which every citizen of Chania has the opportunity to report issues to the municipality and request the appropriate services. For example, every citizen can use the app in order to take photos of malfunctions in the local infrastructure, send them to the municipality of Chania, and request the municipality to act. So far, it seems that 1,500 citizens have downloaded the

app and also use it (C5; C6). However, it should be noted that some interviewees are skeptical regarding the capacity of the municipality to respond
to citizens' electronic requests and deal with local issues efficiently (C4; C7;
C9; C10; C12).

Ambitions leading to innovations can also be found in the field of *local
climate policy*. To commit themselves to innovations in this field, the mayor
became a member of the European Covenant of Mayors in 2015.[9] In this
respect, the municipality has taken, for example, measures to save energy by
promoting the use of environmentally friendly light bulbs.

Another initiative that can be seen as an innovation is the municipality's
effort to *promote the food sector (industry)* of the city and its hinterland. This
is remarkable since the strong economic focus on tourism has made developments in other economic sectors difficult (C1). However, by linking (discursively) innovations in the local food production to the strengthening of
the attractiveness of the city for tourists, the promotion of the local food sector was made possible. An example for this is the beer brewery "Charma,"
the first one in Chania established in 2007. According to its leaflet, it offers
guided tours and beer tasting together with "typical" Cretan meze or "a lav-
ish vegetarian or meat dish prepared with fresh local ingredients." Another
example is the Manousakis Winery which offers "an array of tours and tast-
ings on our beautiful winery grounds" and promises: "Whether you want to
pair wines with delicious Cretan delicacies, or try them on their own, you
will experience a side of Crete you never knew." In concrete terms, the municipality promotes local innovations in the food sector by

- building walking trails to the hinterland where new producers of this
  sector are located;
- organizing an (international) fair for new, high-quality food stuff once
  a year;
- using the municipal market hall more systematically for the promotion
  and selling of these products;
- promoting old crafts (such as pottery) linked to the traditional way of
  agrarian production.

It was emphasized that the Mediterranean Agronomic Institute of Chania
and the Technical University of Crete, mentioned at the beginning of this
chapter, have played an important role in promoting the food sector of the
city and its hinterland (C1 and C2).

In order to cope with social effects of the economic crisis that broke out in
Greece in 2008 (as emphasized by C2; C10), the municipality of Chania also
developed social innovations, which are described in the following.

A "social grocery store" was launched in Chania in 2012. It provides the
most vulnerable members of the local society with means-tested benefits,
which range from food and free meals to psychosocial assistance. The benefits also include school materials for pupils and everyday goods for students,

whether they are studying at the Technical University of Chania or any other university in the country. Those who do not earn more than €4.512 per year are eligible.[10] The beneficiaries can get the products and the goods they need by spending, instead of money, a certain number of points which is dependent on their family status. The more the number of family members, the more points they are entitled to and the more the quantity of products and goods they can get. In 2018, 462 families and 1,082 individuals with 215 children were supported; 17.7% of the beneficiaries were disabled and 9.7% were single parents. Around 150 people in need made use of the offer of free meals every day, 70 people took advantage of the services for students, and 250 pupils took advantage of the offer of school materials provided free of charge. The social grocery store is located in a building provided by a Greek Christian Orthodox monastery and run by the NGO Diastasi. This NGO provides personnel and also uses employees of the Agency for Social Protection, Education, Sports and Culture of the municipality. The free meals are offered in a building of the local orthodox parish, which also provides the staff for the kitchen.

The "social grocery store" is under the supervision of a council committee (C11) consisting of seven members including either the mayor of Chania or a vice-mayor (who presides over the committee), four councilors of the governing party, one councilor of the main opposition party, and one councilor of the minor opposition party.[11]

The "social grocery store" is financed by various sources (C13). In 2018 the municipality contributed €96,183.67 from its budget. The municipality of Chania is also trying to mobilize local organizations and local companies but also individuals through donations of money or goods to finance and provide the services of the "social grocery store"—with great success. It has succeeded in attracting around 40 sponsors, some of whom have been awarded "Gold Sponsors." In 2018, private individuals donated a total of €2,300, while local businesses and organizations contributed a total of €54,000.[12] In addition, almost all supermarkets in the city donate food (C14), the Bank of Chania donates meat, and farmers from the area around the city donate fruit and vegetables.

Another social innovation is the *homeless shelter* that was founded in 2019 and provides temporary housing to 22 homeless people (20 men and 2 women), both citizens of Chania and immigrants, on a daily basis from 7 p.m. until next morning (C10; C11). In particular, the shelter, which is financed entirely by the municipality, provides bedrooms, bathrooms, and laundry services to the beneficiaries (C11).

The municipality of Chania has also created the first *shelter for abused women* in Greece (C11). The shelter, which was founded in 2012, is funded by the European Union (EU) (C13) and it employs psychologists and social workers. It provides psychological and financial support to abused women, while it can offer accommodation to a woman with her children as well.

Another innovation is the *social tutoring school* which started in 2011. It is an initiative taken by the municipality in collaboration with local private tutoring schools. The latter provides to students who are financially unable to pay tuitions the opportunity to study for free (C11). It is estimated that around 30 high school students are beneficiaries of the social tutoring school program (C10). In line with the social tutoring school, the municipality in cooperation with local private technical colleges awards scholarships to those children who do not have the financial ability to pay the fees. Around 15 students have so far benefited from the program (C11).

5.3 Actors, processes, and structuration through local discourses

Asked for typical processes for reaching decisions in Chania in general and on innovations in particular, respondents pointed to the mentioned innovations in traffic and waste management. "These decisions took some time because a broad consensus is seen as the best solution to a problem" (C2). "Listening to people, involving them as early as possible and looking for the best solution" (C2) is quite time-consuming in Chania because the city is seen as dominated by well-organized interest groups (C1; C2; C4; C9; C14)—not least on the level of the 26 districts of the city. For people not integrated or connected to these groups, this characteristic of policy-making in Chania leads to complaints that "there are open-minded people with new ideas, but they are not taken seriously, and their initiatives are blocked" (C1). Moreover, "if you are not part of these networks, it is hard to make your ideas about innovations heard" (C1). Nevertheless, there was ultimately a broad political consensus on the above-mentioned innovations, which is particularly true of the innovations in social services (C10; C11).

The organization of the local community in a large number of associations and organizations is explained (among others by C1 and C14) by the fact that the population of the city—despite the influx of foreigners and Greeks from other parts of the country—consists mainly of people who have known each other for a long time. Furthermore, families of these inhabitants have been living in the city for generations and have "inherited" the ties between them and, not least, with certain associations and organizations. This (as argued, for example, by C1 and C14) leads not only to social ties and solidarity among each other, but also to widespread (normative) standards of appropriate behavior—which has been particularly relevant for the establishment and support of the social services described above (in Section 5.2). The award of certain supporters of the "social grocery store" as "Gold Sponsors" also indicates that in Chania it is important for individuals, but also organizations to show publicly that one ("as a doctor or supermarket" [C14]) is behaving according to these standards of appropriate behavior in order to be socially respected.

As a former local politician (C2) emphasized, well-organized inter-est groups or a "vibrant local civil society" is an advantage—and not a problem—for an effective policy-making process. Well-organized inter-est groups are a precondition for (a) identifying those who are decisive for reaching a commonly or even widely shared solution to a problem (an inno-vation) and (b) being sure ("as much as possible") that an agreement reached will be supported by the public when it has to be implemented. However, well-organized citizens must be convinced of a "good strategic plan" by "good reasons" (C2).

For accepting an argument as a good reason, a reference point in com-municative interactions, which is widely shared in the city, is crucial. In the case of Chania, such a reference point seems to be captured by the following leitmotif: *let's improve the living conditions and keep the old city center intact. This will ensure the attractiveness of the city for tourists and thus provide the economic basis for the well-being of the inhabitants, while securing the future of the city!* This leitmotif is related to communicative interaction and ulti-mately political decisions affecting tourism and the economic well-being of the inhabitants. In terms of relieving the social hardships of inhabitants, it is complemented by the motif of *solidarity within the local community*—with reference to improving the living conditions and well-being of *all* residents.

According to interviewees, innovative ideas are developed in the city, i.e., in local debates about the nature of the city's problems and their potential solutions. Neither the national (Greek) level nor the EU plays a role in de-veloping innovative ideas—although a lot of EU funding is spent in the city (C3).[13] "Athens does not help us! They only take our money, i.e. taxes" (C1). And the EU supported innovations particularly by "forcing us to apply EU regulations, e.g. in dealing with garbage" in line with EU legislation (C1). Furthermore, it was emphasized that Chania is more able than most Greek municipalities to finance its innovations by itself—at least partly (C2).

Another widely shared idea is that *the city can be regarded as a "social enterprise."* This means that the city should be governed like an enterprise. However, this should not be done with the goal of producing profit (in a mon-etary sense) but of improving the well-being of the inhabitants—including local businesses (C2).

In line with other Greek municipalities, the political landscape in the mu-nicipality of Chania was, until the May 2019 local elections and due to the previous electoral systems, dominated by the mayor.[14] The latter controlled the majority in the municipal council and thus the mayor was able to exer-cise almost unrestricted power to promote his policy initiatives and make all the decisions needed to run the municipality. Similarly, in national politics the prime minister controls both the government and the majority in the parliament and thus exercises almost unrestricted executive and legislative power to promote his government policies.

However, in fact the mayor (as well as the prime minister) usually faces the resistance of various organized interests (that can act as veto players) in promoting policy initiatives and particularly innovative policies. The re-action of well-organized interest groups is probably reflected not only in the opposition parties of the municipal council, but also in a part of the majority faction of the municipal council, limiting to some extent the un-restricted power of the mayor. Therefore, it may be appropriate to consider that the mayor might have to engage in a time-consuming deliberation pro-cess (mainly behind the scenes negotiations) with members of his own party in order to build a consensus and thus promote effectively policy plans that are perceived as controversial from certain organized interests. Given that the recent local elections of 2019 were conducted under an electoral system of proportional representation preventing the first party from assuming an absolute majority in the city council, it is expected that the political land-scape will become even more fragmented, increasing the number of veto players and thus delaying further the decision-making process.

In this context, it is possible to argue that in Greek local politics, person-alities play a decisive political role in shaping not only the voting behav-ior of citizens in local government elections, but also influencing (like in other Mediterranean countries characterized by the "Continental European Napoleonic type" of local government) local public debates as "visionary" leaders or even "consensus facilitators" (see Getimis and Hlepas 2006: 186–187; Hlepas et al. 2018: 220–221).

This seems to be particularly the case in Chania where the former mayors (the last one was in office from September 2014 to September 2019 and the one before him from January 2011 to September 2014) clearly fit to the char-acteristics of "visionary" leaders set out by Hlepas et al. (2018: 215)—namely,

- encouraging new projects in the community;
- setting goals for transforming the administrative structure;
- prioritizing the increasing of the attractiveness of the municipality as a place of business and a place for people to live in, by regeneration and development projects, new cultural facilities, improvement of the aes-thetics of the city, etc.; and
- acting as a mediator and facilitator for reaching agreements amongst stakeholders on the basis of persuasion, building trust, and providing information and incentives.

5.4 Key findings

As already mentioned, the core reference point guiding policy choices to achieve innovations in Chania can be summarized by the statement "Let's improve the living conditions and keep the old city center intact. This will ensure the attractiveness of the city for tourists and thus providing the eco-nomic basis for the well-being of all inhabitants, while securing the future of the city!" It is complemented by the widely shared idea that the city can be regarded as a "social enterprise" and that solidarity is required to ensure the well-being of all inhabitants.

Based on these reference points a particular understanding for doing things became dominant, even though the local community is fragmented and at the same time well organized. That despite these structures, a dominant understanding for doing things has emerged due to the fact that the previous mayors acted as "visionary leaders" and (partly) also "consensus facilitators," i.e., with leadership styles giving emphasis to a broad consensus which is seen as a precondition for solving local problems. These styles also imply that it has been a high priority to listen to people, involving them as early as possible in the policy-making process and looking for the best, i.e., a broadly accepted solution. For such leadership styles well-organized interest groups are not a problem per se. Instead, well-organized interest groups are perceived as a precondition for (a) identifying those who are decisive for reaching a commonly or even widely shared solution to a problem (an innovation) and (b) being sure that an agreement is supported by the public when it has to be implemented.

Notes

1 http://www.haniotika-nea.gr/atmomichani-o-tourismos-gia-tin-ikonomia-tis-kritis/ (last check November 12, 2020); http://www.statistics.gr/statistics/-/publication/SEL57/- (last check November 12, 2020).
2 https://www.maich.gr/en/about/ciheam-iamc (last check October 6, 2020).
3 https://www.tuc.gr/index.php?id=5397 (last check October 6, 2020).
4 https://chanianews.gr/aisthiti-meiosi-tis-anergias-ton-fevroyario-stin-kriti-i-mikroteri-anergia/ (last check November 12, 2020).
5 This was the first case where the European Court imposed a fine against a member state for non-compliance with EU legislation (see http://curia.europa.eu/juris/liste.jsf?language=en&num=c-387/97; last check October 6, 2020).
6 See http://www.chania.gr/dimos/erga-espa/SmartCities.html (last check November 12, 2020).
7 http://backoffice.chania.gr (last check November 12, 2020).
8 http://www.librarychania.gr (last check November 12, 2020).
9 "Signatory cities [which are members of the European Covenant of Mayors] pledge action to support implementation of the EU 40% greenhouse gas-reduction target by 2030 and the adoption of a joint approach to tackling mitigation and adaptation to climate change" (https://www.covenantofmayors.eu/about/covenant-initiative/objectives-and-scope.html; last check October 6, 2020). For the European Covenant of Mayors, see, for example, Benz et al. (2015: 323–324).
10 This and the following information about the "social grocery store" is based on statements of two interview partners (C10 and C11) and https://www.cretalive.gr/crete/gematos-o-apologismos-toy-koinonikoy-pantopoleioy-chanion (last check November 12, 2020).
11 https://www.chania.gr/katoikoi/koinpolitiki/koin-pantopoleio.html (last check November 12, 2020).
12 https://www.cretalive.gr/crete/gematos-o-apologismos-toy-koinonikoy-pantopoleioy-chanion (last check November 12, 2020).
13 Unfortunately, data for EU funding is only available for the region of Crete and not for the city of Chania.
14 For the institutionally determined strength of mayors in Greece in comparison to other European countries see Heinelt et al. (2018: 36–37).

6 Elefsina

Panos Koliastasis

6.1 Introduction

The city of Elefsina is located around 20 km outside Athens, in the western part of Attica, and it has approximately 30,000 inhabitants.[1] It is at the crossroads of several land transport networks, with its own industrial harbor and in proximity to the container harbor of Piraeus.[2] As a result, Elefsina is regarded as an "urban village" (E4). In parallel, it is considered as one of the most important cities in the region of Attica. The first reason supporting this view is its ancient history. Elefsina was among the five holy cities in ancient Greece. It is the city where the ceremony of the Eleusinian mysteries took place.[3] Elefsina was also the homeland of the famous tragedian Aeschylus. The second reason is its modern industrial history. From the end of the 19th century onward, the city has gradually turned into the main industrial hub in the wider Attica region.[4] The Charilaos soap factory, as well as other soap factories and mills, all of which were founded in the second half of the 1890s, is located in Elefsina. The Titan cement factory was founded in the early 1900s. This was followed in 1922 by the establishment of the Kronos distillery and in 1925 by Iris, the first varnish and paint factory in Greece.

Due to its industrial development, thousands of Greeks and particularly refugees coming from Anatolia moved to Elefsina in the 1920s to be employed and to improve their living standards. Moreover, in the aftermath of World War II and the Greek Civil War (1944–1949), the industrial growth accelerated. Next to the old industries, new factories were established including the Chalevourgiki steel factory (1953), the Aspropyrgos refinery (1955), the shipyard of Elefsina (1969), the Petrola refinery (1973), and a number of smaller industries. The constant need for workers together with the high rates of poverty in post-World War II Greece contributed to a second wave of internal immigration. Consequently, the population of Elefsina increased rapidly.[5]

However, from 1980 onward, a trend of deindustrialization began since many factories closed down, while only smaller new ones were established. In addition, storage places and logistics facilities were developed. Hence, Elefsina has been transformed into a hub for logistics, transport, and minor industries. Nevertheless, there are several metal and chemical industries and

DOI: 10.4324/9781003084006-6

important shipyards. A number of logistics enterprises in the wider area cooperate closely with the Chinese Cosco company running the container harbor of Piraeus.[6] As a result, the economic sector of the city is largely dominated by the services sector which, according to 2015 data, accounts for 61.7% of the local gross added value, while the secondary (manufacturing) sector accounts for 37%.[7]

A crucial implication of the concentration of so many factories was the air and water pollution, which in turn had negative consequences on the population's health. As one local politician in charge of social services puts it, "Elefsina was the wounded child of the 20th century" (E6). Yet, the strong protests and opposition of the inhabitants as well as grassroots environmental movements led to pro-environmental policy measures which, together with the deindustrialization process, resulted in a significant reduction of pollution.[8] In addition, Elefsina has faced new challenges since it has been hit after 2008 by the fiscal and economic crisis. It is indicative that the unemployment rate exceeded 20% and the poverty rate has increased substantially.[9]

Elefsina is seen by locals as well as outside observers as a left stronghold because left-wing political ideas prevail due to the strong presence of trade unions and environmental organizations. It is characteristic that from 1975 (i.e., after the end of the last dictatorship in Greece), four mayors were left-leaning, while only two were supported by the New Democracy (ND), a center-right party. The current mayor, backed by ND, is right-leaning for the first time in many years. He was elected in the first round of the May 2019 local elections, taking 54.6% of the vote. Although the local election took place under the electoral system of pure proportional representation that usually leads to fragmented municipal councils favoring coalition local governments, the Elefsina poll generated a stable local government since the newly elected mayor and his party received more than 50.1% of the vote and 15 out of 27 seats in the municipal council.[10]

6.2 Issues of Innovations

The municipality of Elefsina developed innovative social policies to strengthen social cohesion. The main pertinent innovations were the social grocery, the social tutoring school, the local medical clinic, the social pharmacy, the center for employment support, the popular university, the counseling center for abused women, the local vegetable garden, and the movement without intermediaries.

The municipality of Elefsina has developed these innovations to react to demands of local people and to ensure and strengthen social cohesion in the face of the social impact of the financial and economic crisis—as underlined by the following statements of local actors:

- The economic crisis has been the main reason for the foundation of social structures since 2011. It is indicative that there were more requests for help to the social services of the municipality of Elefsina" (E1).

- People coming from the middle class had been severely affected by the crisis and thus they were asking for social support" (E3).
- The implications of the crisis forced the municipality to improve and implement policies of social support more effectively in order to protect the most vulnerable members of the local society" (E6).

Against this background, the *social grocery store* was founded in 2011 by the municipality in order to provide means-tested benefits, food, and other goods to the most vulnerable (E1; E2). Currently the beneficiaries are approximately 140 families and around 470–480 individuals, while a few years ago the number had reached 900 recipients (E6). The fall in the number of beneficiaries is not attributed to an improvement of the local economy and the living standards of the recipients (E1). Rather, it is due to stricter selection criteria applied to the evaluation process to increase the provision of goods to those who are in dire need (E6). The *social grocery* is run by *Faros*, a non-governmental organization (NGO), under the supervision of the municipality of Elefsina and particularly of its Agency for Social Affairs (E1; E2). *Faros* provides the personnel (E15) and is financed by the EU Structural and Investment Funds. The provided food and other goods are financed from both the municipality (from which the larger part is paid; E9) and contributions of local industries such as Hellenic Petroleum and Titan that seem to be interested in promoting the concept of Corporate Social Responsibility and thus providing social assistance to a neighboring community like Elefsina (E11). In particular, according to the director of Corporate Social Responsibility of Hellenic Petroleum, the latter purchases products on a monthly basis and offers them to the social grocery store (E11). In sum, it spends approximately €40,000 annually.[11]

Another innovation in the field of social cohesion refers to the *social tutoring school* that was founded in 2012. Its aim is to provide additional educational assistance to students of both elementary and high school coming from socially vulnerable families (E5) or facing serious medical problems (e.g., the disabled). Classes are staffed by teachers working on a voluntary basis (E5). Students at the social tutoring school come also from nearby settlements. It should be mentioned that in 2012 the school received 18 applications, while in 2019 the number increased, reaching 119 applications. The latter might be related to the fact that many former students at the school succeeded in exams allowing entrance into public universities (E9).

A third social innovation is the local *medical clinic* that was established in 2014. It provides free of charge healthcare services to all citizens of Elefsina (E6). Specifically, the provided services include primary healthcare services, a system of electronic prescription of medicine to those lacking health insurance or low-income citizens, as well as provision of nursing care services. It includes a physician, a general surgeon, a pediatrician, a gynecologist, and an orthopedist. The medical equipment of the clinic and the pharmaceuticals are fully funded by the municipality of Elefsina. Patients' visits to the local medical clinic are estimated at about 12,000 a year, while the operating costs of the clinic do not exceed €100,000 on an annual basis (E14).

Another innovation is the *social pharmacy* (κοινωνικό φαρμακείο) that was founded in 2017 and provides free medicine and medical supplies to the poor, unemployed, homeless, and immigrants as well as their family members residing in Elefsina (E1). It is financed by the municipal budget and the EU Structural and Investment Funds, while it distributes medicine and medical material provided by pharmaceutical companies and local private pharmacies. In line with the case of the social grocery, the social pharmacy is run by *Faros* and includes one pharmacist and one social worker (E15). The latter are supervised by a special municipal committee (E6).

A fifth innovation is the *popular university* (λαϊκό πανεπιστήμιο). It was established in 2015 and it is led by a committee that consists of local government officials and ordinary citizens. In the popular university of Elefsina, which is located in a building provided by the municipality, various academics are invited to give lectures on a weekly basis on a number of subjects including philosophy, culture, history, and Byzantine music. Academics lecture on a voluntary basis, although some are given the symbolic amount of €100 for their travel expenses. The number of students participating each year at the popular university is 130, 60 to 70 of whom attend classes on a regular basis (E16).

Another innovative policy initiative that has been promoted by the municipality of Elefsina is the creation of the *local employment service*. It was founded in 2003 in order to provide social assistance to unemployed citizens of the city looking for work because the National Employment Service was seen as ineffective to provide such services in times of growing unemployment. The local employment service has created a database including the CVs of the unemployed and the jobs offered by the local businesses (E17). As an employee of the local employment agency illustrates (E17), depending on the profile of the employees the companies are looking for, the service sends them the corresponding CVs to select those who wish to be hired. About 80–120 people a month seek the help of the service. However, only 10 out of the 20 available jobs per month are filled since a large segment of the local workforce is considered underqualified (E17).

A seventh innovation is the *local vegetable garden* which was established in 2012. The municipality provides residents with limited income, with land (1 acre in total) to cultivate various products for their own consumption (E6). Apart from the land, the municipality also provides the infrastructure, fertilizers, and support from agricultural scientists. It is estimated that around 25 families have taken part so far in the program and cultivate their own products.

Another innovation is the initiative called *movement without intermediaries* (κίνημα χωρίς μεσάζοντες), which was previously active in other parts of the country and started for the first time in Elefsina in 2012. According to an interviewee (E6), the municipality called agricultural producers from all over the country who were interested in taking part and selling their products. Today, it is estimated that approximately 25–30 agricultural producers take part in the initiative of selling their products at lower prices compared to supermarkets and local markets. Probably this is the reason why the initiative has elicited critical reactions by local supermarkets and local agricultural producers who are afraid of losing their market share. It should be noted that the market takes place at a particular place provided by the municipality of Elefsina, and at the end of the day the participating producers offer some of their products for free to the municipality, which in turn gives them to those suffering from extreme poverty as well as to local daycares.

The most recent innovation in the area of social policy is the foundation of the *counseling center for abused women* in 2017. It is staffed by a sociologist, a lawyer, a psychologist, and a social worker, while it is supervised by the Research Center on Gender Equality. According to the latest available data, from May to December 2019, 51 abused women have approached the center. They came not only from Elefsina but also from other neighboring areas (E13). Although many of them turn to the center for legal advice, the center also offers these women the opportunity to have sessions with both the social worker and the psychologist (E13).

Apart from these innovations, the municipality has promoted innovative policy measures on environmental protection. In particular, in 2005, it created the *center for collection of recyclable materials*. The latter was planned and implemented by the mayor who was in office from 2002 to 2011 and for whom (with the expertise as a chemical engineer) the establishment of a local recycling system in Elefsina was high on his political agenda. According to interviewees, it is the only local recycling system in Greece and thus it is seen as a major local innovation (E7; E8). The center collects, with metal bins placed around the city, the massive pieces of garbage (including waste from excavations and demolitions) and recycles them. Furthermore, it has been estimated that the center manages to recycle 80% of the total locally produced waste (6,000–7,000 tons per year).

In parallel, it has become apparent that in Elefsina, activities in the area of culture have been intensified in order to improve the image of the city. It is thanks to these activities that the city was successful in its application for becoming the *European Capital of Culture for 2021* which has now been postponed to 2023 due to the pandemic. The initiative was promoted by the then mayor who ruled the municipality until 2019 and his majoritarian party in the municipal council despite the opposition's critical reaction. However, it is seen by a majority of the locals as an opportunity for the city to rebrand itself as a clean, viable, and dynamic city aimed at attracting tourists and developing permanent cultural infrastructures in favor of its citizens (E9). Thus, the initiative might also contribute to a new narrative about Elefsina (E10). Certainly, according to an interviewee (E12), there were also financial reasons for applying for the project of the European Capital of Culture since the municipality would be awarded €1.5 million from the EU Creative Europe program,[12] which would be used to finance several public works. However, financial support is now at risk because the implementation of the project has faced many obstacles and delays. Therefore, the completion of the project is regarded with skepticism since many local officials as well as journalists and members of the local community claim that Elefsina might not manage it effectively (E12).

6.3 Actors, processes, and structuration through local discourses

In line with other Greek municipalities, in Elefsina the type of local government until May 2019 was mayor-centered. Against this backdrop, the mayor discusses his policy ideas with his party that represents the majority in the municipal council, makes the decisions, and promotes his policies to the municipal council to be voted. Opposition parties, though they usually resist the mayor's policy initiatives, can hardly exert real influence in the decision-making process. This structure is further strengthened, in the context of the Greek political culture, by the extreme party-politicized character and the ideological orientation of Greek politics (Featherstone 2005; Teperoglou and Tsatsanis 2014).

However, politicization does not necessarily mean polarization. It is indicative that there was a consensual political debate in Elefsina considering the design and implementation of the social innovations outlined above (in Section 6.2) that facilitated their effectiveness. In addition, the social innovations were implemented together with NGOs and local industries. Nevertheless, opposition parties expressed their skepticism about, for instance, the particular role of *Faros* in running the social grocery store and the social pharmacy (E15).

Despite the political consensus on social innovations, several disputes became apparent concerning the application for claiming the European Capital of Culture project and the organizational capacity of the municipality. However, the reaction of the opposition hardly prevented the former mayor and his dominant party from promoting their plans in the area of culture, since, as is argued by the former mayor, most citizens were in favor of the project (E9).

In Elefsina the innovations were brought about in two ways.

• First, an initiative can be taken by the mayor and his party. These are the cases of the recycling system and the activities in the field of culture which finally led to the application for claiming the project of the European Capital of Culture. However, long-term success in implementing such initiatives requires public support, which must be underpinned by a broad consensus that can only be achieved and stabilized through political debate.

• Second, an initiative can be initiated either by the municipal administration or by the collaboration of the municipal administration with NGOs. That is the case of the social innovations and particularly the social grocery store and the social pharmacy, which are typical examples of the collaboration of the Department of Social Services of the municipality and the NGO *Faros*. However, public support is needed in these cases as well, because those who are in social need cannot articulate the demand for such innovations. As a result, others have to do it on their behalf—namely, well-meaning sections of the local administration or NGOs.

With regard to the communicative mechanisms contributing to the promotion of innovations in Elefsina, it seems that the city followed the example of other cities to deal with the implications of the economic crisis. By applying the mechanism of *observing others and orienting at them*, good practices are put in place that had previously been implemented successfully by other municipalities around Greece. That was the case with the social grocery store, the social pharmacy, the social tutoring school, or the "movement without intermediaries." All these measures strengthened social cohesion and ensure that an effective social safety net has been put in place to protect the most vulnerable.

Moreover, the choice of Elefsina to engage in a process of becoming the first city in Greece establishing a local recycling system can be related to the *discursive development of a reference point for communicative interaction* through the epistemic authority of a local—namely, the former mayor, who not only served the city for nine consecutive years but also had expertise as a chemical engineer.

6.4 Key findings

In terms of the dominant image of the city of Elefsina, it could be argued that it is perceived as a center for recent industrial history of Greece, while at the same time it emerges as a symbol for environmental pollution caused by industry. In addition, the city was hit hard by the economic crisis that broke out in Greece in 2008. As a result, it had to deal with two huge challenges. On the one hand, addressing the severe economic and social repercussions reflected in the rise of unemployment and impoverishment by designing, financing, and implementing effective innovative policies aiming to strengthen social cohesion and protect the most vulnerable. On the other hand, it has to deal with the challenge to turn itself from an industrial and highly polluted area to a new, services-based, clean city advancing cultural development. In other words, Elefsina faces the challenge of creating a new narrative for itself through the promotion of the initiative of becoming a European Capital of Culture by connecting the past, the present, and the future.

So far it is apparent that the city has managed to put in place and effectively run social innovations, while it remains to be seen whether the challenge of promoting a change in the overall image of the city by cultural innovation and particularly the European Capital of Cultural project will be met successfully.

Notes

1 https://elefsina.gr/el/sintomo-istoriko (last check November 12, 2020).
2 https://www.elefsina.gr/sites/default/files/epix.pdf (last check November 12, 2020).
3 https://eleusis2021.eu/wp-content/uploads/2019/03/ELEUSIS21_BID_BOOK_2016_GR_outline-1.pdf (last check November 12, 2020).
4 See on the economic development of the town and the companies mentioned below https://www.elefsina.gr/el/biomixaniki-epanastasi (last check November 12, 2020).
5 https://eleusis2021.eu/wp-content/uploads/2019/03/ELEUSIS21_BID_BOOK_2016_GR_outline-1.pdf (last check November 12, 2020).
6 https://www.elefsina.gr/el/biomixaniki-epanastasi (last check November 12, 2020).
7 http://www.statistics.gr (last check November 12, 2020).
8 https://eleusis2021.eu/wp-content/uploads/2019/03/ELEUSIS21_BID_BOOK_2016_GR_outline-1.pdf (November 12, 2020).
9 http://www.statistics.gr (last check November 12, 2020).
10 https://ekloges.ypes.gr/current/d/home/municipalities/9229/ (last check November 12, 2020).
11 Initially, it appeared that such donations were seen with skepticism from the opposition in the municipal council since these firms have been regarded as responsible for the pollution of the city (E6). However, this criticism has weakened over the years (E12).
12 https://ec.europa.eu/programmes/creative-europe/actions/capitals-culture_en (last check November 12, 2020).

7   Frankfurt

Hubert Heinelt and Max A. Kayser

7.1 Introduction

The city of Frankfurt is the center of the Rhine-Main metropolitan area and the economic powerhouse of this prosperous region (Lackowska 2011; Heinelt and Zimmermann 2012: 77–87). The former "freie Reichsstadt"[1] has historically always been a center for trade and fairs at the national as well as the international level. The city is well interconnected with the surrounding area by means of public transport and functions as a hub for international flights, high-speed trains, and supply chain logistics. A special feature of Frankfurt is its steadily growing skyscraper skyline, something which is unique among German cities. Because of the conglomeration of skyscrapers, which are among the highest in Europe, Frankfurt is sometimes called "Mainhattan" by local people with a sense of self-irony.

Frankfurt is very densely populated and the number of residents is steadily growing, having reached 753,000 at the end of 2019. Furthermore, the flow of commuters is high because, on the one hand, the city provides a large number of jobs but, on the other hand, it is quite small in relation to the size of the territory it serves: there are more than 387,000 commuters on a daily basis, who account for about two-thirds of all employees in Frankfurt.[2]

As in Offenbach (see Chapter 11), the percentage of residents of Frankfurt who either immigrated themselves or have a parent or grandparent who immigrated to Germany is high: about 45% of the city's inhabitants belong to this group (Stadt Frankfurt 2017: 34). However, in Frankfurt this is not seen as a major problem—as shown in 2018 and 2019 by surveys of the biggest urban problems from the perspective of the people of Frankfurt: in 2018 only 6% of the respondents considered relations between German and foreign residents to be problematic and in 2019 only 5%, far behind housing and transport, which are perceived as problematic by 54% and 58% and 23% and 34%, respectively, by the locals participating in the survey.[3]

As an international financial center (where, for instance, the European Central Bank is located) the tertiarization of the local economy is rather

DOI: 10.4324/9781003084006-7

high (89.4%).[4] The same applies to the average income per capita (€4,085, compared with the national average of €3,133) as well as the fiscal revenue per capita (€3,518).[5] The latter is twice as high as the average for the German federal state of Hesse (€1,606) in which Frankfurt is located.[6]

Nevertheless (as already mentioned), Frankfurt is quite small in territorial size in comparison with its population. As a result, its population density makes it easier for actors to meet and exchange ideas, but also makes it harder to ignore problems, since there is not much room to overlook them. This high population density distinguishes Frankfurt from other large metropolitan cities and is sometimes expressed by locals in the saying that they live in a "global village" (Stadt Frankfurt am Main 2018).

As already mentioned, Frankfurt's population is very diverse and multicultural. However, in contrast with Offenbach (see Chapter 11) the city's job market attracts a workforce that is primarily highly skilled—which originates not only from Germany, but also especially from abroad. Consequently, unlike Offenbach, Frankfurt resembles a global metropolis hosting a large number of mobile cosmopolitans.

The municipality of Frankfurt is a unitary authority (combining the competencies of the first and second tier of local government) with a broad range of responsibilities in social welfare, public health, infrastructure, and economic development. Local government in the German federal state of Hesse is characterized by a collective form, which means that the municipality is governed by an executive board (the "Magistrat") headed by a directly elected mayor. Both the Magistrat and the municipal council have been dominated by a coalition of Social Democrats, Christian Democrats, and the Green Party since the local elections in 2016. Prior to that (since 2006), the dominant parties were the Christian Democrats and the Greens. In 2012, a Social Democrat had already replaced a Christian Democrat, who had been in office since 1995, as the directly elected mayor.

Both the success of a Social Democrat in the election of the mayor in 2012 and 2018 and the Social Democrats' gains in votes and the CDU's (the Christian Democrats) and Greens' losses in votes in the 2016 council elections are related to the increased public attention given to housing problems and a controversial debate about how to solve them (Schipper and Heeg 2020: 126). This results in a high average rent price because living space is scarce in Frankfurt and the average rent for apartments is very high (at almost €15 per m^2 and month in 2020).[7] Local elections were held in Frankfurt on March 14, 2021, after which the Greens became the strongest group in the council. They formed a new coalition with the Social Democrats, Liberals (FDP), and Volt (a national section of Volt Europe). It is unlikely that this new coalition will bring about fundamental changes in the innovations described below. However, it is also questionable whether (innovative) solutions to the housing problems mentioned will be found.

7.2 Issues related to Innovations

Frankfurt is not only one of the economically strongest cities in Germany; it also has the image—among both locals and observers from the outside—of being a frontrunner in innovations in a variety of policy areas. This applies to the local drug policy, the integration of foreigners, the preservation of green areas in the city, and the local climate policy (Heinelt and Lamping 2015a: 73–132 and 2015b: 288–295), which will be outlined in this section.

After years of permanent escalation of the drug problem, a pragmatic and tolerant drug policy approach has gradually been developed in Frankfurt since the late 1980s. The drug policy of Frankfurt regards (a) the protection of the citizens as well as (b) the reduction of harm for drug users as important. Furthermore, suppression measures that are directed exclusively against trafficking in illicit drugs and not against the drug users themselves are closely linked to and aligned with health and social policies aimed at helping drug users. Accordingly, drug policy in Frankfurt is based on the four pillars: (1) prevention, (2) counseling and therapy, (3) survival aids for drug addicts, and (4) suppression. In this sense the drug policy in Frankfurt is guided by the insight: *help and suppression—they can only work together.* The "help" dimension is characterized by the first methadone substitution program in Germany (in 1988) as well as the first public drug consumption rooms in Germany (in 1994) and syringe exchanges in all drug aid facilities. The integration of "help and suppression" is carried out through coordination in the so-called Montagsrunde, i.e., regular biweekly Monday meetings of the municipal offices dealing with drug problems and aid for drug users with public prosecutors, police, and schools which are held under the direction of the municipal health department and its drug unit. The "Montagsrunde" was formed as early as 1988 and the drug unit was established in 1989. The *Frankfurt way in drug policy* became a role model for many cities in Germany and abroad for years,[8] although when first introduced there were fierce public debates about it in Frankfurt (as emphasized by F22).[9] And there is also currently controversy about the Frankfurt way in drug policy because it reveals difficulties in dealing with the problems of drug addiction, which have become particularly obvious in the wake of the Corona pandemic—especially in the area around the central railways station.[10]

In 1989, the "Amt für multikulturelle Angelegenheiten"/AmkA (Office of Multicultural Affairs) was established in Frankfurt by a decision of the Magistrat. This decision was initiated by the Greens in the municipal council immediately after the local election—as stated by Daniel Cohn-Bendit[11] (Stadt Frankfurt 2009: 10), the first head of the AmkA.

> The Office for Multicultural Affairs (AmkA) deals with all issues concerning integration, migration, anti-discrimination and living together in our city. Whether language and education, immigration and residence, religion and worldview, LSBTIQ, associations or everyday issues:

The AmkA provides basic work and advice, it works in cooperation and its own projects and has its own support activities.[12]

This means that, in collaboration with other municipal offices, welfare organizations, and civil society group, the AmkA offers a variety of services for people migrating to Frankfurt.[13] Furthermore, the AmkA facilitates local events and networks focused on migration and the different cultures present in Frankfurt as well as issues its own publications on intercultural topics in Frankfurt. As argued by the AmkA, "successful integration and good living together is based on the fact that Frankfurt's citizens, regardless of their origin, can shape the future of the city" (Stadt Frankfurt 2009: 120). Petra Roth, the mayor of Frankfurt from 1995 to 2012, emphasized in 2009 that in 1989 the Office of Multicultural Affairs

> was a nationwide novelty. As a "Frankfurt model" [it] inspired many other municipalities who also wanted to break new ground in integration work. Frankfurt was one of the first major German cities to recognize the political necessity of promoting local integration measures in a sustainable way and to anchor it in all districts of the city.
>
> (Stadt Frankfurt 2009)

By the 19th and early 20th century, Frankfurt had already developed a Green Belt of parks and open green space around the city center. As a result of the development of the city, these green spaces were transformed (e.g., into a busy, highway-like avenue). However, in 1991 the current Green Belt ("GrünGürtel") was established by a unanimous decision of the municipal council (Stadt Frankfurt 2011; Prigge and Lieser 1992: 61–68). It is a ring around the core city of Frankfurt covering about 80 km^2, which is about one-third of the territory of the municipality of Frankfurt. At the request of the municipal council, Frankfurt's GrünGürtel has been protected since 1994 by an ordinance of the state of Hesse as a nature conservation area.[14] Through a decision of the municipal council taken unanimously in 1991, the so-called *GrünGürtel Verfassung* (Green Belt Constitution) was established in 1991.[15] It determines the goals and the boundaries of the Green Belt as well as the obligation of the municipal council to adopt all measures necessary for safeguarding the Green Belt. This obligation implies that in the case of a council decision on using parts of the Green Belt for other purposes (streets, buildings, etc.), an area equivalent in size and kind has to be added to the Green Belt elsewhere in order to preserve its overall character. Frankfurt's *GrünGürtel* was one of the first such Green Belts to be established by a constitution of this kind anywhere in the world. Tom Koenigs[16] from the Green Party, who was the head of the Environmental Department of the municipality of Frankfurt from 1989 to 1999, played a leading role in setting up the GrünGürtel in 1991. He argued: "I did not invent the Green Belt, but I pushed it through and excited many people for it" (Stadt Frankfurt

2011: 6). Current leaders in the municipal administration still acknowledge the GrünGürtel as a success story, but also stress the importance of it as a "never-ending program" (F3). Hence, there is no guarantee that the GrünGürtel will remain in its present form. However, there is an obligation to maintain and further develop it, which is based on a common vision shared by the actors in the municipal council and administration and the citizens of Frankfurt (as emphasized by F2 and F3, for example).

Tom Koenigs also played a crucial role when key decisions on local climate policy were being made in Frankfurt.[17] The mayor at the time, Volker Hauff (SPD), who was in office for a short time (until 1991), and Tom Koenigs were able to rely on a Red-Green majority in the municipal council and regarded the fields of environmental protection and increasing energy efficiency as highly relevant—the latter not only in terms of energy policy, but also and foremost in terms of climate policy. Both topics were reflected in the 1989 coalition agreement between the SPD and the Greens. Not only was the GrünGürtel a part of this agreement, but also the establishment of the Energy Unit within the municipal administration, "which should try to promote energy efficiency above all, but also emission protection" (F19). Together with the establishment of the Energy Unit, the powers of the Environmental Office were expanded. During this time, Frankfurt was co-founder of the Climate Alliance of European cities in 1990 (Kern and Bulkeley 2009)[18] and became the first German city to join the Alliance. The "climate offensive" enacted by the municipal council in 1991 and the decision to build combined heat and power plants set the four paradigmatic cornerstones of Frankfurt's energy and climate protection policy (see Stadt Frankfurt 1991; 1993; 1996): (1) stricter standards for energy-efficient construction, (2) expansion of energy-saving combined heat and power generation (decentralized combined heat and power generation as a "particularly successful method of saving energy"; Stadt Frankfurt 2010: 82), (3) reduction of heat and power requirements in residential, office, and industrial buildings, as well as (4) an increase in the share of renewable forms of energy. In February 2005, the municipality was awarded the Climate Star 2004 by the Climate Alliance of European Cities[19] for its efforts to expand decentralized co-generation of heat and electricity. Reduction of the demand for heating and electricity in residential, office, and industrial buildings has been a key element of Frankfurt's climate protection policy since that time. This key element is related to a standard for a "passive house" ("Passivhaus"), which

> was developed in Germany in the early 1990s. According to the definition of this technical standard, the heating demand of passive house buildings has to be less than 15 kWh per square meter per year—meaning the heating requirement in a passive house is reduced to the point where a traditional heating system is no longer considered essential.
>
> (Heinelt and Lamping 2015b: 299)

Thus, by passing the Passivhaus resolution of 2007, a course of activities was formally defined which constitutes political continuity rather than an innovation. However, the Passivhaus resolution bundles previous activities in the building sector. This resolution thus had the character of a codification of a particular approach in local climate policy focused on the urban building stock. According to an administrative employee, the Passivhaus resolution is "the flagship of what we have developed here [in Frankfurt] in terms of energy policy in the toolbox for climate policy" (F19). This particular focus of local climate policy in Frankfurt is justified in the line of argument of local actors (see, for example, Stadt Frankfurt 2008: 9–10) by the fact that Frankfurt's building structure is strongly characterized by skyscrapers and office buildings, i.e., by a type of buildings which are characterized by relatively high energy consumption and associated CO_2 emissions. Nevertheless, it was not until December 2009 that—based on a joint motion by the Christian Democrats and the Greens—a climate protection concept was adopted by the municipal council which is intended to further interlink, intensify, and develop all individual measures of the municipality's climate policy. On March 1, 2012, the municipal council approved a joint motion introduced by the CDU and the Greens to update the Frankfurt energy and climate protection concept with the aim of covering 100% of the city's energy demand with renewable energies by 2050 at the latest and reducing CO_2 emissions by 50% by 2030. Finally, the current coalition formed by the SPD, the CDU, and the Greens agreed in September 2019 on a municipal "climate package" which included the premature phase-out of coal from a combined heat and power plant, municipal CO_2 pricing, more charging stations for electric vehicles, climate-friendly urban development, and more greenery. The Magistrat has officially approved this program through which the city of Frankfurt wants to become climate neutral by 2050.[20]

The emphasis given to climate-friendly urban development and more greenery in this programmatic renewal of Frankfurt's climate policy indicates a challenge for innovations in another policy—namely, housing policy. As already outlined in the introduction to this chapter, Frankfurt is facing a severe problem of housing in general and of affordable housing in particular. As emphasized by a partner of a local planning office (F2), it was possible to use office buildings for housing (particularly in the Niederrad district) and to carry out several building projects in a short time and with high quality of life (such as the "Europaviertel") despite resistance by local residents (such as at the Riedberg). Furthermore, a new and so far unique phenomenon in Germany is the boom in construction of luxury residential skyscrapers, which can be observed in Frankfurt. "Currently, 5,000 apartments in 22 high-rise residential buildings are under construction or at an advanced planning stage, i.e., every fourth new apartment in Frankfurt is in a high-rise building" (Schipper and Heeg 2020: 124; translation by the authors). This new phenomenon is unique in Germany and fits Frankfurt's image of "Mainhattan." However, it can hardly be seen as an improvement in the housing sector because average prices of €10,000 per m^2 and peak values of over €14,000 per m^2 are being reported (Schipper and Heeg 2020: 124). In addition, existing instruments of housing policy are already being used to a greater and greater extent—such as municipal housing subsidies, the requirement to construct social housing when a building permit is issued, and attempts to prevent the displacement of the resident population through special permits for changes in the use of buildings in certain parts of the city. However, these instruments have not had noteworthy effects (Schipper and Heeg 2020: 124–125 and 132ff.), but their introduction and use has led to fierce debate.[21] There is also a heated debate on whether and how the municipal housing company should be used to create affordable housing and reduce rents.[22]

"With the hard club" was the headline of an article in the Frankfurter Allgemeine Zeitung/*FAZ* (February 20, 2020),[23] in which it was reported how the city is acting against cases where houses have been approved as a residential building, but apartments in these houses are rented like hotel rooms without permission. In October 2019, the head of the planning authority, Mike Josef (SPD), announced that he wanted to take stronger action against this misuse of residential building (called "illegal residential living" ["illegales Residenzwohnen"]). According to an interim report, 395 apartments have been regained for the housing market from October 2019 to mid-February 2020. The municipality "charges the providers for regulatory offenses and takes away the profits. The municipality has collected one million € in this way—in three and a half months." The municipal building inspection identified such apartments by "searching relevant internet sites." "If the rooms are only rented on a daily or weekly basis, at least for less than three months, the building inspectorate will assume that it is actually an accommodation business." This "misuse of residential buildings" is different from holiday apartment brokers such as Airbnb. However, the use of holiday apartments was rearranged by the municipality in a charter in 2018. On the basis of these statutes, the use of a person's own home as a holiday home is allowed with the permission of the municipality

> for a maximum of eight weeks a year. It is often tenants who apply for this permission. However, the providers of residential apartments are usually owners of entire buildings, in which several apartments are offered as furnished rooms in a hotel-like manner.

Finally, it is generally acknowledged that areas for new buildings must be designated in land use plans. However, this contradicted specific interpretations of what climate-friendly urban development and more greenery in Frankfurt entail, and led to a decision-making blockade not only in the council but for many years also in the current coalition of the SPD, the CDU, and the Greens. A formal compromise was reached by the "Integriertes

Stadtentwicklungskonzept 2030+" ("Integrated Urban Development Concept 2030+"). However, the goal for building 60,000 new apartments and in particular an entire new district consisting of between 8,000 and 12,000 apartments, called "Josefstadt," [24] is still causing heated political debate. These debates are taking place not only within Frankfurt, but also between the city and the neighboring towns,[25] and have culminated in two contrasting concepts (F8): according to one of these concepts, new settlement areas are to be designated and built on in Frankfurt. This concept is primarily being pursued by the Social Democrats and Frankfurt's Planning Authority. According to the other concept, new settlement areas and thus housing opportunities are to be created outside Frankfurt—in communities from which the city center of Frankfurt can be reached by public transport in no more than 30 minutes. This concept, called the "Große Frankfurter Bogen" ("Great Frankfurt Arc"), was proposed by the Hessian state government and its Minister of Economics, Tarek Al-Wazir (a member of the Green Party).[26]

Moreover, there are conflicts between the goals of saving energy and reducing CO_2 emissions through the construction of passive houses and the cost incurred with such buildings for owners and tenants. However, the passive house standard is still justified through the lowering of heating costs and thus the lowering of the "second rent"—as the municipal housing company, the ABG, had already done in the past: "Apartments in Frankfurt must remain affordable. In times of persistently rising energy prices, the company began years ago to upgrade the energy performance of buildings in order to sustainably reduce additional costs for tenants."[27]

7.3 Actors, processes, and structuration through local discourses

Compared to the neighboring city of Offenbach, Frankfurt is not struggling with the negative consequences of deindustrialization, although the once significant chemicals industry sector has decreased over the last decades. Instead, Frankfurt is benefiting from economic globalization due to the city's strong financial sector, but also due to logistics and trade. This is especially true concerning the airport, where more people are employed than in Frankfurt's banking sector. The airport is therefore seen as "an economic engine of the city" (F2).

However, these economic circumstances have not led only to a strong financial basis for the innovations outlined in the previous section.[28] They have also resulted in two dominant local perceptions regarding innovation and the problems the city is encountering. First, the city is seen as a frontrunner in innovation and, second, problems are defined as the drawbacks of the city's success. The Amt für multikulturelle Angelegenheiten argued for example that "The reasons for the increasing immigration to Frankfurt are manifold; one of the most important reasons is the economic attractiveness of Frankfurt as a 'global city' and the associated social and infrastructural networks as well as job opportunities."[29]

Both perceptions are expressed in certain beliefs about how the city functions, namely, that it is fast-paced and always changing. In this respect, Frankfurt is seen by locals not as a "laid-back city"—like Munich (Barbehön and Münch 2014: 159). Instead, problems arise quickly in the city as a result of its dynamic changes, and social problems are clearly visible. However, they are perceived as part of the city's success and characteristic of its spirit expressed in a "can-do mentality" resulting from a high level of confidence in its own problem-solving capability (Barbehöhn and Münch 2014: 159f.). Consequently, problems are seen in Frankfurt not only as the flip side of success, but also as challenges the city can and should deal with. Against this background, they are transformed into something that is an inevitable part of a positively perceived dynamic development of the city. This also means that the way the city is developing is generally not being contested. And as a result of the dynamic changes in the city that have been emphasized, solutions can and have to be found quickly.

The belief that solutions must and can be found quickly and only your own proposals make quick solutions possible also plays a role in the dispute about how new housing construction should be made possible that has already been mentioned—either primarily in the city of Frankfurt or in neighboring municipalities.[30] Those who focus on the Josefstadt and other inner-city areas (such as F8) argue that this is the only way to build thousands of new apartments in a short period of time, while supporters of the Große Frankfurter Bogen emphasize that this would be the only way to address the housing issue quickly and without uncertain legal disputes over development plans.

These widespread perceptions are also expressed in the attitude to upper levels of government (the state and the federal level): "The basic conviction [is] that the city is the mistress of its problems and can process them adequately itself, and above all quickly" (Barbehöhn and Münch 2014: 159; translated by the authors). Or as stated in the Frankfurter Rundschau (June 24, 2010): "If you orient yourself to the state government, then you cannot make any progress: the pace set by the people of Wiesbaden [where the state government is located] is much too slow."

This dominant perception is combined with a widespread understanding that strong leaders in local politics or the municipal administration are not solely responsible for and capable of solving the problems, but the local society itself—as shown by Barbehöhn et al. (2015: 70–78) and asserted by a number of our respondents. One of them (F20) even said: "This city is successful *despite* [emphasis added] the politics of city hall." Thus, the local society is seen in Frankfurt as a dynamic field of public discourse as well as interactive practice in which there is a struggle for predominant understanding of the problem and solutions are discussed. Against this background, criticism is accepted, but at the same time critics are expected to have confidence in the ability to solve problems or conflicts through communicative interaction. Otherwise, critics run the risk of being marginalized as eccentric lone fighters. Nevertheless, difference, especially cultural difference, is not only tolerated, but is in itself positively regarded.[31]

As a result, it is not surprising that most respondents emphasized that a shared or even dominant understanding of a problem in the local society was necessary for the innovations outlined in the previous section. Such an understanding of a problem forms the foundation for willingness to compromise and acceptance of innovations. Consequently, the municipality tries to anticipate possible resistance from the citizenry and to integrate their ideas in policy proposals through dialogue processes and other forms of participatory governance (as pointed out in detail by F8). The most recent expansion of the airport caused protest, but it was limited through compromises as a result of dialogue processes seen as typical for Frankfurt (e.g., by F2).

Respondents (see F1 for example) linked these observations to the city's egalitarian culture which becomes obvious in the "Eppelwoi Wirtschaften" typical to Frankfurt, where people from different parts of the local society meet and sit down at long tables to drink "Eppelwoi" (a kind of cider) together and to eat local dishes.

At these—but also at other similar—places in Frankfurt, strangers easily establish contact with locals and this contributes to a particular "localization" of cosmopolitans (F2).[32] The integration of foreigners into (urban) society in this way fits Frankfurt's image or self-perception of having always been international—nowadays especially regarding people who live in the city for professional reasons for a certain time and leave again after that. These people are usually young and well educated, want to experience urban life, and can afford high housing prices (F2).

It is easy for strangers to make contact with locals at the places just mentioned, particularly during the international fairs that have been hosted by Frankfurt for centuries. These fairs still shape the yearly routines of citizens and urban life in Frankfurt (F2).

However, within this cozy picture and the widely accepted growth policy, there has been one highly controversial issue for some years—namely, housing and rental prices. They are a particularly severe problem for residents with lower and even middle incomes. Closely linked to this issue are debates about segregation and the use of urban space. This situation might challenge the image of Frankfurt as a city which is not only able to apply solutions which are seen as the opposite of what is perceived as its success but is nevertheless still willing to implement all the same—and even more: to do so quickly. However, (at least) the following must be kept in mind. First, all growing major German cities are confronted with this issue and so far not one has found a remarkable innovation which is seen as both a novelty and an improvement by locals as well as by outside observers (Rink and Egner 2020; Egner and Grabietz 2018). Second, the successful innovations presented above were not without controversy at the time they were introduced. This applies particularly to the *Frankfurt way in drug policy* (as briefly mentioned in Section 1 of this chapter). Furthermore, Frankfurt's emphasis on climate mitigation in local climate policy has been criticized for years by those who have been more in favor of climate adaptation (Heinelt and Lamping 2015b: 295f.). Third, it might be correct to say

> that the current housing policy in Frankfurt is characterized by opposing tendencies and forces. The municipal planning authority is making efforts to supplement private-sector housing construction projects with alternative approaches in the areas of public, cooperative and/or communal housing construction. At the same time, however, there are equally strong forces within the governing coalition in Frankfurt that oppose these efforts based on the argument that only new construction by the private sector will solve the housing shortage.
>
> (Schipper and Heeg 2020: 135; translation by the authors)

However, that is what is meant by a "struggle over ideas" (Stone 2012: 13). And such a "struggle over ideas" is inevitable in order to (eventually) arrive at a common or even dominant understanding not only that there is a serious problem that needs to be solved as soon as possible, but also regarding the measures to be taken to address it in a way that is considered appropriate. That this kind of understanding is necessary to achieve innovations (in the sense of "new ideas that work") is a common feature in discussions in Frankfurt, and it is typical for Frankfurt that these discussions take place in public with strong input from the local society—and not only among political parties in the municipal council. Admittedly, these debates last a comparatively long time by Frankfurt standards. However, this may be due to the particular policy issue—namely, the "Rückkehr der Wohnungsfrage" (the return of the housing question) in the urban growth centers of Germany for which so far no convincing answer has been found anywhere.

Finally, the tradition of protest movements in Frankfurt should be considered, because the city was not only a center of the protest in 1968 (and later on) and an important place for the development of the Green Party in Germany but also for more recent left-wing protest—such as the Occupy movement. Nevertheless, Frankfurt seems to have lost its radical political heritage as occupied houses or autonomous projects—such as the "Institut für vergleichende Irrelevanz" ("Institute for Comparative Irrelevance")—have disappeared. This might be due to a growing relevance of different extended forms of citizen participation at the local level (since the 1990s), but may be also because a particular part of civil society has been pushed out of the city by high rents.

7.4 Key findings

One key finding from the case study on Frankfurt is that cities are in a good position to achieve innovations when there is a "can-do mentality" resulting from a high level of confidence in their own problem-solving capability. In Frankfurt this "can-do mentality" is also a result of a dominant understanding that problems are just the reverse side of the success of the city which enables it (ultimately financially) to solve them—and to that can be added: to solve them alone without waiting for help from others (particularly upper levels of government). In addition, the "can-do mentality" in Frankfurt involves not only a political elite but the local society as well.

Nevertheless, the current housing crisis shows that the ability to innovate can take time or is even limited. This observation is related to the fact that it is easy to agree that not only something but something new has to be done. However, it is not so easy to agree that a particularly novel approach and the way to achieve it are appropriate. This can take time—especially in the case of a policy issue for which no widely accepted solution can be found elsewhere.

Notes

1 Frankfurt was an imperial city during the time of the Holy Roman Empire (*Sacrum Imperium Romanum* or *Sacrum Romanum Imperium*; since the late 15th century occasionally used with the addition *Nationis Germanicæ*, i.e., of German nation). This meant that between 1372 and 1806 the city was a self-ruling entity and subordinate only to the Emperor of the Holy Roman Empire and not to one of the many territorial rulers of the Holy Roman Empire.

2 Dates from June 2019. See https://statistik.arbeitsagentur.de/DE/Navigation/Statistiken/Interaktive-Angebote/Pendleratlas/Pendleratlas-Nav.html (last check September 11, 2020).

3 See the article "Frankfurter Sorgen" ("Frankfurt's worries") in the *FAZ*, September 23, 2020.

4 https://www.wegweiser-kommune.de/statistik/frankfurt-am-main+beschaeftigung+2015–2018+tabelle (last check September 11, 2020).

5 https://www.wegweiser-kommune.de/statistik/frankfurt-am-main+-finanzen+2016–2018+tabelle (last check October 20, 2020).

6 https://www.wegweiser-kommune.de/statistik/frankfurt-am-main+finanzen+2016–2018+land+tabelle (last check October 20, 2020).

7 See https://www.bbsr.bund.de/BBSR/DE/WohnenImmobilien/Immobilienmarktbeobachtung/ProjekteFachbeitraege/mieten/start.html?nn=446432 (last check March 18, 2020).

8 For the information provided in this paragraph, see https://frankfurt.de/themen/gesundheit/drogen-und-sucht/der-frankfurter-weg-in-der-drogenpolitik/das-saeulen-modell; https://frankfurt.de/themen/gesundheit/drogen-und-sucht/der-frankfurter-weg-in-der-drogenpolitik and https://frankfurt.de/themen/gesundheit/drogen-und-sucht (all checked October 07, 2020).

9 See also the article "Umstrittene Pionierin" ("Controversial pioneer") in the *FAZ*, January 18, 2020, on the occasion of the 80th birthday of the former head of the Health Department under which this drug policy was introduced.

10 See, for example, the article "Zähes Ringen um den Frankfurter Weg" ("Tense struggle for the Frankfurter Weg") in the *FAZ*, September 02, 2020.

11 Daniel Cohn-Bendit was a prominent leader of the French student protest in May 1968. After his expulsion from France he was active in social movements in Frankfurt and published the city magazine *Pflasterstrand*. Between 1994 and 2014 he was a member of the European Parliament. From 2002 he was co-chair

of the Group of the Greens/European Free Alliance. He ran alternately for the German Greens and the French Les Verts and Europe Écologie-Les Verts.

12 https://amka.de/organisation (last check October 07, 2020).
13 For a full overview see https://amka.de/veranstaltungen (last check October 07, 2020).
14 http://web.archive.org/web/20181125030710/ and https://www.frankfurt.de/six-cms/media.php/738/lsvo_052010mitkarte.pdf (last check October 08, 2020).
15 https://frankfurt.de/themen/umwelt-und-gruen/orte/gruenguertel/gruenguer-tel_az/gruenguertel_verfassung (last check September 16, 2020).
16 From 1993 to 1997 Koenigs was also the treasurer of the municipality of Frankfurt. He took part (along with Joschka Fischer) in Frankfurt in the 1970s in the student movement and in squatting and street fighting. In 1973 he donated his heritage to the Viet Cong and Chilean resistance fighters. After he left office in the municipality of Frankfurt he worked for the United Nations—for instance, (from 1999 to 2002) as Deputy Special Representative of the UN Secretary-General in Kosovo, where he was responsible for setting up the local public administration, and (from 2006 to 2007) as UN Special Envoy for the United Nations Assistance Mission in Afghanistan (https://www.bundestag.de/webar-chiv/abgeordnete/biografien18/K/koenigs_tom-258568; last check November 04, 2020).
17 The following description of innovations in climate policy is mainly based on Heinelt and Lamping (2015a: 76–86).
18 https://www.climatealliance.org/about-us.html (last check October 08, 2020).
19 https://www.climatealliance.org/municipalities/climate-star.html (last check October 30, 2020).
20 See the article "Frankfurt stellt kommunales Klimapaket vor" ("Frankfurt presents municipal climate package") in the *FAZ*, September 26, 2019.
21 See, for instance, the article "Rezepte für den Wohnungsmarkt" ("Recipes for the housing market") in the *FAZ*, September 12, 2019.
22 See the articles in the *FAZ* from October 31, 2019; February 11, 2020; February 12, 2020, and February 13, 2020.
23 The following quotations in this paragraph are also taken from this article and from an article also published on February 20, 2020, with the title "Stadt schöpft eine Million Euro ab" ("City collects one million euros").
24 In local debates this planned new district is called "Josefstadt," named after the head of the municipal planning authority, Mike Josef, who is also the chairman of the SPD in Frankfurt.
25 See, among others, the following articles in the *FAZ*: "Kein Konsens darüber, wie Frankfurt wachsen soll" ("No consensus on how Frankfurt should grow") of May 15, 2019; "FDP und Grüne sehen Josefstadt kritisch" ("FDP and Greens look critically at Josefstadt") of October 26, 2019; "SPD in der Region wird für Josefstadt stimmen" ("SPD in the region will vote for Josefstadt") and "Wettbewerb für Stadtteil an der A5" ("Contest for district on the A5 motorway") of October 31, 2019; "Den großen Schinken ins Fenster gehängt" ("The big ham hung in the window") of December 13, 2019; "Weichgespülter Wachstumsplan" ("Soft-washed growth plan") of December 30, 2019.
26 https://wirtschaft.hessen.de/presse/pressemitteilung/al-wazir-startet-initiative-fuer-grossen-frankfurter-bogen (last check October 30, 2020).
27 http://www.abg-fh.com/unternehmen/wir-ueber-uns (last check July 15, 2020).
28 Respondent F3 emphasized that the annual budget of the municipality of Frankfurt is as high as states like Uganda. In fact, the annual budget of Frankfurt reached an amount of about €4 billion in 2019. But to balance the budget, about €160 million of debt had to be taken on (https://frankfurt.haushaltsdaten.de/2019/zahlen-und-fakten; last check October 30, 2020).

29 https://www.vielfalt-bewegt-frankfurt.de/sites/default/files/medien/downloads/ amka-monitoring15-final-02.pdf (last check October 08, 2020).
30 See the article "Wir brauchen Schnelligkeit bei der Planung" ("We need fastness in planning") in the *FAZ*, December 28, 2019.
31 This is also emphasized by Barbehön et al. (2015: 96) and D'Antonio (2015: 527–535).
32 https://www.zeit.de/entdecken/reisen/merian/frankfurt-main-metropole-wohnort/komplettansicht (last check October 08, 2020).

8 Kalamata

Alexia Timotheou

8.1 Introduction

Kalamata is a city in southwestern Peloponnese, the capital of Messinia sub-region, and an important port of Southern Greece. It lies 239 km far from Athens. The city extends to 440.3 km^2, while its population reached 69,849 citizens according to the 2011 census. It offers a tranquil scenery, an urban landscape directly connected to the waterfront, embraced by the imposing mountain of Taygetos and is, in respect to finance and commerce, a significant urban center of the Peloponnese Region, the administrative center of Messinia, and home to several Schools of the University of Peloponnese.

From the late 19th until the first decades of the 20th century, Kalamata made a substantial financial, social, and cultural development. The footprint of the period 1860–1914 is still evident in the city of Kalamata. These were the years when the commerce was liberalized and Kalamata was evolved into a large productive, commercial, and financial center, thanks to its proximity to the sea and fertile lands. That was the time when significant public and municipal works were constructed and keep on defining its image until this day.

During the interwar phase, the city's dynamic decreased due to immigration to the USA. Following World War II and the Civil War Kalamata did not manage to make a comeback to its former economic prosperity. Even worse, the deindustrialization of the period between 1960 and 1980 weakened even more the economic basis of the city financially because large industrial sides such as factory of wines, spirits, agricultural products, and the cylinder mills "Evangelistria" stopped working. At the same time, the military dictatorship (1967–1974) induced limitations to municipal initiatives, while cultural creativity suffered from extreme conservatism and even from different kinds of censorship (Makaris 2017).

This decline started to reverse with the tenure of Mayor Stavros Benos (1978–1990), who envisioned a new perspective for the city while preserving its particular identity and was therefore crucial for the development of the Master Plan and cultural activities of the city (outlined in the next section).

DOI: 10.4324/9781003084006-8

Mayor Benos managed to crack a long-standing dominance of the conservative Right in the city. Since then, the city has been changing hands between the two dominant parties (Nea Dimokratia/ND and the socialist party/PASOK). PASOK's influence collapsed after the outbreak of the economic crisis, while ND managed to sustain its local forces. After 13 years in office for ND politician Panagiotis Nikas (for three consecutive terms from 2007 to 2019), the mayorship passed to his former deputy mayor, Thanasis Vassilopoulos, while Nikas was elected as governor of the Peloponnese Region. But the reform of the election system that calls for proportional representation in local government left the new Mayor Vassilopoulos without a supporting majority of council members.

Despite the efforts of Mayor Benos, the 1980s marked a further decline of the thin industrial base of the whole area around the city characterized by a limited number of plants that were focusing on traditional industrial activities (e.g., textiles). This deindustrialization, later on, followed by the economic crisis since 2008, led to high unemployment and badly affected the level of social cohesion and social capital in the city.

Nevertheless, there were also some quite promising economic developments in the wider area of Messinia. It is estimated that the flagship of the tourist sector, the luxurious complex of Costa Navarino, has, directly and indirectly, contributed to the economy of Messinia with more than €2 billion in the last 10 years, since its construction in 2010.[1] The immediate effect on the area's gross domestic product (GDP) is at 3.02%, while the total impact on Messinia's GDP surpasses 8%. Almost 70% of the employees are from Messinia, while 2,508 indirect new jobs were created in the sub-region. The new investments of €1.2 billion are expected to create 11,200 direct and indirect jobs. The complex "fuels" several other sectors, such as transports, agriculture, food, fishing, and others, creating a new economy of 80 separate services with an emphasis on alternative tourist forms.

Kalamata's airport is connected with more than 30 international destinations, which increased its connectivity by more than 15 times in the period 2009–2019.[2]

With regard to the image of the city, Kalamata wants to make the best use of the new opportunities that have risen thanks to the new highway and the international airport, to become an example of a strong regional resistant city—and this in a country where everything is concentrated in the capital. It wants to be acknowledged as an extrovert city achieving sustainable development, giving emphasis on culture and arts, environmental protection, and urban renovation. To this end, its natural attributes are of enormous assistance, with the picturesque landscape, the renowned agricultural products (particularly extra virgin olive oil), and the good food, available almost everywhere, offering a comparative advantage. On top of that, the vivid artistic and cultural life makes the city a unique place to live in and visit.

8.2 Issues of Innovations

Greek cities are, in most of their parts, the unplanned products of historic and social development. The city of Kalamata claims to be the only city that managed to alter its form based on human-centered urban planning, based on two priorities, environment and culture.

It all started a few decades ago, when a visionary mayor, Stavros Benos, along with a team of inspired scientific associates envisioned a better future for the city. The planning process finished in April 1986 with an integrated Master Plan, which proved the most powerful weapon against the city's biggest disaster in its modern history: the earthquake of the following September. In dealing with the disaster, self-organization, innovation, knowledge, and learning capacity were evident throughout the whole period from emergency response to reconstruction (Dandulaki 2018).

The earthquake destroyed almost 25% of the built-up areas. The municipality's first reaction was to maintain Kalamata's historic and cultural identity. All actions were based on their belief that earthquakes afflict humans even more than buildings, and therefore all efforts were oriented to save the city through a process framed by the Master Plan which was the city's compass toward economic and social reconstruction.

> On the night of the earthquake, although in anguish, I felt calm and optimistic about the future of my town. Thanks to the recently completed planning, we knew exactly where the new buildings and services would be placed. [...] For our city, the earthquake was our savior.
>
> (Ka1)

Since the city already had a detailed Master Plan, it was much easier to ask for financing from the Greek government's Program of Public Investments, as well as from European Funds (European Investment Bank and Reconstruction Fund of the Council of Europe).[3] It was the first time that European funding procedures bypassed central government and money flew directly into the municipality's accounts (Ka2).

Another challenge was the bunch of smaller or bigger interests trying to defeat the planned rebuilding of the city (see Section 8.3). It was not easy, and the conflicts were relentless. However, local authorities managed to stick to their original planning, and, finally, the reconstruction of the city was carried out in accordance with the plan at hand. The overall long-lasting efforts of urban reconstruction were awarded by the European Commission, the European Council of Town Planners, and EuropaNostra (an organization for saving and giving prominence to the city's monuments).[4]

Shortly before the earthquake, The Master Plan was adopted shortly before the earthquake of 1986. The Municipal Enterprise of Cultural Development of Kalamata (DEPAK) had been established in 1985, focusing on three fields: dance, music, and visual arts (painting and sculpture). Right after the earthquake, significant efforts were made not only to keep these activities going but also to boost the established cultural structures even more, as the citizens' way out from these desperate times. This handling positively affected the morale of the inhabitants in those difficult times and laid the foundation for a unique cultural identity for the city and the generations that came along. New institutions were established and cultural associations were supported, rendering the city an exemplar for the country.

Later on, taking advantage of the National Cultural Network of Cities initiated in 1995 by the Greek Ministry of Culture, the city of Kalamata stepped up on its existing cultural activities and chose to be further promoted as "the city of dance." Of course, "the initiative came from the Ministry of Culture, but the response of the city was bold and decisive" (Ka3). This resulted in the creation of the International Centre of Dance, whose main activity is the *International Dance Festival.*

Since 1995, the Festival attracts visitors from Greece and abroad. The Festival is considered as one of the most significant dance events in Europe, due to the professionalism that characterizes its planning and the presence of internationally renowned artistic groups, as well as new talented artists, whose later course has proven their rightful selection by the Festival.[5] The International Dance Festival has helped to build bridges with international choreographers, boost creativity of young artists, and, of course, provide financial resources to the city.

In addition to this cultural innovation, about 30 more associations dealing with cultural aspects emerged over the years. This "confirming that the establishment of strong municipal institutions, such as the Dance Festival, not only do not undermine the operation of other associations but on the contrary, they fully support them" (Ka3). In 2008, DEPAK was merged with three other municipal organizations—the Vocational Training Center, the Municipal Theatre, and the Municipal Enterprise of Tourist Development—to a newly established organization entitled FARIS (the name of a local mythical demigod), which continues the cultural activities of the city.

Kalamata also applied to be the European Capital of Culture for 2021. Although it eventually lost to the rival city of Elefsina, Kalamata wanted to claim the title of European Capital of Culture for 2021, projecting its comparative advantage as the "only example of a city implementing the ideal of cultural decentralization. It's a typical provincial Greek city functioning as a stronghold of contemporary European civilization."[6] Citizens practically showed how they care for their city, drafting a cultural strategy and actively engaging in working groups for the common cause, proving that they need and ask for innovative actions.

After the announcement of Elefsina as the European Capital of Culture for 2021, the former Mayor Nikas spoke about "an unfair decision, which certainly has political background."[7] However, Kalamata's candidacy left behind a valuable legacy ready to be exploited for the benefit of its people. In fact, citizen-based projects ("Art from Citizens," "Citizens Today—Citizens

Tomorrow") resulted from activating about 400 people in Kalamata, which is quite a remarkable number for a small Greek city. Another proposed project was the "Culture Pass," a map of culture in the city, which offered a more detailed cultural strategy and specific ways of attracting visitors. In general, Kalamata's candidacy included some key elements that could contribute in the mid-term to the city's cultural strategy, and according to the European Capital of Culture selection committee, the energy, commitment, and participation of citizens were worth further development.[8]

Local businesses supported the city's efforts with their own funds, financing the second phase of the contest for becoming the European Capital of Culture with €180,000.

Although Kalamata was not hit by the economic crisis of 2008 as severely as the big agglomerations in Greece, the city still had to deal with a high percentage of citizens in need. Against this background, new municipal social services were established, namely, the municipal grocery, the medical center, the social pharmacy, the offering of free meals, and the local vegetable gardens. These structures are mainly financed by the municipality and supported by volunteers, the Church, and private donors.[9]

Emphasis is also given to the Κέντρα Δημιουργικής Απασχόλησης Παιδιών, i.e., centers targeted at the harmonization of family and professional life of parents. With the cooperation of several actors (e.g., FARIS, the center for environmental education, the World Wildlife Fund, the municipal unit of health, the community library, the municipal conservatory, and gallery), these centers aim at the physical, emotional, mental, and social development of children.

Another innovation in Kalamata is the renovation of the old hospital to the new city hall, a new modern public building. It is one of the few public buildings in Greece to be cooled and heated with geothermal energy. The new city hall houses almost all municipal departments and services, thus saving money from paying rents to other buildings. Additionally, the CO_2 emissions have dropped to one-third, while there is no further need for oil or fossil fuels. Regardless of the outdoor conditions, the operation costs have dropped by 30%. As far as the social impact is concerned, the new city hall has revived the degraded western side of Kalamata, after the old hospital's removal, whilst new jobs have been created around the area.[10] For this reconstruction, the city was awarded the "Oikopolis" award in June 2017, an award for environmental awareness.[11] And in the same year the city also received the panhellenic award for buildings' energy efficiency.[12]

An inextricable part of Kalamata's and Messinia's history and economy are olive groves and olive oil. After an initiative of George Karampatos, former President of the Messinian Chamber of Commerce, the organization "Olive Tree Routes" was established and after a few years (in 2003) they were unanimously recognized by Unesco as "World Cultural Route of Intercultural Dialogue and Sustainable Development." The Routes of the Olive Tree are itineraries aimed at promoting intercultural dialogue and heritage awareness based on the olive tree, a universal symbol of peace. In 2005, the Routes of the Olive Tree were certified as a Cultural Route of the Council of Europe. This certification enables the "Routes" to act as a gateway to new cooperation between territories and bring together organizations, inter alia, universities, actors of civil society, scientists, artisans, and artists from several olive-growing countries, as well as Chambers of Commerce, companies, and also other Euro-Mediterranean networks.[13]

This was the official acknowledgment of an idea that started and expanded thanks to an initiative outside of the municipality. The municipal authority has not supported this effort in any way. The organization was initially supported by individual people, who implement various activities, among them, olive tree feasts, short itineraries for the discovery of olive-growing regions, information days and seminars around the olive tree culture and cultural tourism, studies and researches on the Mediterranean products, and traditional gastronomy, but also actions aiming at hosting and integrating refugees from olive tree countries.[14]

One must keep in mind that in former times the tourist policy was only limited to some fragmented efforts to attract tourists in the wider area. The statement of the former Mayor Nikas is characteristic of the pertaining understanding of this issue that the "tourist policy is not listed in the municipality's responsibilities."[15] For the first time, the current municipal leadership announced a new program (funded with €170,000) to promote tourism in the next years. The new strategic plan emphasizes new technologies, the city's promotion in different events and exhibitions, and the need for prolongation of the tourist period. During the deliberations of the respective municipal council, councilors also referred to the plan as a dynamic procedure, which will be evolving, adapting, and improving.

Among the tourism activities of the former city government, the installation of technical equipment should be mentioned, which enables disabled people to have easy and autonomous access to the sea.[16] This initiative developed disability tourism since disabled persons can visit Kalamata and get the chance for rehabilitation in the water.

Technology-oriented companies showed particular interest to assist in new digital practices. Via "DigiKa" (Digital Kalamata), the municipality's effort was to create a new mentality of using electronic tools, a digital culture that would contribute to saving time and money and developing long-distance cooperation with other actors. Furthermore, Kalamata has been trying to become a "smart city," operating a wireless network for the city areas of great financial importance and high visibility. "DimosKalamatas-WiFi" is free for all and it uses a fiber network and open software technologies. The wi-fi network, apart from its obvious advantages, offers visitors and inhabitants the possibility to get acquainted with Kalamata and its history, use its transportation means, get informed about cultural events and other activities in the city, get an overview about entrepreneurship in the city by a webGIS map, and, more importantly, receive administrative services from the municipality, submit requests (by a platform called "citizens' observatory"), and get informed about the municipal bodies' activities and decisions. Finally, a digital observatory for climate change provides information publicly on the consumption of energy and water of all municipal buildings and infrastructure. The overall goal of all these measures is to highlight the historic and tourist wealth of the city, support tourism, and improve the services of the municipality through a new digital environment.

Finally, a new Sustainable Urban Mobility Plan (SUMP)[17] is under deliberation now. It is

> a strategic plan designed to satisfy the mobility needs of people and businesses in cities and their surroundings for a better quality of life. It builds on existing planning practices and takes due consideration of integration, participation, and evaluation principles.

There is a special section on the municipality's website, where citizens may submit their views, as foreseen.

8.3 Actors, processes, and structuration through local discourses

The tenure of Mayor Benos (from 1978 to 1990) brought great changes for the city and a new narrative of the city's development potential. New institutions were established in the sector of culture, while with the help of renowned figures of the time, Grigoris Diamantopoulos, a well-known urban planner, and Manos Hatzidakis, a famous composer and man of culture, the issues of environment and culture were incorporated into the new urban planning (Ka1). Grigoris Diamantopoulos was the one who convinced Mayor Benos that their work would be successful "only if we can persuade citizens that their benefit coincides with the city's benefit" (Ka1).

Moreover, the economic and political context in the country was accommodating for a visionary reconstruction. With the access of Greece in the EC in 1981 and a political era starting at the Greek national level with the victory of the PASOK in the election in the same year, promoting "change," forward-thinking, and comprehensive solutions did not seem outlandish. Nonetheless, the new approach to reconstruction was not automatically and effortlessly introduced (Dandulaki 2018).

In fact, the implementation of the plan proved to be quite difficult. The new law 1337/1983 was about to set a brand-new framework for town planning. This development at the national level, however, heated up the debate in Kalamata on the Master Plan. During the session when the municipal council of Kalamata was to vote on the levies on the inhabitants, in the form of land and money which were to be paid in connection with the plan,[18] outraged citizens who felt their interests were being touched invaded the city hall and attacked the mayor and his advisers. These citizens of Kalamata were supported by many citizens from all over Greece who had come to Kalamata because they also saw their interests affected by the new planning law. This incident had nation-wide implications, boosting awareness and sympathy for innovative planning efforts.

The disaster caused by the earthquake was the window of opportunity for Kalamata's reconstruction. Thanks to the completed Master Plan a few months earlier, the municipal authority had a carefully designed strategic plan to rebuild the city and maintain social cohesion.

Thus, Kalamata became a role model in Greece. It was one of the few times when a natural disaster was dealt with in such an organized and integrated manner, and it was also the first time that the level of credibility of the local authority (due to the well-documented plan) was rewarded by the EU with direct cash-outs to the municipality (as already mentioned in Section 8.2).[19] The municipality's role from emergency response throughout reconstruction was an outcome of innovation and self-organization, as there was no institutional outline of specific responsibilities and tasks in disaster management (Dandulaki 2018).

Moreover, culture was the element that was used by local authorities to enhance social cohesion. Although some opponents considered the support of culture to be "a kind of luxury" (Ka2), no one from the responsible leadership of the municipality did ever think to envisage it as a secondary issue on the municipal agenda (Ka2). The priority in reconstructing historical buildings and the organization of cultural events consisted the framework in which leadership dealt with the disaster. Even today, this particular cultural identity of the city makes it stand out in the country, rendering it a successful show-case. Although the International Dance Festival is not financially sustainable ("culture is never financially sustainable"; Ka2), its positive side effects in attracting tourists and making the city famous on the cultural world stage are, however, considerable.

Nevertheless, interviewees (Ka3, Ka4) have expressed complaints about the management of existing assets in this field, such as the newly constructed dance hall. The new hall was inaugurated in 2019 with the ambition to become a hub of culture for the whole region of Peloponnese, focusing not only on dance but on theater, music, visual arts, and additional events, such as scientific conferences, lectures, and expositions, giving a boost to Kalamata's sustainable development.[20] However, municipal authorities only use the hall for a small number of events, which is the reason for critical voices to argue that its true potential is not exploited (Ka3). The same interviewee argued that both the dance hall and the International Dance Festival were not appropriately used in Kalamata's candidacy for the European Capital of Culture.

Although it lost to its rival city Elefsina, Kalamata has managed to activate and bring together several actors in the city and pull together an important work that could be used to further improve the city's infrastructure and institutions. However, although efforts were made to start a dialogue in the municipal council (from actors other than those acting in city hall), no discussion ever started, and the municipal leadership is to be blamed (Ka3).

> One of our city's biggest disadvantages is that the local authority [refer- ring to the former mayor Nikas; the author] does not support new initi- atives, neither gives the floor to other actors to express their views [...] although we have remarkable human capital with new ideas and will- ingness to help the city, and we really have the infrastructure and es- tablished institutions as a background [for further innovations], the municipality suffocates these voice.
>
> (Ka3)

In general, Greek society is not characterized by active participation in mu- nicipal issues. Despite the activities described above, this is also true in prin- ciple for Kalamata. This is demonstrated by the Επιτροπή Διαβούλευσης. It is a committee overseen by law (L. 3852/2010) for municipalities of more than 10,000 citizens in which societal actors and citizens are involved, who thereby have the chance to discuss and find solutions along with the munici- pality for issues concerning the local community. This committee has only a small number of actors (Ka2, Ka3, Ka4), and in the last years there have not been any attempts to reverse this situation. There are societal actors with a strong voice, such as the Chamber of Commerce and the University of Pe- loponnese, which have made several proposals to the municipal authorities (the previous leadership). However, as per an interviewee (Ka4) if the mayor does not agree with these suggestions nothing can advance: "During my tenure as the Chamber's president, I had sent approximately eighty thou- sand letters addressed to the mayor [the former mayor Nikas] with different proposals. I never got an answer, not once" (Ka4).

And regarding the SUMP (mentioned at the end of Section 8.2) an inter- viewee admitted that besides the formal process, no systematic efforts were made to promote this action, and therefore the people's response is not what one would expect. "We are not having any dynamic relationship with the people" (Ka2).

Finally, the system of simple proportional representation that was intro- duced by the former SYRIZA (leftist) government has made it more diffi- cult for local leaders to push through innovations. In the past, mayors (like Benos) could expect that their ideas would be supported by their majority party and that new ideas could be pushed through in the municipal council even against resistance—although of course, even then this was accompa- nied by a struggle over ideas, whose successful outcome, i.e., a dominant understanding of what has to be done why, would make implementation easier. Nowadays, a success in such struggles over ideas is even more im- portant when no clear majority exists in a municipal council. A characteris- tic example for Kalamata for such a constellation was the case of blocking the installation of a 5G wireless network in the city. The municipal council decided to suspend the 5G pilot program which would have made Kala-mata the first city in Greece to have such a network. The majority who were against this wireless technology claimed that it would possibly cause serious repercussions on public health.[21] After a heated, three-hour-long debate, the decision to suspend the program was carried by 16 votes to 13 (13 votes were in favor of the mayor's suggestion to wait until the experts' tests and measurements). The mayor, Thanasis Vassilopoulos, lamented, "I have nine municipal councilors and can count on as many as 16 on specific issues out of a total of 41,"[22] showing his disappointment. This case did not only demon-strate problems caused by the proportional electoral system, it also demon-strated that innovative measures can only be successfully implemented if it is discursively clarified (and not just by counting the votes cast) why some-thing new should be introduced—something new that is recognized as an improvement. A consideration of the communicative mechanisms presented (in Chapter 2) and their application with reference to the narrative patterns prevailing in Kalamata would probably have helped.

8.4 Key findings

Kalamata has been developing into a modern urban center, a reference point in southwestern Peloponnese. The city is endowed with a beautiful natural landscape, which along with the new infrastructure, attracts not only tour-ists, but business potential as well.

Forty years ago, Mayor Benos managed to create a new narrative for the city. Stepping on two basic pillars, environment and culture, he laid the foundation for transforming Kalamata into a city of culture and a role model for the rest of the country. Of course, this did not happen overnight. It took many years and the active contribution of multiple actors (municipal enterprises, private companies, local cultural associations, and groups of citizens). Municipal administrations after Benos' leadership also cultivated this mentality (some more and others less) and even though today's cultural activities are not characterized by the same dynamic as before, Kalamata has managed to rebrand itself, standing out as a culturally renovated city with flagship events such as the International Dance Festival.

This is quite unique for a small Greek city like Kalamata, but since local society has benefited from culture-related services and infrastructure, it is now an inseparable part of the city's identity. As one of the interviewees admitted,

> [...] our children had the chance to participate in such activities [attend-ance in DEPAK's courses for dance, music and visual arts; the author] and from my perspective, for my two kids, these courses defined them even more than the everyday school [...] Today they can distinguish what is worthy and what is not.

(Ka2)

Moreover, apart from micropolitics and rather usual conflicts in everyday local political life, there seems to be unanimity in the role that major stakeholders play in the development of Kalamata.

In the end, the city's reframing from a small provincial coastal town to a rising center of modern culture seems to be sustainable, since Kalamata has experienced to a great extent the benefits of innovative changes.

Notes

1 https://www.tornosnews.gr/epixeiriseis/hotels/39997-costa-navarino-sta-2-diseyro-h-symvolh-toy-sthn-topikh-oikonomia.html (last check November 18, 2020).
2 https://www.tornosnews.gr/epixeiriseis/hotels/39997-costa-navarino-sta-2-diseyro-h-symvolh-toy-sthn-topikh-oikonomia.html (last check November 26, 2020).
3 https://www.ekdd.gr/ekdda/files/ergasies_esta/T4/030/10305.pdf (last check November 26, 2020).
4 http://www.benos.gr/Articles-Container.asp?Article=020 (last check November 26, 2020).
5 https://kalamatafaris.gr/%ce%ba%ce%b1%ce%bb%ce%bb%ce%b9% cf%84%ce%b5%cf%87%ce%bd%ce%b9%ce%ba%ce%ad%cf%82-%ce% b4%ce%bf%ce%bc%ce%ad%cf%82/%ce%b4%ce%b9%ce%b5%ce% b8%ce%bd%ce%ad%cf%82-%ce%ba%ce%ad%ce%bd%cf%84%cf% 81%ce%bf-%cf%87%ce%bf%cf%81%ce%bf%cf%8d-%ce%ba%ce%b1%ce% bb%ce%b1%ce%bc%ce%ac%cf%84%ce%b1%cf%82/ (last check November 17, 2020).
6 https://www.news247.gr/koinonia/etsi-tha-ginei-i-kalamata-politistiki-proteyoysa-tis-eyropis.6453853.html (last check November 18, 2020).
7 https://www.messinialive.gr/nikas-gia-politistiki-protevousa-kalamata-eprepe-echei-epilegei-dystychos-adikithike/ (last check November 18, 2020).
8 https://eleusis2021.eu/wp-content/uploads/2016/12/ecoc-2021-greece-selection-report_9.12.2016GR.pdf (last check November 18, 2020).
9 For similar local innovations in the provision of social welfare services see particularly the chapters on Chania and Elefsina in this book.
10 https://www.tharrosnews.gr/news/content/%CE%B-D%CE%AD%CE%BF-%CE%B4%CE%B7%CE%BC%CE%B1%CF%8 1%CF%87%CE%B5%CE%AF%CE%BF-%CE%BA%CE%B1%CE%B-B%CE%B1%CE%BC%CE%AC%CF%84%CE%B1%CF%82-%CF%83% CE%B5-%CE%AD%CE%BD%CE%B1-%CE%BA%CF%84% CE%AE%CF%81%CE%B9%CE%BF-%CF%8C%CE%BB% CE%B5%CF%82-%CE%BF%CE%B9-%CE%B4%CE%B7%CE%BC% CE%BF%CF%84%CE%B9%CE%BA%CE%AD%CF%82-%CF% 85%CF%80%CE%B7%CF%81%CE%B5%CF%83%CE%AF% CE%B5%CF%82-%CE%BC%CE%B5-%CE%B1%CE% BD%CE%B1%CE%B2%CE%AC%CE%B8%CE%BC%CE%B9%CF%83%CE% B7-%CF%84%CE%B7%CF%82 (last check November 18, 2020).
11 https://kalamatain.gr/new/to-vravio-ikopolis-2017-sto-dimo-kalamatas/ (last check November 18, 2020).
12 https://www.messinialive.gr/dimos-kalamatas-proslipseis-7-kathigiton-gia-kdapmea/ (last check November 18, 2020).
13 https://olivetreeroute.gr/whoweare-en/history-en/ (last check November 18, 2020).

14 https://olivetreeroute.gr/whoweare-en/history-en/ (last check November 18, 2020).

15 https://www.tharrosnews.gr/2020/01/%CE%9F%CE%B9-%CF%80%CF%81%CE%BF%CF%83%CE%B4%CE%BF%CE%BA%CE%AF%CE%B5%CF%82-%CF%83%CF%84%CE%B1-%CF%8D%CF%88%CE%B7-%CE%B3%CE%B9%CE%B1-%CF%84%CE%BF-%CF%83%CF%87%CE%AD%CE%B4%CE%B9%CE%BF-%CF%84/ (last check November 18, 2020).

16 https://seatrac.gr/en/about-seatrac/ (last check December 28 2020).

17 https://ec.europa.eu/transport/themes/urban/guidance-cycling-projects-eu/policy-development-and-evaluation-tools/sumps-and-cycling_en (last check November 18, 2020).

18 http://www.benos.gr/0020-Stuff-Speeches/Seismoi-002-003_DialexiKontopoulou.pdf.

19 https://messiniapress.gr/2018/09/13/gr-diamantopoylos-o-poleodomos-poy-allaxe-tin-kalamata-meta-toys-seismoys-toy-1986/ (last check November 18, 2020).

20 https://eleftheriaonline.gr/stiles/apopseis/item/169634-gia-to-polypatho-megaro-xoroy-kalamatas (last check November 18, 2020).

21 https://greece.greekreporter.com/2019/12/05/sterilization-fears-force-greek-city-of-kalamata-to-suspend-5g-network/ (last check November 18, 2020).

22 https://www.messinialive.gr/apli-analogiki-kai-i-steirosi-evalan-telos-sto-5g/ (last check November 18, 2020). Although the municipal council of Kalamata consists of 41 members only 29 participated in the vote of the council because some councilors left the meeting after the discussion without casting their vote, and some were absent.

9 Kassel

Melina Lehning

9.1 Introduction

With 205,481 inhabitants (by the end of 2019),[1] the city of Kassel is the only large city in the northern part of the German state of Hesse. Kassel lies both in the center and on the edge: in cultural, economic, and geographic terms the city is the center of northern Hesse. However, compared with other larger German cities it plays a less pivotal role and is located far away from urban centers (Schroeder 2016: 14). Nevertheless, Kassel has good connections to the rest of Germany and Europe by motorways and high-speed trains. The significance of Kassel's location is expressed, above all, by its current economic structure based on transport, mobility, and defense industry: it is the second largest production site for VW (Volkswagen) in Germany and is also home to smaller Daimler, Bombardier, and Krauss-Maffei Wegmann production sites. The economic structure also has an industrial heritage, which is why the city is described as a "working-class city" (Flemming 2016).

The industrial heritage led to a situation described by an interview participant as follows: Kassel was "really in a downward spiral" with hardly any positive dynamics or forecasts (K8). Nevertheless, over the past 10–15 years there has been a transition from a purely industrial city to an industrial as well as cultural one (K3). This development started with the reunification of Germany. While Kassel had a peripheral location before 1989, late in that year German reunification shifted the city to the center of Germany (if not Europe) starting in 1990. This made the city more attractive as a location for industry and logistics and led to a dynamic economic development in the region around Kassel (Hessisches Ministerium für Wirtschaft, Energie, Verkehr und Wohnen 2012: 13). In addition to the increasing economic attractiveness of the city, Kassel has benefited from the changed role of the university since the 2000s (K3), because its expertise has been used to strengthen the potential of Kassel and the region (K6). The University of Kassel is now a "dynamic motor that can send development impulses in various directions" (K3). As emphasized by the Hessian state government, "modern industry, cross-company and cross-cluster innovation approaches based on close cooperation with an application-oriented university

DOI: 10.4324/9781003084006-9

landscape are the fundamental success factors for the region" (Hessisches Ministerium für Wirtschaft, Energie, Verkehr und Wohnen 2012: 5). These approaches are pursued around Kassel (as elsewhere) "to increase regional competitiveness, to offer sustainable, high-income jobs and to promote the balance between the rural regions and the center" (Hessisches Ministerium für Wirtschaft, Energie, Verkehr und Wohnen 2012: 57). A growing number of small and medium-sized enterprises, so-called hidden champions (Schroeder 2016: 16; translation by the author), not only contributed to economic growth but also improved the image of the city both internally and externally.[2] The result was a

> significant increase in industrial production in the city of Kassel, where the initial figure in 2000 was exceeded in 2006 by almost 40%. Over the course of the financial and economic crisis of 2008, however, industrial production also weakened significantly in the city of Kassel, but in 2009 it was still 15% above the starting level of the year 2000.
> (Hessisches Ministerium für Wirtschaft,
> Energie, Verkehr und Wohnen 2012: 15)

The city of Kassel also registered a surplus of almost 4,000 commuters per day (Hessisches Ministerium für Wirtschaft, Energie, Verkehr und Wohnen 2012: 9) and a population increase of 13,522 people between 2008 and 2019 (Schroeder 2016: 16).[3] The unemployment rate, which for a long time was above the national average, has fallen to 5.9% by 2018 (Stadt Kassel 2019: 38). Per capita income increased from €2,383 per month in 2006 to €3,342 per month in 2016 and at the same time "Kassel is the only city in the region to record an increase in the number of people in employment" (Hessisches Ministerium für Wirtschaft etc. 2012: 9). The demographic change is also a result of an increasing number of students at the University of Kassel.

However, despite the increase in population, housing prices are still modest compared with Frankfurt (see Chapter 7) and Bensheim (see Chapter 4), but also Offenbach (see Chapter 11). In 2018 the average rent for an apartment with up to 40 m^2 was approximately €9.60 per m^2 and for an apartment with up to 80 m^2 about €7.40 per m^2,[4] while in 2018 the average price for purchasing an apartment was €2,250 per m^2.[5]

Besides the economic and demographic transformation just outlined, the city stands out due to its image as a cultural center. The "reorganization of the cultural sector" (Schroeder 2016: 15; translation by the author) is related to a changed local (self-)perception which has contributed to shaping the image of the city in the "outside world" as well. The municipality has supported this change, above all, by providing suitable framework conditions such as rooms or corresponding funding portfolios (K2).

As in all German cities, local self-administration also plays a crucial role in Kassel (Stadt Kassel 2019). The city council is the supreme organ of the municipality (Stadt Kassel 2019),[6] and the magistracy acts as the executive body. The magistracy is a collegiate governing body chaired by the mayor as "collegial leader" (Heinelt and Hlepas 2006: 36). Since 2005, this position has been held by Social Democrats (Bertram Hilgen from 2005 to 2017 and Christian Geselle since 2017). From 1993 to 2005 the post was occupied by a Christian Democrat (Georg Lewandowski). Nevertheless, the Social Democrats form a central component of Kassel's everyday political life, and the city has long been one of the strongholds of the Social Democratic Party of Germany (SPD), even though its proportion of the vote is declining in Kassel, as in Germany in general. From 2006 to 2016, the SPD ruled in a coalition with the Green Party (Bündnis 90/Die Grünen). In the 2016 local elections neither party won enough seats in the council to continue this government, which is why the SPD formed a coalition with the Green Party and the Free Democratic Party (FDP). After the local elections in March 2021, the Greens became the strongest group in the council and formed a coalition with the SPD. This suggests that the council will continue to promote the development of the city as described below.

9.2 Issues related to Innovations

From a historical perspective, a wide variety of innovations can be identified. These include the first pedestrian zone in Germany, which was opened in 1953 (Eckardt 2014). Another innovation involving the physical construction of public space was the raised curbstones at bus stops, the so-called Kasseler Busborde ("Kassel's bus curbstones"; K11).

More recent institutional innovations are related to the fact that most companies are not located in the city but in the surrounding area, something which makes close cooperation among the municipalities necessary. This cooperation takes place at various levels in the form of networks. One example is the Zweckverband Raum Kassel,[7] which was founded for this purpose in the 1970s. However, as a result of changes following the reunification of Germany, the Regionalmanagement Nordhessen GmbH[8] now plays a more important role (Hessisches Ministerium für Wirtschaft, Verkehr und Landesentwicklung 2012: 24). This regional development agency is a public-private partnership established in 2002. It is owned by the city of Kassel and five Landkreise (counties), on the one hand (together owning 50% of shares), and, on the other, by the regional Chamber of Commerce and Industry, the regional Chamber of Crafts, and a business association called *Pro Nordhessen* (owning 30%, 15%, and 5% of the shares, respectively; K1).[9] The agency coordinates partnerships in clusters to develop and implement measures for strengthening and safeguarding jobs and general economic growth and, through this, the national and international competitiveness of the region. In addition to commercial site marketing, main areas of activity are mobility, health, decentralized energy production, and tourism, which are "the cornerstones of competitiveness and innovation" (Hessisches Ministerium für Wirtschaft, Energie, Verkehr und Wohnen 2012: 54).[10] What is unique here, as one respondent said, is the way in which problems are perceived and possible solutions are developed—namely, through shared awareness of regional problems and willingness to find the appropriate "set of levers" to solve them together (K1). This understanding of collaboration under the umbrella of the Regionalmanagement Nordhessen GmbH is reflected in various working groups (e.g., the German-Chinese business network; K1) and is expressed in the particular narrative providing the basic understanding of what development policy means in the region. The core of this narrative is that decisions on the promotion of the region are made "at the same table" and that "competition among participants would only produce losers" (K1). And, in fact, this form of cooperation with a "high number of exchanges and networks" (K2) made it possible for Kassel to make the cultural and economic turnaround together with the surrounding municipalities and Landkreise (counties).

Another example is the competence network *dezentrale Energietechnologien e.V.* (deENet. E.V.; an association of experts and companies that specialize in decentralized energy technologies), which was founded in 2003 to develop and implement sustainable lighthouse projects together with research institutions, municipalities, and companies in the Kassel region (K13).[11] With its more than 100 members, the key objective of deENet e.V. is networking and integration of companies in the region, which is also reflected in the number of members in the association. Although the initiative came from industry, trade associations, and research, the region was involved in the topic of renewable energies from the very beginning in order to strengthen industry and trade. The goal is

> [...] to develop the region into an internationally recognized location for future energy supply and efficiency. To this end, sustainable lighthouse projects are being developed and implemented together with companies, research institutes and local authorities. Precisely to increase the regional added value and competitiveness, for jobs with sense and of course for a high quality of life in our beautiful North Hessen.[12]

In 2016, deENet e.V. was integrated into the clusters of the Regionalmanagement Nordhessen GmbH. Today, despite the innovation potential emanating from deNEet e.V this network no longer has a strong position, as the topics covered by deENet e.V. have increasingly been taken over by the Frauenhofer Institute for Energy Economics and Energy System Technology (K8).[13]

Further innovations can be found in the context of the university. The University of Kassel was viewed critically by the citizens, especially in the beginning when it was established as a "Gesamthochschule," i.e., a combination of a university and a university of applied sciences. One respondent said:

> They have always said "What is this? We are here between Marburg and Göttingen and we are given a pseudo university, which is actually not

a real university at all." In this respect, this university was never really admitted into the city community.

(K3)

Another respondent (K10) added:

> In the beginning it was more a rural university, where mainly people from northern Hesse and southern Lower Saxony studied. And now it is a nationally and partly also internationally recognized university, which brings more and more new people to this city with new ways of life.

As a result of being renamed as university, a process of change took place in which the university is now defined as an important element of the city, because Kassel "went from a city with a university to a real university city" (K9). In addition to the increasing number of students who have shaped the cityscape and the society, there is also a pool of ideas and young start-ups that contribute significantly to the perception of the city of Kassel as an innovative center in the region. A task of existing companies is now seen as coordinating the implementation of new ideas through so-called partnership platforms and, particularly with start-ups, to offer them a home and to exploit regional potentials (K4; Bieber 2016: 145). Another symbol of this kind of institutional innovation is the opening of the Science Park located on the university campus that provides office and workshop space for young start-ups in an area covering over 6,000 m^2. As a limited liability company, the Science Park belongs half to the city and half to the university. One respondent described it as a nationally perceived project which, as a university start-up and innovation center, offers a possible contact point for all those who have a connection to the university (K8). This contact takes place primarily via transfer organizations such as UniKasselTransfer, for the purpose of making competencies and new ideas "actively usable for society."[14] Since 2015, the

> professional and creative environment as well as the proximity to the university [...] have made Science Park Kassel the location for innovative start-up companies from all areas of the university... it offers space... experienced specialists... start-up consulting and start-up financing [... It] increases the attractiveness of the city as a business location.[15]

The changes in the region meant that cooperation between the actors and site marketing became more important. The Zweckverband Raum Kassel as a planning body was strengthened as a result. One interviewee pointed out that it was nevertheless the creation of the Science Park as an interface between research and application that succeeded in bundling the dynamics that had emerged since the beginning of the 1990s (K8). People who would normally have gone elsewhere now returned to Kassel and remained in the city or the surrounding region. The Science Park thus contributed not only to the concentration of innovative ideas, but also to a more favorable perception of the improved quality of life (K8).

Despite the strengthening of the regional economy with the help of innovations such as the Science Park, a clear social dividing line can be seen within the city. While in half of the city there is a more middle-class and expensive residential structure with a high degree of gentrification, the neighborhoods around the so-called Nord-Holland are characterized by social housing and high unemployment as well as a significantly higher proportion of people with an immigration background than the rest of the city. "Industry started here" (as emphasized by an interviewee [K1]). In order to meet the associated social challenges, the "Zukunftsbüro" ("Future Office") was founded in 2008. Since then, the city of Kassel has been working together with the Landkreis and the Evangelische Akademie Hofgeismar (Protestant Academy Hofgeismar) to find solutions to the shortage of skilled workers and to increase civic engagement.[16] The Zukunftsbüro falls under the responsibility of the mayor and acts as "a link between the municipal administration, the functionaries in organizations and the citizens, in order to develop perspectives together and actively shape the future."[17] But there is still great need for action. For this reason, local actors are trying to cope with the consequences of demographic and economic changes through their own initiative. Due to rising rents, the proportion of affordable living space is also declining in Kassel. This is leading to a high proportion of empty shops in some parts of the city which gave some students the idea of breathing new life into vacant buildings and making it possible for residents to interact with each other by changing the use of the former shops. Under the name "Kontaktlabor" ("Contact Lab") they organize encounters that should offer space for a renaissance of neighborhood meetings even in times of increasing digitalization.[18]

A connecting and at the same time characteristic element in the city apart from industry is culture. While the industrial sector was neglected for a long time, the cultural scene has developed strongly since reunification, also through the establishment of associations (K6). In the meantime, it is precisely the cultural sector that shapes the image of the city to the outside world and thus also its political action (K2, K4, and K8). As one respondent (K6) stated, culture is "sacred" in Kassel and much more important than anything else. However, as another interviewee (K3) emphasized, it has to be kept in mind that in Kassel cultural activities in general and cultural innovations in particular follow a kind of predetermined path. Manifestations of this are the United Nations Educational, Scientific and Cultural Organization (UNESCO) world cultural heritage "Bergpark Wilhelmshöhe" and the UNESCO world heritage site Grimmwelt. Another cultural figurehead of the city is the "documenta,"[19] which has been critically evaluated over a long period (K7). It is now perceived in the city as something special and an expression of the "uniqueness of this city," since it has "created an independent cultural world market-oriented basis" (K3). This is also expressed in the name "documenta Stadt," which has been in use since 1999 (Klaube 2013). Everything is now "staged and culturalized" and this has led to the creation of "an independent, cultural, world market-oriented basis" (K3). As a result, the last documenta, which was held for the first time in Kassel and in another city, namely, Athens, was the subject of heated debates. Not just because costs were higher. Rather, many people had the feeling that "our silverware" was being taken away (K3). It becomes clear that the citizens are more open to culture, which is now also perceived internationally. One interviewee (K2) said:

> The documenta was not popular from the start. For decades there were massive discussions and now the people of Kassel say "This is our documenta and we identify with it." It's a development that is not all that old. In other words, establishing such an innovative and sometimes provocative format in the urban society in this form involved a long, long journey.

Nevertheless, culture has become a strong identifying feature about which people are proud and which they do not want to share with others. Citizens increasingly perceive culture as an important feature of their city, which is also reflected in a young and "vibrant, free culture scene" (K2). Inhabitants have been particularly committed to various initiatives such as the operation of the KulturBahnhof,[20] whose halls are also home to CARICATURA. Further examples are the KulturNetz,[21] the Kasseler Kultur Forum e.V.,[22] and the "Junge Kultur Kassel" initiative,[23] which was founded in 2009 to preserve public spaces such as outdoor swimming pools or to use the former Salzmann areas (an industrial monument) as an intercultural meeting place for the younger generation. The significance of art to the city of Kassel is also evident in the way the Kunsthochschule ("academy of art"; K13) is viewed. It was integrated into the University of Kassel at an early stage. Since then, however, its status has been controversial; it is actually only a faculty. Because it possesses a certain degree of autonomy, the art academy finds itself in an undefined intermediate position[24] and connects institutionalized culture and the independent cultural scene. It has become clear that culture has been transformed from a "foreign object" (Fremdkörper) into an integral part of the cityscape (K7).

As in the industrial sector, an open planning process can also be identified in the field of culture. The "Kulturkonzeption"[25] (cultural concept) plays a decisive role in these developments. This was developed in the course of Kassel's application to become the "European Capital of Culture 2025," because the preparation of a cultural development plan was required by the European Union (EU) as a prerequisite for a successful application.[26] In the period from July 2017 to June 2018, citizens and actors, especially from the field of culture, had the opportunity "to work out the potentials, challenges and guidelines for the further development of culture in Kassel against the background of social transformation processes."[27]

Although the application was withdrawn at an early stage, in the sense of a cultural strategy the concept represents an important milestone in promoting cultural potential on the one hand and in using culture as the flagship of the city on the other, in order to create a nationally as well as internationally visible identity (K1 and K2).

By combining a critical review of the status quo and planning a coherent set of future activities (rather than individual and isolated measures), more attention was paid to areas that should be strengthened (K2). Especially in the field of culture, this led to an increased identification of the inhabitants with the city, for example, through recognition of the documenta as "our documenta" (K2). A follow-up project, the so-called Kulturkonzeption Kassel 2030, serves as a further measure to keep this process alive.[28]

9.3 Actors, processes, and structuration through local discourses

In general, the city has seen increased involvement of civil society. Although there are some closed networks, regular cross-sectoral meetings are an essential feature of a relatively homogeneous urban society and at the same time an important prerequisite for the development of innovations (K6). The municipality helps develop measures to ensure the participation and integration of interest groups. In this context, culture builds a connecting link (K2). "Dense civil society structures," especially in the field of culture, are "anchored in the DNA of the city" (K3). Consequently, pluralistic and active civil society participation represents an important element of policymaking in Kassel (K2), but also leads to a variegated critical mass, making it difficult to steer projects in one direction (K6).

In particular, structures and processes through which innovations are developed and implemented are often informal in Kassel (K5). Experts and civil society actors exchange views on specific topics and problems in these forums. However, these are usually open networks in which anyone can participate. The networks are also strongly consensus-based (K2 and K9).

Admittedly, one respondent said that it usually takes a lot of "suffering" to get decisions moving (K3). This is expressed not least of all by the fact that it took about a decade to consider and agree on the advantages for the city offered by the reunification of the two German states. The more informal structures and the involvement of a large number of actors also contribute to the fact that problems cannot be dealt with more quickly (K6). According to these particular local circumstances, the first step is to recognize and define problems and to develop perspectives for solving them. This process is then followed by planning based on perceived future challenges, such as those arising from so-called megatrends such as globalization or digitalization (K2). An important factor here is the size of the city. Kassel finds itself in a "field of tension between provincial and world art (documenta)." The city is big enough to discover new things, but small enough to keep track of the big picture. As one interviewee (K2) remarked, exchanges among "the institutions, with business, with industry, with the university and with individual actors" as well as direct contact with artists is readily possible, particularly due to the size of the city. Consequently, an "us versus them" attitude ("Lagerdenken") is not common and bottom-up processes are strongly emphasized:

> And these different actors [...] obviously have very different ideas [...], but also varying impetus which they lend to such a process. The actors introduce creativity, ideas, but also wishes and demands [...]. It is [...] the task of the municipal administration and politics to create structures and framework conditions for the implementation of these wishes and demands. And this is exactly the same process as found with Kulturkonzeption. That parallel worlds are not established [...] but, instead [...] things are linked together.
>
> (K2)

The Regionalmanagament Nordhessen GmbH and the Kulturkonzeption are examples of substantial innovations in Kassel characterized by the fact that they are based on particular forms of networks or working forums that seek to closely examine the status quo and challenges in the respective policy areas while formulating aims and strategies, and implementing activities. Nevertheless, the Regionalmanagement Nordhessen GmbH and the Kulturkonzeption follow "different approaches" (K2). While primarily economic and infrastructure issues are dealt with by the Regionalmanagement Nordhessen in clusters, the Kulturkonzeption encompasses cultural activities developed within the framework of Kassel's application for selection as the European Capital of Culture 2025.

The emergence of the Regionalmanagement Nordhessen GmbH was the result of various workshops which focused on working out core elements of a regional development concept. This also included an analysis of strengths and weaknesses and the definition of specific goals and actions for different sectors. These workshops were initiated by various actors in November 2000, such as the regional Chamber of Commerce and Industry, the University of Kassel, the "Regierungspräsidium" (deconcentrated administration of the Hessian state government for the region), and the business association Pro Nordhessen.[29] This process resulted in the draft of a cooperation and partnership agreement, which was discussed with the Hessian Minister of Economics and finally signed in January 2002. From then on, leading figures in local politics and business dealt with the design of the most efficient forms of cooperation as public-private partnerships.

The Kulturkonzeption evolved in different ways. First of all, it was the result of an extended informal dialogue between actors from the fields of art, education, and culture. However, there was also a stocktaking event to summarize the status quo (Kruska and Pröbstle 2017: 4). A broad-based participatory process ultimately defined the general goal "to develop potentials, challenges and guidelines for the further development of culture in Kassel, and, in particular, the cultural scene, against the background of social transformation processes" and made it possible to translate these goals into more specific targets and recommendations for actions (ibid., translated by the author). To achieve this, everyone had to be aware of the opportunities and constraints of the actions of all actors involved in this participatory process (K2).

One interviewee made it clear that important impetus also comes from the university, in particular from the Science Park with its numerous cooperation networks (K8). The research topics reflect current problems and fields of action. It is important that the problems not be tackled in one single place. Rather, it is also important to take the strong regional disparities into account, and consider the resulting pressure of surrounding municipalities on the Landkreis. Thus, networks play a special role in Kassel. The Science Park seeks to reflect this mindset and by understanding networks as ecosystems and building a "learning system between cooperation networks" so that dynamics and problems that vary from field to field are taken into account (K8).

This view was also expressed when deENet e.V. was established as a network bringing together various actors from the energy sector. The challenge in such collaborations is usually that "some people are not fully aware of their respective roles" and there are isolated "power struggles and fighting behind the scenes" even though there is common ground (K8). For this reason, pioneers are usually needed "to introduce best-practice examples on site" (K8) such as the professor who provided the crucial impetus for founding deENet e.V. (K13).

It becomes clear that Kassel is a city of discontinuities and contrasts, especially from a historical perspective (K8). For a long time, Kassel was—in comparison with other cities—unable to cope with its position in the shadow of the southern part of Hesse. This role was mainly attributable to the geographical distance from the Rhine-Main area and is also reflected in social perception, which is why the region around Kassel is still called "Hessian Siberia." According to one respondent, this situation always ensured that (mainly financial) efforts were modest and "the lesser variant was always chosen, and effort was always limited" (K14). It seems that local actors (particularly in the city hall) have now learned to apply and market this role strategically. This did not happen overnight. A major upheaval was brought about by the reunification of the two German states, in the course of which the economic conditions in and around the city changed. This is expressed both in a change in the discourse and in a change in strategy, which are linked to the identification of opportunities and innovative ways of using them as well as to the development of new leitmotifs or images which function as points of reference for further communicative interaction. While for a long time the image as a workers' city was regarded as a symbol of largely economic problems, the narrative has changed and Kassel now plays an even more important role as an industrial and cultural city, especially as a *Regiopol* (regional center) in northern Hesse (Schäfer 2008).[30] However, the story of the "Armenhaus Kassel" ("poorhouse Kassel"; K11), which is located in the "valley of tears" (K1) and "rose like a phoenix from the ashes" (K8), was essential for the actions of the local actors. It should be borne in mind that individual areas cannot be considered independently. Rather, due to their novelty innovations have usually had an interdepartmental effect which is not confined within departmental borders and related, specific problem perceptions and action orientations.

The renaming and reorientation of the university confronted the city with a larger number of young people. The resulting structural changes and conflicts—for example, in the area of housing supply or the retail vacancy rate—were not seen as a problem but were presented as related to the "increased attractiveness" of the city (K7). People now also wanted to stay, and Kassel is ranked one of the most innovative cities (K7 and K8) in a large number of city surveys.

Developments over the last 10–15 years show that a changed perception of the problem is now shaping policy-making in the city. A financially more or less balanced municipal budget as well as a shifting structural and image have made it possible to turn attention to larger issues such as the consequences of globalization or climate change. The city was thus open to external political questions that needed to be taken into account. In this context, the city began to be marketed as open and international (K11) and tried to break with the image of "Hessian Siberia." An expression of this was the "documenta14" held both in Kassel and in Athens.

Culture plays a special role in this context, although for a long time its significance was not presented as a decisive characteristic of urban life in Kassel. Over the last 30 years this has also changed from an economic perspective. The marketing of culture as a figurehead of the city led to a new external perception. Culture has been increasingly regarded as an economic factor. Furthermore, culture is now seen as a connecting element in the city with an effect on its dynamics, which are claimed to exist as a result of a vibrant, young, and liberal-minded art scene.

9.4 Key findings

Given the economic and demographic changes it underwent after 1989, Kassel needed "new ideas that work" in order to change from a poorhouse to a city of art and culture. Furthermore, the city has capitalized on its position in the shadow of southern Hesse, especially the banking metropolis

Frankfurt and the state capital of Wiesbaden, and is now depicting itself as a "survival fighter" in "Hessian Siberia." It can thus be said in summary that the mentality of tackling and solving problems together in open networks described above can be regarded as a characteristic of Kassel (K1). Various committees are being set up to achieve a "lebendige Vielstimmigkeit" ("lively polyphony"; K4). However, important for this process are (also in view of local actors) so-called frontrunners that spread a "spirit of optimism" and thus motivate all actors involved. If such a frontrunner is in place, this can lead to problems being addressed relatively fast (Kruska and Pröbstle 2017: 4). Concerning innovations in economic development and in arts and culture, it was crucial in Kassel that in local discourses the potentials resulting from the reunification of Germany were recognized: these made it possible to shift the city from a peripheral position directly alongside the Iron Curtain to the center of Germany or even Europe. Resulting changes were both perceived and actively used to make the city more attractive as a logistics location (K6). As a result, many large companies settled in and around Kassel, which led to an appreciation of the region. Kassel developed into a "cultural, administrative, service and knowledge metropolis in northern Hesse" (Schroeder 2016: 16; translation by the author). There was a transition from a purely industrial city (based on metal, electrical, and defense industries) to a city characterized by industrial production as well as culture. This transformation was a long-term process because it took time for something new to be accepted in Kassel. Key improvements cannot be clearly assigned to a particular sector of society or policy. Rather, innovations have been achieved in a collaborative way that made it possible to pursue specific problem perception and approaches to address problems. This may explain the fact that Kassel is often underestimated and that it often appears that the city does not use enough of its potential due to "encrusted structures" (K13).

Notes

1 https://statistikatlas.kassel.de/bericht1/atlas.html (last check October 8, 2020).
2 These "hidden trump cards" are portrayed in the brochure "Hidden champions – Leading North Hessian Companies in Profile." Available online: http://www2.hna.de/bkbackoffice/getcatalog.do?catalogId=186245#page_8 (last check September 11, 2020).
3 https://statistikatlas.kassel.de/bericht1/atlas.html (last check September 11, 2020).
4 https://www.immowelt.de/immobilienpreise/kassel/wohnungspreise (last check September 11, 2020).
5 Although indicators of economic and demographic changes are positive, it must be mentioned that Kassel was part of the Hessian bailout program for over-indebted local governments (Heinelt and Stolzenberg 2014: 234f.). Between 2013 and 2017 the municipality received around €260 million from the state government to reduce its debt. This amount contributed significantly to the consolidation of the municipal budget.
6 https://www.kassel.de/buerger/rathaus_und_politik/kommunalpolitik/inhaltsseiten-gremien/stadtverordnetenversammlung.php (last check September 11, 2020).

7 https://www.zrk-kassel.de/ (last check October 02, 2020).
8 http://www.regionnordhessen.de/start/ (last check September 11, 2020).
9 http://www.regionnordhessen.de/regionalmanagement/ueber-uns/ (last check September 11, 2020).
10 For an overview of the current projects, see http://www.regionnordhessen.de/regionalmanagement/aufgaben-und-projekte.html (last check September 11, 2020).
11 https://www.kassel.de/unternehmen/wirtschaft-inhaltsseiten/deenet.php; https://www.deenet.org/unsere-aktivitaeten/rueckblick/nordhessen-2020-dezentrale-energie-und-arbeit/ (last check September 11, 2020).
12 https://www.kassel.de/unternehmen/wirtschaft-inhaltsseiten/deenet.php (last check September 11, 2020).
13 https://www.iee.fraunhofer.de/ (last check September 11, 2020).
14 http://www.uni-kassel.de/ukt/startseite.html (last check September 11, 2020).
15 https://www.sciencepark-kassel.de/science-park/das-konzept/ (last check September 11, 2020).
16 http://www.landstaerken.de/index.php?id=zukunftsbuero_stadt_kassel (last check September 11, 2020).
17 http://www.landstaerken.de/index.php?id=zukunftsbuero_stadt_kassel (translation by the author; last check September 11, 2020).
18 https://www.kassel-live.de/2019/05/08/mehr-kommunikation-wagen/; https://www.hna.de/kassel/kassel-kreative-lassen-leere-laeden-aufleben-12304502.html (last check September 11, 2020).
19 https://www.kassel.de/buerger/kunst_und_kultur/documenta.php (last check September 11, 2020).
20 http://www.kulturbahnhof-kassel.de/informationen/ (last check September 11, 2020).
21 http://kulturnetz-kassel.de/verein/ (last check September 11, 2020).
22 http://kulturnetz-kassel.de/verein/ (last check September 11, 2020).
23 http://www.ijkk.de/ijkk/ (last check September 11, 2020).
24 https://www.kunsthochschulekassel.de/kunsthochschule/portraet/autonomie/?L=1 (last check September 11, 2020).
25 https://www.kassel.de/buerger/kunst_und_kultur/kulturkonzeption.php (last check September 11, 2020).
26 https://www.kassel.de/buerger/kunst_und_kultur/auf-dem-weg-zur-kuko.php (last check September 11, 2020).
27 https://www.kassel.de/buerger/kunst_und_kultur/auf-dem-weg-zur-kuko.php (last check September 11, 2020).
28 https://www.kassel.de/kulturhauptstadt/https://www.kassel.de/kulturhauptstadt/ (last check September 11, 2020).
29 http://www.regionnordhessen.de/regionalmanagement/ueber-uns/ (last check September 11, 2020).
30 The term "Regiopol" primarily refers to smaller or mid-sized, urban regions lying outside Germany's most densely populated metropolitan areas (such as the largest, the Rhine-Ruhr metropolitan region encompassing Essen, Dusseldorf, Cologne, and Bonn). A regiopolis functions as an economic center within the surrounding region. In order to remain competitive, they usually present themselves as innovative locations with their own development potential (see Aring and Reuther 2008: 8–33).

10 Leipzig

Hubert Heinelt and Max A. Kayser

10.1 Introduction

At the end of June 2020, the city of Leipzig had a population of about 593,000 people.[1] However, it should be mentioned that it had its peak population in 1933, when 713,000 people lived in the city. At that time, the city was compared by locals as well as by people elsewhere (see Steets 2008: 166) with Hamburg, Cologne, and Frankfurt as well as with Barcelona, Lyon, and Manchester. Buildings from the late 19th and the early 20th century, i.e., the time when Leipzig was seen as a European "boom town," are the city railway station (one of the biggest in Europe) and the "Baumwollspinnerei," which was one of the biggest cotton mills in Europe (Steets 2008: 173).[2] The decline of the city started after World War II. In the years between 1980 and 1989 alone, i.e., the years before the unification of the two German states, the population of Leipzig decreased by 30,000 (Steets 2008: 160). One of the reasons for the decline in the city's population was that many houses built in the late 19th and early 20th century had become uninhabitable due to systematic lack of maintenance investment. After the unification of Germany the population of the city decreased further from 530,000 in 1989 to 490,000 in 1999 (Lütke Daldrup 2003: 55; Rink and Kabisch 2019: 843–849) due to economic restructuring in the territory of the former German Democratic Republic and the movement of people to the West, i.e., the "old" Federal Republic of Germany (Bartetzky 2015: 11–19).

As a result of the declining population, about 60,000 apartments were uninhabitable at the end of the 1990s (Rink and Siemund 2006: 52). In addition, 800,000 m^2 of office and commercial space were unused at this time (Steets 2008: 166). And even at the beginning of the 2000s it was emphasized that "there are about 2,500 Wilhelminian style houses [houses built in the late 19th century; the authors] not yet rehabilitated and over 90 percent no longer inhabited" (Lütke Daldrup 2003: 55).

Between 2000 and 2010 the number of inhabitants increased only at moderate average annual rates of less than 1%, but between 2011 and 2017 the population has been growing remarkably by average annual rates of about 2%, which means, in absolute terms, by approximately 10,000 people.[3]

DOI: 10.4324/9781003084006-10

The recent increase in inhabitants can be seen as an indicator of a successful redevelopment of the city. However, this success has led to new challenges which call for new interpretations of what can and has to be done (with priority), i.e., innovations different from those achieved in previous years.

Indeed, the opening of new factories by BMW (in 2005, now with 5,300 employees)[4] and Porsche (in 2002, now with 4,000 employees)[5] as well as of a newly built airport which has developed as a hub for air cargo (with DHL and Amazon logistics centers, for example) have contributed positively to the economic restructuring of the city. The same applies to a newly developed media sector. The economic restructuring of the city has been supported by all sorts of funding from the federal and the EU levels, for which the municipality has applied energetically and successfully (L3; see also Bartetzky 2015: 193–197).[6]

Nevertheless, the unemployment rate remains high (6.3% in 2019), although it is lower than in most parts of the territory of the former German Democratic Republic.[7]

Leipzig has good connections to motorways (A9, A14, and A38) as well as to the German railroad system, particularly to the new high-speed train connection between the south (Munich) and Berlin. Furthermore, the Leipzig/Halle airport has developed remarkably in recent years—however, as mentioned above, more for air cargo than for airline passengers.[8]

Leipzig is the site of several institutions of higher education[9] which have attracted students during the last decades not only from Eastern Germany, but also from Western Germany and elsewhere—not least due to comparatively low rents for housing.

10.2 Issues related to Innovations

In 2003/2004, in a study of the development perspectives of the city in the context of high levels of housing vacancies and decay as well as numerous vacant lots and areas of undeveloped land, the municipal planning director, Engelbert Lütke Daldrup, and a member of a local private planning office, Marta Doehler-Behzadi, characterized Leipzig as a "perforated city" ("perforierte Stadt"; Lütke Daldrup and Doehler-Behzadi 2004: 10ff.; see also Bartetzky 2015: 204–211).[10] At the time, Leipzig was viewed as a "perforated city" because it differed from the image of a densely populated and compact European city due to its high levels of vacant houses and numerous empty and derelict properties. In other words, over recent decades the large number of vacant houses and numerous abandoned building lots have perforated the city, which in the 1930s was a densely populated and compact city (with 713,000 inhabitants in 1933; see above).

The diagnosis of Leipzig as a "perforated city" led to a particular reference point for political measures with two conclusions: on the one hand, further loss in density and compactness of the city should be avoided, whereas, on the other hand, existing—or more precisely, available—vacant and decaying housing as well as numerous vacant lots and areas of undeveloped land should be treated as an asset (see Rink and Siemund 2006: 53).

The expression "perforated city" was not only an innovation in itself, as the expression was new. More importantly, the expression brought an innovative understanding of "de-densification" to bear—namely, more green space, more light, and more opportunities to live without enforced commercial valorization (L2). This understanding of the city questioned discursively the notion of urban life that regards density as a core element of "urbanism" (Wirth 1956) and vacant spaces only as a loss of density and thereby of urbanity.

This notion of urban life has been very important for Leipzig because for many years after 1989 "material or social artifacts which are perceived by observers as both a novelty and an improvement" (Braun-Thürmann 2005: 6) have been related mainly to successful attempts to use vacant housing and vacant lots as assets.

However, the more Leipzig moves in the direction of growth again, the more this notion of urban life is losing its relevance as a reference point for debates at the local level and resulting political decisions. The same applies to the attention being paid to the initiatives outlined in the following as innovations. What has been needed since the beginning of the 2010s is a new reference point for how to deal with urban growth, which requires an answer to the question how to use available land to address the challenges of building new housing (together with private developers or not) and safeguarding space for public infrastructure and green inner-city areas (as emphasized particularly by L14 and L15).

First successful attempts at using vacant housing and vacant lots as an advantage were initially developed independently of activities by the municipality in the 1990s by young people who occupied vacant buildings not only for housing, but also for self-organized parties, clubs, readings, and art exhibitions. Many of these activities were initiated by students at the local institutions of higher education, who tried to use the "free spaces for self-realization" ("Freiräume der Selbstverwirklichung"; KREUZER 2007, No. 5, 12ff.) offered by the city. This gave rise and meaning to a key word in local discourses concerning the city—namely, "Leipziger Freiheit" ("Leipzig freedom"; see also below)—which was later (until 2017) also used for marketing purposes.[11]

Over time, some of the initially self-organized activities and the networks of people carrying them out became legal organizations (nicely described by Silke Steets 2008: 182–211), and contributed substantially to Leipzig's image of having stimulated the rise of the creative class (Florida 2002) of this city (Steets 2008: 14–17). Examples are activities in the former Baumwollspinnerei (mentioned above), where artists and painters especially found space for their work and galleries (such as the EIGEN+ART gallery)[12] and were able to present their work as well as contemporary paintings in general.

This applies in particular to painters of the so-called Neue Leipziger Schule ("New Leipzig School"). The most prominent representative of this kind of contemporary painting is Neo Rauch.[13]

To legalize occupied houses and retention of vacant houses, in 2003 the municipality developed together with an association—named *HausHalten*— the so-called Wächterhäuser (guardian houses; see also Bartetzky 2015: 233–236) as an innovation. Through this scheme people searching for housing or space for other uses (e.g., an art gallery) are allowed to use vacant houses, but they have to take care of the building they are using.

> The *basic principle* of the Wächterhäuser is very simple: house maintenance through use. The use of the house prevents vandalism and limits weather damage, as these are quickly discovered and remedied by the users. "A lot of space for little money" is the maxim[...][14]

The legal basis for the Wächterhäuser is a concession agreement ("Gestattungsvereinbarung"; see Rink and Kabisch 2019: 851) between the owner and the HausHalten association, in which the right of use of the house is transferred to the association for five years (see Rink and Görbing 2019: 6–7). The owner of these houses was and still is not exclusively the municipality (or its housing association, the Leipziger Wohnungs- und Baugesellschaft/LWB). Instead, many of these houses are private property. Contracts between the association and individual users regulate the rights and obligations of users. When the users of a house form a housing community, the contracts are replaced by a direct agreement between the owner and the "Wächter," i.e., the users, as "guardians" of the building.[15]

The HausHalten association also manages another innovation in coping actively and creatively with vacant houses in need of renovation—namely, "Ausbauhäuser" (houses to build up or renovate). In this case, an individually defined standard of reconstruction or renovation is combined with a classic tenancy. To provide a long-term but flexible perspective, the rental agreement is directly between the homeowner and the tenant. Tenants receive living space for individual self-development coupled with stable, favorable rental conditions, while financial investments and maintenance work carried out by tenants are counted toward rent. For the homeowner, this arrangement offers long-term stable, calculable rental income and added value, with comparatively lower levels of capital expenditure on their part.[16]

The basic difference between Wächterhäuser and Ausbauhäuser is that the former are mainly for temporary use (usually until a renovation has been carried out) and the latter for long-term use based on a rental contract.

The HausHalten association is part of the "Netzwerk Leipziger Freiheit." This network is financially supported by the municipality based on a council decision (L15). It supports initiatives to form (small) housing cooperatives and is backed by the housing policy adopted by the municipal council in

2015 (Stadt Leipzig 2015; see below). Through this decision the municipality has committed itself to strengthening such initiatives by making municipal real estate available and offering advice on all matters relating to cooperative building and living.[17] As mentioned on its website

> [...] *Leipziger Freiheit* is an example of the possibilities for development and the creative freedom of this city. The creative... handling of possibilities and spaces... is part of Leipzig's self-image. This has added to the city's reputation in competition with others and confronted the downward spiral of birth decline and job churn.[18]

An innovative initiative, now taken by people in Leipzig as a matter of course, is the form of participatory planning practiced in Leipzig under the motto "Leipzig weiter denken" ("Thinking Leipzig ahead").[19] It involves a broad spectrum of actors in debates on the future of the city and on instruments/measures for reaching agreed goals, and is an expression of the kind of civic-mindedness that characterizes political processes in Leipzig. However, the question remains open whether and how far this initiative can make a contribution to establishing a new reference point for debates in Leipzig on how to deal with urban growth and find an answer to the question of how to use available land to address the challenges of building new housing and safeguarding space for public infrastructure and green inner-city areas.

10.3 Actors, processes, and structuration through local discourses

The following two aspects are basic features of "how things are done" in Leipzig, i.e., of processes of public debate and decision-making.

At first glance a basic feature of "how things are done" in Leipzig is that since 1990 all mayors of the city have been Social Democrats, and the Social Democrats (SPD), the Left, and the Green Party have been collaborating in the council (Brieler and Rink 2019: 834). Consequently, Leipzig is called a "red city." This is seen as a reason why the relationship between local government and the government of the federal state of Saxony is perceived as not an easy one (L1). However, the tensions between the federal state of Saxony and the city of Leipzig are not based on party politics alone, but also on a particular relationship with upper-level government. Leipzig is seen by its citizens as a "city of citizens" ("Stadt der Bürger")—in contrast to Dresden, which is not only the capital of the federal state, but was also the former residence of the King of Saxony. This means that citizens of Leipzig are used to "doing things for themselves" (L7), i.e., without the "patronage" of an upper-level government. This attitude of local people can be seen not only in the way civil society initiates innovations by pushing topics on the agenda of local politics and the administration. It is also expressed by the fact that even today a significant portion of the costs of cultural activities and institutions in the city are covered by local people and not by funds from the federal state. One example of this is the difference between the Semperoper in Dresden and the Gewandhaus in Leipzig. Whereas the Semperoper was built as the royal court theater and still functions as the state opera of Saxony, the Gewandhaus was initially founded by local merchants and aristocrats and is now run as a municipal enterprise (see Gewandhausorchester 2019 and Semperoper 2019). The name Gewandhaus refers to a cloth warehouse run by local merchants where the first concerts took place. This shows that the Gewandhaus was created by and for Leipzig's citizenry—in contrast with the (royal) Semperoper (ibid.).

The second basic feature of "how things are done" in Leipzig is that public debates in Leipzig were and are still based on a widespread sense of justice in the citizenry and a simultaneous willingness of citizens to act autonomously—in keeping with the slogan "Leipziger Freiheit." This does not mean that there are no "Wutbürger" in Leipzig, i.e., angrily shouting, demanding citizens.[20] However, there is a citizenry that not only actively participates in discussions about urban challenges, but is also prepared to take autonomous action to solve identified problems (L2). The result is a habitus expressed in the following way: "We do not have problems! We are confronted with challenges we can solve!" (L3).[21] It also demonstrates that milieus with such an attitude have survived the political regime of the former German Democratic Republic (GDR). But it also means: "You cannot bypass Leipzig's citizenry" (L3).[22] This attitude is expressed in protest movements and a widely shared pride in historical protests—particularly in the context of the regime change in 1989.

> Leipzig, the shabby, dilapidated Saxon metropolis, seemingly robbed of all its former splendor, intelligence and openness, liberated itself and the entire GDR from the shackles of the [communist] SED regime. The narrative of Leipzig as the *hero city* ["Heldenstadt"] was born.
> (D'Antonio 2015: 95)

This widely shared pride about historical protests even refers back to previous centuries (for an overview of historical protest actions in Leipzig, see Krehl et al. 2005).

Important for innovation, especially in the period after the fall of the Berlin Wall and up to the end of the 2000s, was the undisputed understanding in Leipzig, however, that everything must be done to reduce the unemployment rate, which was around 20% during this period. This uncontroversial understanding was also supported by otherwise rather reluctant actors. This was the case, for example (with regard to the Protestant parish, among others), for the sale of land in order to be able to establish new sites for companies such as Porsche, DHL, BMW, and Amazon. In addition, the noise of aircraft, which are also allowed to use the airport during the night, was accepted against the background of this shared understanding. Things are different now due to the better situation of the local labor market (as emphasized by L7 and L11; see also further below).

Another basic shared understanding of challenges and perspectives for action in Leipzig until the end of the 2000s has been captured in the expression "perforated city." It meant (as described in the previous section) that a further loss of density and compactness of the city needed to be avoided and that the existing vacant housing and numerous unused plots of land needed to be regarded as assets for the development of the city. This understanding guided decision-making in urban development, with respect to the use of vacant housing and vacant lots in the inner city as well as to the development of industrial sites and similar other activities on the outskirts of the city area.

Both strategies complemented each other in the understanding of local actors (as emphasized by interviewees). Furthermore (as will be shown at the end of Section 10.3), the complementarity of (a) stimulating business and similar developments on the outskirts of the city and (b) the use of vacant housing lots in the inner-city area was also supported by the organizational structure of the municipal administration.

Against the background of a widely shared understanding of what should be done (and a related reference point), it is not surprising that operational decisions were taken quite quickly and without resistance during the first two decades after the unification of the two German states in a city that was used to lively debates (L2). The establishment of sites of Porsche, BMW, DHL, and Amazon in the 2000s are examples of rapid operational decisions handled as a top executive priority ("Chefsache"), i.e., decided by the mayor (L2).

Although from an outside perspective conditions with respect to urban development may have seemed favorable, the debate in Leipzig about existing housing vacancies and areas of undeveloped land shows that identifying a particular solution depends on the collective interpretation of given circumstances. The diagnosis of Leipzig as a "perforated city" and the resulting perspectives on innovation are an example of this.

Nevertheless, debates during this time also usually revealed the existence of controversial elements because this is what debates are about. In this respect, political debates can be seen as an expression of a process aiming at a collective choice of knowledge and interpretation ("Wissenswahl" and "Deutungswahl"; Nullmeier 1993: 186) by which reference points for further debates and operational (policy) choices ("Handlungswahl"; ibid.) are (or can be) defined, which eventually lead to innovations. Consequently, lively public debate on the one hand and rapid operational decisions on the other were not seen as a contradiction in Leipzig. The city seems to be an example of how lively public debates can contribute to shared understanding of "what has to be done" (a collective choice of interpretation) and what the challenges and opportunities are, and from what perspective policy choices should be made. This has been the precondition for developing the ability to decide quickly when a choice of action has to be made in a specific situation.

It might be argued that fast decisions are possible in Leipzig because of the collaboration of the Left, the Green Party, and the SPD, which have a majority in the council. However, local politics is characterized by the "Leipziger Modell" (Brieler and Rink 2019: 835–837). This means flexible majorities are formed in the municipal council. In other words, council members of the individual parties do not pursue a clear party line, but decide on a case-by-case basis. This approach emerged in the 1990s precisely to make rapid decisions (L3).

The "Leipziger Modell" can also encourage bottom-up agenda-setting because councilors in Leipzig are open to new ideas, as long as they are perceived as beneficial to the city (L9). To determine whether an idea or measure is beneficial to the city is of course easier when a shared understanding of what can and should be done has been reached. Open-mindedness, particularly concerning experiments, is especially the case for the innovation already mentioned such as the Wächterhäuser or the free spaces used by the creative art scene. Such open spaces were described as one of the main assets of Leipzig and the reason why people move to Leipzig in order to have space and possibilities to do things the way they want to (L9). The reason why Leipzig could offer those possibilities in contrast to Dresden cannot be explained by cheap rents and vacant buildings alone, but is also a result of the very different attitudes of the local societies, the political parties, and (at least during the first two decades after unification of the two German states), the municipal administrations.

Today, the debates in Leipzig on the current challenges posed by growth in general and gentrification in particular are much more controversial—not only in terms of how these challenges can be effectively addressed, but also in terms of what is perceived as normatively appropriate (L3; see also Bartetzky 2015: 274–277; Rink and Kabisch 2019: 858–860). This is not surprising because there is a lack of collective agreement on the interpretation of these challenges.

Given that a collective interpretation of the challenges is lacking, a vast number of not only new but also contradictory ideas have been articulated in public debates and by the political parties in the municipal council in recent years. Under such circumstances, consent (or even a compromise) is hard to find, and when a decision is taken it often turns out to be difficult for the municipal administration to implement and put into practice against resistance (such as an ambitious local climate policy; see Büttner and Rink 2019). It is not surprising that under such conditions actors (L9, L10, and L14) perceive the municipal administration as "too slow," arguing that "innovations happen *despite* the administration" or emphasizing that in 1905 the architect of the "new city hall" already referred ironically to the slow municipal administration by putting snails on the doorknobs of the main entrance. Although the people with whom interviews were conducted broadly highlighted that the administration of the city of Leipzig has been open-minded, particularly concerning experiments, it is also emphasized that changes in this behavior have been observed since the end of the 2000s (L12, L13, L14, and L15).

Furthermore, the Leipziger Modell is being criticized now to a greater and greater extent because it gives too much power to the mayor and the municipal administration as they initiate policy proposals and seek a majority for their proposal in the council (L3).[23]

Moreover, the Leipziger Modell, which is based on changing majorities in the council, is called into question by the fact that it is part of the "habitus of the city" (Lindner 2003) that local actors, even in the context of highly controversial debates, ultimately want to bring about a decision—and not simply wait until a consensus or compromise has been found. In certain situations, this attitude implies that stable alliances are ultimately formed in order to be able to act. Such an alliance was formed by the SPD, the Left, and the Green Party for enacting a new municipal housing policy in 2015 (Stadt Leipzig 2015; for details see Rink 2020). And in view of the foreseeable, never-ending controversies surrounding the question of how to deal with urban growth—and, above all, the lack of affordable housing—"a stable and resilient red-red-green constellation or design majority ['Gestaltungsmehrheit'] has been established [in housing policy] in contrast to the practiced 'Leipziger Modell'" (Rink 2020: 193). Despite the ongoing controversies, the council's 2015 decision on a new housing policy was prepared both with a commission of experts (composed of representatives of all party groups in the municipal council, housing cooperatives, some private housing companies, civil society organizations, academics, and representatives of other cities) and with broad citizen participation. "For the implementation of the housing policy, the *Netzwerk Leipziger Freiheit* [mentioned above in Section 10.2] was founded with a coordination office" (Rink 2020: 188).

The fact that an organization called Netzwerk Leipziger Freiheit was entrusted with the implementation of the new housing policy and above all with the support of new forms of housing and living may have been a coincidence. However, whether consciously or unconsciously, it expresses a discursive recourse to a widespread image of the city. As already mentioned, the term "Leipziger Freiheit" was not only used for city marketing, it also expresses a certain attitude toward life in general and politics in particular.

A widespread perception or self-image in Leipzig is also that the city has potential "that cannot be taken away from the city"—namely, its size, land, and buildings (as one of the interviewees [L13] emphasized). This perception is related to particular causal assumption (or interpretation of given constraints and possibilities) and reproduced by a particular narrative. It does not matter if observers from outside take it for true or as a (fairy) tale (Czarniawska 2002). What is important is the impact of this perception on actions. A widely shared self-image in Leipzig is that the city has potential which merely needs to be recognized and applied. This may be the huge number of old buildings—although (particularly in the 1990s and 2000s) often dilapidated and vacant—or buildings constructed for a bigger number of users than those actually using them—such as the main railway station and the stadium. The latter (now named Red Bull Arena) had until its re-building in the early 2000s a capacity of 100,000 seats and at that time the second largest stadium in Europe at the time.

The perception that the city has potential which merely need to be used leads to the image that the city is a "sleeping beauty" (Steets 2008: 162ff.). This image can lead to two choices of action.

On the one hand, it can lead to a passive attitude which means that it is simply necessary to wait for the prince to awaken the "sleeping beauty" with a kiss. Such a "prince" was the real estate investor and developer Jürgen Schneider, who did a lot for the renovation of historical buildings in Leipzig before he filed for bankruptcy in 1994. Another example is the Red Bull Company which founded the football club *Rasen Ballsport Leipzig e. V.*—or RB Leipzig—in 2009, now using the Red Bull Arena. However, such a pas-sive attitude can hardly be found in Leipzig.

On the other hand, locals themselves can try to awaken the "sleeping beauty." This applies to young people who occupied and still use vacant old buildings as well as local politicians—such as, in particular, former Mayors Lehman-Grube and Tiefensee—who not only succeeded in restructuring the Leipzig Fair and the airport as well as attracting new fairs (such as the Games Convention, which took place in Leipzig from 2002 to 2008) and particularly the sites of BMW, Porsche, DHL, and Amazon, but also tried to bring the 2012 Olympic Games to the city.[24]

Although the interpretation of how to treat the "sleeping beauty" is widely shared—namely, in an active and autonomous way (i.e., not waiting for the prince to awaken the "sleeping beauty" with a kiss)—there have been changes in the understanding of *how the world is functioning* in general and what this means for actions to be taken in Leipzig (*what has to be done*). In the 1990s and 2000s there was a more or less hegemonic understanding which was expressed (a) in the general orientation toward taking action, of doing anything to improve the employment situation and (b) the diagnosis of a "perforated city" which resulted in a particular orientation toward ac-tion. Instead, today there are various causal assumptions. The debate on how to deal with current developments in the housing sector (gentrification) is an example of this situation. Another one is the struggle over ideas about the use of land still owned by the municipality. At best—as during the first two decades after unification—different causal assumptions are relevant to activities which are taking place in parallel. This applied to "traditional" strategies and measures for attracting commercial settlement (e.g., Porsche, BMW, the newly built airport) and the innovations for using house vacancy and vacant land in a strategic way (mentioned in Section 10.1).

This seems to have changed since the 2010s in respect to standards of appropriateness (of *how the world should function*) underpinning collective action in Leipzig. As mentioned before, a basic standard of appropriate-ness widely shared in the city is the belief that there are no problems, but challenges which can be solved in an active and autonomous way. However, when it comes to concrete decisions, standards of appropriateness can differ. This leads to controversies—such as in the case of the current developments in the housing sector and the resulting question if something like gentrification is happening in Leipzig and how to deal with it.

Nevertheless, there are some discursive patterns in Leipzig which explain not only why having lively public debates on the one hand and fast operational decisions on the other is not a contradiction. The following quotation might also capture a particular discursive pattern which explains the optimism present in controversial debates, which seems to be distinctive for Leipzig:

> The path from the label "hero city" to "boom town" was short. It was simply declared to exist. For, where you tore down borders and walls with candles and prayers, many other things, if not *everything*, seemed possible.
>
> (D'Antonio 2015: 96)

Furthermore, it is deeply grounded in discursive practices in Leipzig—as emphasized by interviewees (particularly by L4 and L11)—that it is expected by all those participating in public debates that they want *to make a contribution to achieving a better future for the city*—and not just criticizing something without outlining a solution for the issue addressed. Again, a similar attitude in public debates was detected by Barbehön et al. (2015: 69–70 and 94–95; 2016: 243) for Frankfurt (and confirmed in Chapter 7 of this book).

However, there are (at least) two further characteristics of public debates in Leipzig. First, only those are accepted as "Leipziger," i.e., people living in the city, who are trying to contribute to an improvement of the city. This means on the one hand that "new arrivals" can be quite easily accepted as equals—which was explained by interviewees (L2 and particularly L4) by reference to the history of the city where trade fairs have been taking place for centuries and a lot of people from elsewhere were not only coming to the city occasionally but also staying.

Second, in contrast to Frankfurt the expectation of making a contribution to achieve a better future for the city was connected with a clearer image of what this better future of the city should look like—namely, the claim that the "human being is at the center" ("Der Mensch steht im Mittelpunkt"; L4; see also Brieler and Rink 2019: 842).

As mentioned above, the understanding of the citizenry is deeply connected with the willingness to act autonomously, which in essence is what "Leipziger Freiheit" means. Actors in political parties and councils as well as in the city administration made use of this potential by being receptive to initiatives from the local community, supporting and institutionalizing innovations and mediating between the actors. This was done in order to improve the general living conditions in Leipzig and to seek solutions to problems that the city would otherwise hardly be able to solve. The use of vacant buildings by Wächterhäuser is a good example.

However, this example also shows that bottom-up innovations in using vacant buildings are under pressure due to rising rents and a growing shortage of open space.

Furthermore, the attitude of actors in Leipzig has changed since the early 1990s, together with the way decisions are made. "Today some miss the former dreams and their 'pompousness' and criticize the political 'commitment to normality', while the political leaders of the city claim that they won't be 'never again boundless'" (D'Antonio 2015: 99).[25] Or as one of the interviewees (L11) emphasized:

> In the past, ideas were implemented quickly and opportunities were exploited immediately. At the most, attention was paid to compliance with legal regulations. Today, everything takes longer, because policy objectives have become more controversial or just unclear, more attention is paid to compliance with formal procedures, and fear of resistance has grown. This can strengthen the influence of the administration, which is more focused than other actors on formal procedures.

In addition, citizens who are active in the multitude of innovative initiatives have become more pragmatic. The more their initiatives are successful, the more they try to protect their achievements. Furthermore, tensions and "ideological differences" (L12) have become more apparent since the limits of the positive effects of innovative initiatives have been discussed— particularly in the context of growing pressure on the housing market and the debate about gentrification.

Finally, clear reference points for collective actions were no longer protected by authority within the municipal administration. From 1995 to 2005, Lütke Daldrup was the head of the building authority, which was at the same time responsible (with two separate offices) for urban development and economic development on the one hand and city planning on the other. These joint responsibilities made it possible to ensure the complementarity of economic development and inner-city development by attracting new enterprises to the edges of the city and using empty buildings and areas of undeveloped land for innovative activities in the city center. This complementarity was forfeited to a greater and greater degree (see Rink and Siemund 2006: 56) as the struggle over space became more intense due to population growth. At the same time, the municipal land registry office ("Liegenschaftsamt"), directly under the responsibility of the mayor, became more powerful because municipal land is under its authority.

10.4 Key findings

As shown by the case of Leipzig, the mix of an active and self-confident local civil society, political leaders, and a council able to capture diverse ideas and a hands-off mentality within the municipal administration can result in an open and flexible policy-making style. Under such conditions citizens can participate actively in agenda-setting, develop innovative ideas, and initiate innovative solutions.

The "Leipziger Modell" is typical of the constellation of actors in the council and between the local parties, which means that pragmatic decision-making is preferred, focusing on "what is best for the city." This limits party-politicized politics and the influence of individual parties and their representatives. However, focusing on the "best for the city" requires a common understanding of what this means. Such a reference point for decisions has been increasingly lost in Leipzig since the end of the 2000s.

The crucial lessons to be learned from the case of Leipzig are the following: first, innovations can be so successful that they solve the challenges that contributed to their creation, but this can then lead to new challenges. Second, to achieve agreement on novel improvements under changed conditions, these conditions have to be interpreted in such a way that new reference points for political actions are established which make it possible for the concerned local community to identify what can and must be done. Leipzig is a successful and innovative city, but it is still unclear how the new challenges of urban growth are to be met again with innovations that are widely regarded as factually and normatively appropriate. Nevertheless, local actors in Leipzig display the habitus that they want to and can make decisions—and do not block each other in an environment of uncertainty about what is the right path forward. This is shown by the 2015 council decision on housing policy.

Notes

1 https://statistik.leipzig.de/statcity/table.aspx?cat=2&rub=1&per=q (last check October 02, 2020).

2 For more details on the historical development of the economic structure of Leipzig, see Rink (1996a: 57–90) and Brieler and Rink (2019: 820).

3 https://statistik.leipzig.de/statcity/table_print.aspx?cat=2&rub=1&tim=36,35,34, 33,32,31,30,29,28,27,26,25,24,23,22,20,19,18,17&per=y (last check October 02, 2020). See also Rink and Kabisch (2019: 856–860) and Rink (2020).

4 https://www.bmwgroup-werke.com/leipzig/de/unser-werk.html#ace--1044412540 (last check October 02, 2020).

5 https://www.porsche-leipzig.com/porsche-in-leipzig/meilensteine/ (last check October 02, 2020).

6 Since 2014 the city of Leipzig has received €205.4 million from the European Regional Development Fund (EFRE) and European Social Fund (ESF) (Staatsministerium für Wirtschaft, Arbeit und Verkehr 2019: 3).

7 https://arbeitsmarktmonitor.arbeitsagentur.de/faktencheck/regionalstruktur/tabelle/312/2019/unemployrate/?r= (last check April 11, 2021).

8 On the limited direct connections to other airports see https://www.mdf-ag.com/reisende-und-besucher/flughafen-leipzig-halle/ (last check October 02, 2020).

9 https://www.leipzig.de/wirtschaft-und-wissenschaft/studium-und-forschung/universitaet-und-hochschulen/ (last check October 02, 2020).

10 On the debate about the "perforated city" in Leipzig and in urban restructuring in general, see Rink and Siemund (2016).

11 See http://www.leipziger-freiheit.de/ (last check October 02, 2020).
12 See http://www.spinnerei.de/galerie-eigen-art-119.html (last check October 02, 2020).
13 Some of Rauch's paintings can be seen on https://www.youtube.com/results?-search_query=neo+rauch (last check October 02, 2020).
14 http://www.haushalten.org/de/waechterhaeuser_modell.asp (last check October 02, 2020).
15 http://www.haushalten.org/de/waechterhaeuser_modell.asp. On the history of "Wächterhäuser" and the association *HausHalten*, see http://www.haushalten.org/de/haushalten_chronik.asp (last check October 02, 2020).
16 http://www.haushalten.org/de/ausbauhaus.asp (last check October 02, 2020).
17 https://www.netzwerk-leipziger-freiheit.de/wir/ (last check October 02, 2020).
18 https://www.netzwerk-leipziger-freiheit.de/wir/ (last check October 02, 2020).
19 https://english.leipzig.de/services-and-administration/opportunities-for-residents-to-get-involved-and-make-a-difference/thinking-leipzig-ahead/ (last check October 02, 2020).
20 Nevertheless, the right-wing "Alternative für Deutschland" ("Alternative for Germany") won 11 out of the 70 council seats in the last local election which took place in 2019 (https://www.leipzig.de/buergerservice-und-verwaltung/wahlen-in-leipzig/stadtratswahlen/stadtratswahl-2019/wahlergebnis-stadt-leipzig/; last check October 02, 2020). In 2014 this right-wing party had won only four seats (https://www.leipzig.de/buergerservice-und-verwaltung/wahlen-in-leipzig/stadtratswahlen/wahlergebnisse-2014/; last check October 02, 2020).
21 This habitus shows similarities to what has been detected for Frankfurt by Barbehön et al. (2015: 69–70 and 94–95; 2016: 243) and is confirmed in Chapter 7 of this book.
22 For the survival of particular social milieus during the period of existence of the German Democratic Republic, see Rink (1996b).
23 Furthermore, it is argued (for instance, by L14) that citizens could not clearly identify who (which party) had the initial idea for a decision.
24 As we know, the 2012 Olympic Games did not take place in Leipzig. However, Leipzig won the competition among the German cities of Düsseldorf, Frankfurt, Hamburg, and Stuttgart but did not become one of the official "candidate cities"—which included London, Madrid, Moscow, New York, and Paris—from which London was finally chosen as the city where the 2012 Olympic Games took place.
25 "Never again boundless" ("Nie wieder maßlos") refers to a statement by Leipzig's Lord Mayor Burkhard Jung with an identical title in DIE ZEIT on July 12, 2012, to an article about Leipzig published in this weekly German newspaper on June 28, 2012.

11 Offenbach

Max A. Kayser

11.1 Introduction

The city of Offenbach is located in the south of the federal state of Hesse, which is in the center of Germany. Offenbach is part of the prosperous Frankfurt/Rhine-Main region, which has about 5.55 million inhabitants in total and is one of the most densely populated metropolitan areas in Germany. Offenbach itself has 138,933 inhabitants.[1] The population has increased by over 10% since 2011.[2] The city has very good connections to national motorways, railways, and the international airport of Frankfurt, as well as numerous local and regional public transport lines.

Historically, Offenbach was characterized by large-scale factories, especially in the leather and printing industries, whose most important German production sites were situated in Offenbach. The shift from industrial to service industries in recent decades has resulted in extensive job losses for low-skilled workers.

Like in other former industrial cities, the Social Democratic Party (SPD) is still a dominant party in Offenbach. Although the council was dominated by a so-called Tanzania coalition consisting of the Christian Democrats (CDU), Greens, Liberals (FDP), and "Freie Wähler" ("Free Voters," a list of people participating in an election without having the status of a registered political party), the mayor of Offenbach is still a Social Democrat. After the local elections of March 14, 2021, a coalition was formed in the municipal council between the Social Democrats, the Greens, and the Liberals, which will undoubtedly continue the innovations presented in the next section.

Offenbach can be viewed as a diverse, open-minded, and unique city. The attention the city recently received at the 15th International Architecture Exhibition in Venice as a showcase of an "arrival city" (Saunders 2011),[3] as well as several appreciations in local and national news media, marks a turning point for the city's image.[4] In recent decades, the city, which had previously been regarded as the "problem child" or an "island of poverty" ('Armutsinsel'; O4) of the region, has become a pioneer in terms of migration, local labor market policy, and reforms of the municipal administration. Due to the developments on the housing market which have caused prices

DOI: 10.4324/9781003084006-11

to explode in Frankfurt, as well as in the surrounding area, Offenbach has suddenly become attractive—as emphasized by an interview partner (O7): "Here, construction activities have been increasing during the last three or four years." Nevertheless, several issues still need to be addressed which could otherwise undermine the momentum gained in recent years.

11.2 Issues involving Innovations

In Offenbach, the challenges to be addressed through innovations are seen in the context of the economic and social consequences of deindustrialization. Even more, today local actors have recognized that in Offenbach "all political parties in the 1970s and 1980s ignored the signs of the times [...] and slept through the [economic] development. [...] Unemployment then gradually built up because simple jobs in industry disappeared" (O7). Against this background, it has become evident to local actors in the meantime that "something has to be done" (O2; O4) in order to create stable growth in employment, income, and local tax revenues for the city. Consequently, locals in Offenbach see it as crucial to critically reassess if an innovation is really tackling one of these main issues—or if it is "just polishing the surface." In this regard the city still suffers from the sharp decline in industrial production in the 1970s, which led not only to an unemployment rate higher than the Hessian average (8.7% in Offenbach vs. 4.6% in all of Hesse in February 2020)[5] but also to a transition to a low-skilled service sector and a high municipal budget deficit (O4).[6] One of the most notable features in Offenbach is that it has the highest proportion of residents with a migration background in Germany. In total, 61.6% of Offenbach's population has migrated to Germany (Magistrat der Stadt Offenbach 2017: 38).[7]

Innovations that have been observed in Offenbach in recent decades can be attributed to three areas: *social cohesion, economic development,* and *culture.* In each of these areas, developments that are perceived by citizens as new and an improvement to the status quo took place.

The first area (*social cohesion*) refers in particular to the integration of people arriving in Offenbach and enabling them to take part in everyday life as well as in the political decision-making process. By offering incoming migrants a social and economic perspective, the city is trying to reduce fluctuation and keep more people in Offenbach. This is an important issue because otherwise people who move to Offenbach and receive language courses, special job-search support, or health services there will move to another city if such integration measures have a positive effect, which is perceived as problematic by officials in the municipal administration (O1).

The most important steps taken by the municipality to improve integration processes and facilitate social cohesion include the issue of integration being given highest priority ("Chefsache") in Offenbach (Hessisches Ministerium der Justiz, für Integration und Europa 2012: 23). This has meant that the topic is placed at the top of the municipal administration's agenda and the mayor takes direct responsibility for the issue. Offenbach was one of the first municipalities in Germany to seriously recognize the scope of the challenge posed by integration of people with foreign origin, and has worked on it beyond department structures through regular exchanges between different offices (O3; Schulze-Böing 2018: 56). By 1998, the municipality had already established the "Leitstelle Zusammenleben," i.e., a central office for "Living together," and adopted a comprehensive integration concept in 2004 (Hessisches Ministerium der Justiz, für Integration und Europa 2013: 50–51; Stadt Offenbach 2004). Not only does the integration concept connect previously established projects and set the goals for various integration measures, but it also outlines the way local administration has to deal with the topic of integration:

> Due to the high proportion of citizens of non-German origin, at the municipality level integration policy in Offenbach is [...] an interdepartmental task and not a special topic of individual departments. In an increasingly international city in the center of the Rhine-Main area, the administration is also becoming more international and intercultural, as it is responsible for a clientele that, to an ever-increasing extent, has different origins and cultural backgrounds. This development requires a leadership task due to the overall social significance and complexity of the topic.
>
> (Stadt Offenbach 2004: 54)

The importance attached to integration is also expressed by the establishment of the position of an integration commissioner ("Integrationsbeauftragter")[8] responsible for the development of key guidelines for integration in the city. Furthermore, the municipality strives to bring actors together and exchange ideas about the issue beyond its own local administration tasks. The so-called integration competence team ("Kompetenzteam Integration") works with the head of the integration department and the head of the local migration council ("Ausländerbeirat") on future integration measures and evaluates the ongoing integration process in the city.[9] Besides members of the municipal administration, the team consists of representatives from several local civil society organizations, particularly those from migrant communities, but also from the local employment agency ("Agentur für Arbeit").

In addition to measures taken on the initiative of the municipality, Offenbach is very keen to attract and implement federal support and pilot projects for integration management.[10] Especially within the federal program of the so-called pilot projects for integration, the municipality supported various smaller civil society groups and enabled them to organize themselves, exchange information, and become active in the city (Hessisches Ministerium der Justiz, für Integration und Europa 2013: 51–52). The focus on networking various communities, offering administrative capacities to embed societal actors, and strong political leadership regarding this issue are the key factors behind Offenbach's success in this area. As the former head of the department for integration and social services, Peter Schneider, pointed out: "It's all about feeling that you belong somewhere—without pulling up your roots. Integration is not about assimilation. The moment you feel respected, you feel at home."[11]

The second area of innovation in Offenbach, *economic development*, refers to attracting new businesses and generating not only economic growth but also sustainable jobs outside the low-skilled service sector. As already mentioned, Offenbach still has a high unemployment rate and needs a stable labor market to meet the challenges of fluctuation and migration. The city has taken several steps to develop a comprehensive strategy for promoting economic development and creating new jobs and prospects for employments of residents and newcomers.

One of the first comprehensive approaches to strategic economic development was the "Masterplan Offenbach 2030" (Magistrat der Stadt Offenbach und "Offenbach offensiv" 2015). The work on the master plan was inspired by a unique way of thinking—namely, that "it is more important to look at what potential we have, not at what went wrong, [...] look into the future [and ask] what potential we have and how we can better apply it" (O4). Above all, space was seen as having the greatest potential not capitalized upon earlier: space, "which is not available anywhere else in the Rhine-Main area in such a concentrated form [and above all] with such excellent [infrastructure] connections" (O4).

The master plan was developed by the newly founded "Offenbach offensiv" association, which coordinated actors from civil society, business, and the local University of Art and Design (Hochschule für Gestalting/HfG Offenbach) as well as from the municipal administration. The plan combined various strategies and projects which already existed in the city (O4) and focused on several key projects for enhancing economic development and quality of life in the city (Magistrat der Stadt Offenbach und "Offenbach offensiv" 2015: 156ff.). The ultimate goal of the plan is to attract new businesses. In addition to this, the aim is to develop higher-priced housing in order to change the composition of the city's population, "because you cannot change a population structure through displacement. Instead, you have to try to attract higher earners and the well-off to Offenbach" (O7). Particularly as a result of the establishment of businesses, the income of the municipality should rise due to the business tax proceeds (i.e., a tax which German municipalities may levy on businesses), which was also a central point in the agreement with the state government within the framework of the bailout agreement of the state of Hesse.[12] The "Masterplan Offenbach 2030" is considered a significant success for the city. The plan seems to be making Offenbach especially attractive to investors and, indeed, new real estate projects—such as the harbor district—are seen as positive examples demonstrating that Offenbach offers good investment opportunities compared to its expensive neighbor Frankfurt (O4).

Another key project within the Masterplan Offenbach 2030 (one of ten) is the *innovations campus* planned on the brownfield site of a former paint factory. In order to purchase, develop, and market the site, the city has founded its own company, Inno Innovationscampus Ltd & Co. KG. This company received €6.95 million from the municipality to buy the 35-hectare site from the Swiss chemicals company Clariant and €3 million as a capital advance for developing and marketing the site. The municipality wants to carry out the development and marketing through the company itself in order to have direct influence over the settlement of new, future-oriented companies on this largest, contiguous inner-city development area in the entire region and thus have influence over further structural economic development of the city and further consolidation of the municipality's finances.[13]

In this way, the master plan has contributed to changing the city's image. Enhancing the city's profile "was also a reason for developing the master plan and the fact that the local community could accept such a change in Offenbach's image" (O8; similar statements were made by O9).

In addition to the measures under the master plan, the city is offering funding and support for small businesses and freelancers in the creative economy.[14] However, as with measures related to the issue of integration, these measures were also supported by external funding, which the municipality obtained from 2010 to 2015. This applies, for example, to the program "Local economy—the creative economy in local neighborhoods" ("Lokale Ökonomie—Kreativwirtschaft im Quartier") funded by the European Regional Development Fund (ERDF) focused on local businesses in the creative or cultural sector.[15] Businesses were able to apply for funding of up to 50% for advertising, online platforms, or hardware and software.[16] Moreover, the local energy supplier EVO AG is supporting start-ups with a co-working space on their company premises. Although "Startwerke," the first facility for promoting start-ups in the cultural and creative industries, suspended its work (mainly because the name was legally protected by another company),[17] the number of businesses in the creative economy based in Offenbach more than doubled from 1,345 in 2007 to 2,967 in 2013 (Magistrat der Stadt Offenbach 2015: 4). Or as an interviewee (O1) put it: "We're now the city with the most start-ups in Germany."

The third area of innovation is focused on *culture* and deals mainly with the longstanding negative image of Offenbach in the German media and the Rhine-Main region.[18] As already mentioned, the city was seen as a "problem child" in otherwise prosperous Hesse. Media reports which portrayed rundown districts and emphasized high crime rates and dangerous neighborhoods shaped the image of Offenbach as a less livable city. In order to attract investors and new businesses and make citizens feel welcome, it seemed obvious that something about the image of Offenbach needed to change. This has been done in a remarkable way. With regard to the city's cultural image it was emphasized that the city is

> colorfully mixed. Offenbach is also a city of studios. [...] This artistic aspect is still very much alive, and I think that these different lifestyles and living styles complement each other to some extent and create a

positive overall image [...]. The city is not just a trendy city, but is also not a degenerate and disorderly city.

(O6)

A fundamental change is the reframing of the migration issue by referring to the "arrival city" concept of Doug Saunders (2011). This was done through an exhibition entitled "Offenbach is almost alright" at the 2016 Biennale di Venezia together with the Deutsche Architekturmuseum (DAM; German Architecture Museum) and its presentation on "Making Heimat" which shed light on different forms of migration in Germany. The image of Offenbach as an "arrival city" was strongly promoted by Kai Vöckler (2017), whose professorship at the local University of Art and Design is to a large part funded by the municipality in order to analyze and facilitate the creative and cultural scene in Offenbach.[19] The designation of Offenbach as an "arrival city" had a huge positive impact on the city and fundamentally changed the way the city is perceived today (O2; O3; O4).[20] The reframing of migration by (re-)labeling Offenbach as an "arrival city" shaped the modes of communication regarding this issue. Offenbach was no longer seen as a city dominated by the issue of migration but as, by definition, diverse, multicultural, interesting, and authentic. The negative image of an entrance gate to Germany and a city of passage for newly arrived migrants consisting of a temporary and unskilled workforce was transformed into the positive image of the "arrival city" in global migration movements which brings the past to life again and connects it to present-day migration. By doing this, migration became something like the DNA of the city throughout the ages.

In contrast to Frankfurt, the issues of immigration and fluctuation could not be seen as mere side effects of the success and the "dynamics" of the city (see Barbehön and Münch 2014: 158; Barbehön et al. 2016: 242).[21] However, with the term "arrival city" Offenbach was in a position to explain why local society functions the way it does and show that the city is fulfilling a purpose—namely, integration of new arrivals on a daily basis. This turned what was once a problem into an advantage, which not only makes Offenbach appealing to the cosmopolitan art scene but it also creates a unique selling point for the city itself. This shift in the public image of Offenbach changed the reputation of the city and made it attractive to people from elsewhere who might otherwise have considered moving to Frankfurt/Main. One interview participant (O2) put this also into the context of increasing rents in Frankfurt:

Well, we're no longer seen as the underdog or the problem child of the Rhine-Main area, but as a city where you can live normally like anywhere else. And this was a stroke of good fortune: people can now see that nothing is possible in Frankfurt and think—let's look at Offenbach.

Another remarkable cultural change is related to hip-hop culture emanating from the region and from Offenbach itself. However, unlike the late 1990s, the raw image of the city presented in rap videos and song texts is not seen as a flaw, but as a source of creativity and a genuine part of urban life (Vöckler 2017).[22] Although the development of the scene is detached from most of the "official" art and culture scene in Offenbach, individual actors and networks have contributed to the overall image of the city.

Besides the three main areas of innovation—social cohesion, economic development, and culture—it is also worth looking at some of the *past issues related to innovation* in Offenbach, still affecting local politics: the reforms of the municipal administration and the local labor market policy. Both were part of the New Public Management (NPM) reforms carried out throughout Germany, but were implemented in Offenbach earlier than elsewhere. Faced with a constantly tight municipal budget and difficult local labor market, the city was eager to cut costs and get the most out of public services. This resulted in rigorous measures to optimize public administration or, as one of the interview participants put it: "The city knows how to manage the little we have" (O2). And another interview participant confirmed this by emphasizing that in the 1990s Offenbach was regarded as a "leading city regarding public administration reforms due to the fiscally difficult situation" (O1; see also Barthel and Spiegel 2008). The budget deficit was not necessarily seen as a restriction of capability but instead as an opportunity to come up with new ways of establishing more efficient municipal administration. In this context one interview participant (O1) emphasized that "around this time, what was innovative was the new steering model [the German version of NPM; the author] and we had some quite innovative approaches regarding our human resource policy." More specifically, this meant deliberately recruiting personnel from the private sector in order to achieve a more management-oriented approach and to "stir up the administrative structure" (O1). The overall goal was not only to introduce more economical procedures in administration, but also to implement a quality management system (QMS) for public administration (Barthel and Spiegel 2008: 281). In 2005 Offenbach was the first major city in Germany to be certified with an extensive QMS for all administrative departments (Barthel and Spiegel 2008: 291). This streamlining process is seen as a very positive achievement by the municipality and as an advantage over other cities:

> […] we are still the city with the lowest staffing ratio, thus with the highest efficiency of our administration. […] To my knowledge, Offenbach is significantly more efficient compared with Darmstadt or Frankfurt or any other municipal administration in Hesse.
>
> (O1)

Unsurprisingly, this argument is contested by parts of the local society, which claim: "The public administration is dysfunctional and processes take far too long due to the poorly staffed offices. The only way to get things done in a timely manner is via personal networks. […] This works far better in Frankfurt" (O5). Others (such as O2) see this as the normal downside of a lean administration, and argue that it is a question of capacity, and that peaks in workload always occur. The problem is more fundamental. The high fluctuation among citizens constantly increases administrative work regarding registration and other services for new arrivals (O2).

Perpetual budget deficits in the municipality explain why Offenbach became the very first city to be included in the bailout program for local government of Hesse's state government (Heinelt and Stolzenberg 2014). The aim of the program is not only to support local government through financial help, but to consolidate its budget in a sustainable way. Therefore, what happened in Offenbach under the bailout program can be seen as the support for a further streamlining process of the municipal administration.

Around the same time as NPM reforms were being implemented in Offenbach, the city was trying to reduce the high unemployment rate and create more jobs (Magistrat der Stadt Offenbach 2017: 39). The municipality collaborated with the local branch of the Federal Labor Office and introduced new management styles in its own employment services. In this regard "Offenbach has always been a trendsetter. Along with a few other cities we have always been the role model for the rest of the Republic" (O1). And the same interview participant emphasized that regarding local labor market policy: "we [also] began very early to collaborate transnationally. In 1995/96 for example, we built the first municipal employment service with support from colleagues from the Netherlands."

Although those reforms might be contested and are not seen as innovations in themselves,[23] local actors in Offenbach perceive these changes as an improvement and a step in the right direction in order to be capable of dealing with other issues faced by the city.[24] As an interview participant (O1) puts it:

> Those things are not totally new. However, what we did and still do is to constantly assemble known ways and elements in a new way. I would say this is something that distinguishes Offenbach and made it possible to implement something like an integrated management against all the odds.

The early and constant pressure for the municipality to adapt to the difficult budgetary situation could be a reason why actors in Offenbach sought out innovations and implemented reforms earlier than most other German municipalities. This is underlined by some who claim that "Offenbach faced all the problems every other city encounters today, but ten to fifteen years earlier" (O2). These circumstances may have resulted in certain advantages in managing constraints and developing innovation capabilities.

Nevertheless, Offenbach still has a higher unemployment rate than other cities in the Rhine-Main area (as outlined at the beginning of this chapter). But what is striking is the will to tackle this issue and address it in a straightforward manner, whereas other municipalities may be tempted to downplay economic downturns or to fatalistically blame upper-level authorities and point to general societal developments. This results in open-minded cooperation which works quite well compared to other cities. The way in which Offenbach used what was initially perceived as a particular local restriction on action to implement reforms and initiate new cooperation can be seen as a specific approach to develop a new understanding of local possibilities for action and to interpret or relabel previously perceived restrictions as opportunities. An example of such a reinterpretation of challenges is the new way of addressing migration with the labeling of Offenbach as an "arrival city."

11.3 Actors, processes, and structuration through local discourses

In order to analyze the decision-making processes in Offenbach, it seems useful to look at what is perceived and dealt with as Offenbach's "attributes of the community" (Ostrom et al. 1994). For locals as well as for external observers it is clear that "Offenbach is simply different from the rest of the Frankfurt/Rhine-Main area. […] Offenbach is the first German city in which migrants are in the majority. This [means] that Offenbach is a special case even in the ['multicultural'] Rhine-Main area" (O4). However, this widespread observation leads to emphasis on different structural characteristics of the city. For some local actors (e.g., a senior local government official [O1]) the fluctuation of people in general and migration in particular results in a weak local civil society. In their view, members of society are missing who not only look after the interests of individuals or particular groups, but general concerns, too. However, other local actors (e.g., a representative of a local welfare organization [O6]) emphasized: "There is a strong culture of networking in Offenbach. That is a culture of cooperation which makes meetings possible where we discuss how to get along together in a good way." This view is confirmed by the broad membership of the competence team integration (mentioned in Section 11.2) which, in addition to officials of the public authorities, consists of about 30 representatives from different migrant organizations.

Regardless of how these different interpretations of mobility and migration are assessed as structural characteristics of the city, one thing is undisputed in local debates: Offenbach is highly inclusive. The city not only integrates more than 163 different nationalities[25] with their different cultures and religions, there are also very ambitious attempts to offer opportunities for participation in local decision-making and to create inclusive networks for different actor groups. A good example is *Masterplan Offenbach 2030*, which applied a step-by-step approach to create a shared understanding of key challenges in Offenbach as well as ways of addressing these issues. This was, in part, achieved on the basis of inputs from citizens, who then joined experts in smaller working groups. The findings of the working groups were later discussed in public, and the feedback considered again in the working groups. In total, the process to create Masterplan 2030 took three public sessions and three sessions in the working groups. Furthermore, online participation tools available for use by anyone were created (Magistrat der Stadt Offenbach und "Offenbach offensiv" 2015: 16).

A remarkable feature of Offenbach is that, despite highly inclusive and egalitarian participatory processes, the city is capable of making quick decisions and implementing new ways of doing things. The development of the master plan again provides a good illustration of how quickly things can be achieved in Offenbach (although the master plan was initially viewed quite skeptically by many political actors). After the cooperation agreement between "Offenbach offensiv," which organized and financed half the cost of the master plan process,[26] and the municipality was signed in July 2014, the participation process started in March 2015. The entire process took only nine months, and the city council adopted the final version of the master plan in February 2016 (Magistrat der Stadt Offenbach und "Offenbach offensiv" 2015).

Much like other cities, Offenbach is described as a city of "short distances" where problems and issues can be solved quickly and easily. This not only describes physical density; the phrase also refers to the close relationship between decision-makers and the local community within the city (O4). This is made possible by, on the one hand, the relatively small size of the city and, on the other, by the small number of people belonging to the core group of local decision-makers, a group that is easier to "grasp" compared with larger cities such as the neighboring city of Frankfurt (O1). People know each other and "distances" to the local decision-makers are in fact "short." This may explain why some processes go more quickly in Offenbach than elsewhere, while a certain level of argumentative exchange in the decision-making process is maintained (O1; O3; Magistrat der Stadt Offenbach und "Offenbach offensiv" 2015: 16). Willingness to make quick decisions is also a mentality shared in some leadership circles in the municipal administration, which sometimes goes hand in hand with a "can-do attitude" perceived by some local actors (O1). However, this "can-do attitude" is limited to smaller groups of very active leaders and is not a widespread perception of problem-solving capacity among the citizenry, as seems to be the case in Frankfurt or Bensheim (see Barbehön et al. 2016: 242 and Chapters 4 and 7 in this book). This is underpinned by the general view of residents that Offenbach's ability to "get something done" by relying on its own means is very limited. This attitude results in a more cautious approach to "doing something" and emphasis is placed on external support, as O2 puts it: "Maybe one could say that [Offenbach] has a laid-back approach on how to deal with things. Everybody knows that money is short and therefore things will not be perfect. You rely on external funding."

Aside from this view, the municipal administration and leading politicians are eager to form and cultivate networks of decision-makers across all administrative units. According to one interview participant (O1), the former mayor, Gerhard Grandke, played a crucial role in overcoming the "silo mentality" (Silomentalität') typical for a public administration (O1) organized in a fragmented way according to specific responsibilities. Under the leadership of Grandke in the mid-1990s, the municipal administration was streamlined and forced to accept a different, more open management style (see above). However, the innovations made during that period cannot be attributed solely to the leadership of Mayor Grandke, but also stem from the reform spirit in a municipal administration focused on being innovative in tackling budgetary problems faced by the municipality. Or, as one interview participant put it, "leadership is one factor. The second factor, however, is, of course, financial resources and tax regulation" (O1). But this person added: "The third factor involves the processes we developed, in other words, management roundtables and project structures, which are to some degree alien to public administration, especially at the interorganizational level" (O1).

In addition, willingness to compare the city with others played a crucial role in innovation processes in Offenbach. The idea of comparing, evaluating, and trying to create "islands of excellence" ("Exzellenzinseln"; O1) is considered typical for the city of Offenbach.

In this regard, a certain pride becomes apparent in local discourses on how to deal with pressing challenges, particularly concerning the provision of jobs or the integration of migrants. Unemployment and the integration of migrants are clearly seen as problems which are more serious in Offenbach than in other cities, but are being managed in the best way possible. Local government actors in Offenbach are very confident that they are doing a good job in these policy fields. This self-perception is also connected with the habit of comparing: "We can be bad sometimes, but we always have to be better than Frankfurt. That is what we have done over the last thirty years, [for instance] in all aspects of the employment service" (O1). Such a high level of self-confidence may be contradictory, considering the overall unfavorable condition of the city and its former (self-)image as a "problem child" as well as realizing the city is to some degree dependent on external support. However, the high degree of confidence in their own ability to solve problems can be seen as a result of the city's ability to master challenges even under high pressure. This is demonstrated by the case of the privatization of public services, which is seen as an option for maintaining the provision of public goods: "Many things have been outsourced [...]. This might also be an Offenbach way of doing things. Finding ways to maintain the provision of public goods and services of the city even in a fiscally adverse situation" (O2).

Importing ideas and people and the willingness to compare the city with others is beneficial for the development of the city and interactions within the local society. The most prominent example of this characteristic is perhaps the relabeling of Offenbach as an "arrival city." This image was not initially developed by local actors but by a professor from Berlin who moved to Offenbach and by a museum in Frankfurt. Nevertheless, it was gratefully accepted and used proactively to take the place of the former image. This underlines the openness of actor constellations in Offenbach and their willingness to include external ideas in the innovation processes of the city. As mentioned by one interview participant (O2): "We are grateful for initiatives from outside. This is due to the decades during which the city merely managed the [municipal] debt. Whereas now we are happy if people come and say: 'I'm going to do this now.'"

With regard to the relationship between local discourses and innovations in Offenbach, two different aspects can be recognized as new and as improvements: first, the change in how challenges or problems are perceived and, second, how these shifts in the understanding of a particular challenge result in a new approach to that issue. This becomes strikingly visible when considering the three areas of innovation in Offenbach (outlined in Section 11.2) and the way these areas are interconnected. Taken together, the new actions and storylines make it clear that the new visions of an arrival city, a creative businesses sector, and a culturally vibrant city have replaced the former narrative of a poor city whose core features were mainly seen as negative (O4). The city managed to reframe its negative image in a positive way and create a vision for the future by presenting a plausible story about itself. What makes this story about Offenbach as an arrival city authentic is the way the past, the present, and the future of the city are related. One of the main arguments regarding the arrival city discourse is that Offenbach has always been an arrival city, but nobody told them this until recently (O1; O3). The city has been welcoming migrants looking for work and refugees looking for a place to live since the 17th century, when the first Huguenots settled in Offenbach.

The development of the arrival city idea can be seen not only as the construction of a new narrative, but as the *discursive development of reference points for further communicative interactions*. This also holds true for the development of the Masterplan Offenbach 2030. Both innovations were brought about by a combination of external experts, recognized expertise in the city, and results of local public debates.

On the basis of this new thematicization of migration, a substantive reorientation of decisions took place in the following time through the communicative mechanism of *framing*.

However, other mechanisms also contributed to this reorientation. In comparison with others (*observation of others and orientation to them*), actors in Offenbach view the city as unique in the region. This is sometimes described in a negative way: "Offenbach really struggles with some of its structural problems and you have all these placid cities close by—this stands out" (O2),[27] which leads to a feeling of inferiority in the city. On the other hand, in local discourses the same unique features are turned into positive attributes by artists, creatives, and students alike, who are looking for a more raw and authentic urban life (O4). Furthermore, the city sees itself as a pioneer in terms of social integration and NPM reforms (O1).

The strong emphasis in the local discourse on the creative sector and culture as well as the integration of culture as an economic factor for the city can be seen as a form of *issue relabeling*. What is not unique to Offenbach, but is in fact a common trend in urban development, is taking greater account of so-called soft factors for economic development.

The communicative mechanism of *immunization* is less frequently used, although it is popular in the local discourse in the form of references to the limited fiscal capability of the municipality—which means that no more can be done than is being done.

Through these communicative mechanisms actors in Offenbach have been able to benefit from changes in the "attributes of the physical world" (Ostrom et al. 1994). These changes can be seen first of all in a nationwide trend toward urbanization and also toward rising rent prices in the Rhine-Main region. Based on the innovations achieved in Offenbach, many people who are looking for a place to live but do not want to pay or cannot pay the high rents in Frankfurt have been moving to the city for a number of years (O3; O4). This influences the social dynamic within the local community and leads to a more "hip" image of Offenbach, where people still have the chance to use open urban spaces for social or cultural activities which would not be possible in neighboring Frankfurt (O4).[28] Consequently, the mechanisms that actors in Offenbach have used in communicative interactions and the innovations brought about by them are important for many positive developments in the city. Not only has the perception of the city by both local people and those not living in Offenbach changed in a positive way, but numerous steps have also been taken to improve the lifestyle of the inhabitants of the city. The changes become visible in several projects, which were unimaginable a few years ago. One is the new harbor area[29] with a now new prominent location for the HfG (Offenbach 2010). The new harbor area highlights a strong focus on the creative sector, which has consistently grown in recent years (Magistrat der Stadt Offenbach 2015). The architectural shift that accompanied the new investments in the city demonstrates the transition of Offenbach and manifests the new guiding narrative, which has taken the place of focusing on earlier deficiencies and dependencies.

11.4 Key findings

What lessons can be learned by analyzing the local discourse on innovation in the city of Offenbach? First of all, it becomes clear that Offenbach is a place where local actors are constantly able to reshape the city. The old days of the industrial sector and the famous leather goods are gone, although not forgotten. Something new was needed to define the city without the former image of a proud working-class city. The narrative of an "arrival city" seems to embody all the different positive and negative features of the city and serves as a short storyline to describe life in Offenbach. Apart from the new image of the city, other things in Offenbach are also functioning well. Keeping the distinctive features of the city in mind, it can be said that Offenbach has been able to establish new ways of doing things and making life easier for its citizens by:

- being open for collaboration, external support, new ideas, and people;
- overcoming traditional structures in municipal administration and working on key issues across its departments;
- combining strong leadership with participatory mechanisms for stakeholders;
- being in constant contact with citizen groups and enabling them to have a say in local politics;
- utilizing authentic local features and turning them into a new authentic narrative.

Of course, external factors have offered opportunities for the development of Offenbach and are part of the reason why the city is now perceived as more appealing compared to the early 1990s. However, local actors had to make use of these opportunities. The high rents for apartments and offices in Frankfurt are especially pushing tenants and entrepreneurs out of this neighboring city, but something had to be done to persuade them to regard Offenbach as a livable alternative. This is changing the composition of the local population and might, at some time in the future, level out the differences between Frankfurt and Offenbach. The employees of the European Central Bank who have moved in from abroad can look out over nearby Offenbach from their offices in Frankfurt, but are probably unaware of the city border between the east of Frankfurt and Offenbach's new harbor area.

Notes

1 See https://www.offenbach.de/medien/bindata/of/Statistik_und_wahlen_/dir-18/dir-29/BEV1-2019-Einwohnerstruktur_nach_Stat.Bez._d_nd.pdf (last check September 11, 2020).
2 See https://www.wegweiser-kommune.de/ (last check September 11, 2020).
3 Offenbach was a part of the German contribution to this exhibition under the title "Making Heimat." The full title was "Making Heimat. Germany, Arrival Country." Offenbach was presented at the German pavilion in Venice from May to November 2016. See http://www.makingheimat.de/en (last check September 11, 2020). The name of the Offenbach exhibition was "Offenbach is almost alright" (Vöckler 2017: 102).
4 The *Frankfurter Allgemeine Zeitung* (*FAZ*), one of the largest daily newspapers in Germany, devoted one entire Feuilleton section to the city of Offenbach (FAZ, June 26, 2018).
5 https://statistik.arbeitsagentur.de/Navigation/Statistik/Statistik-nach-Regionen/Politische-Gebietsstruktur/Hessen/Offenbach-Nav.html (last check September 11, 2020).
6 See https://www.wegweiser-kommune.de/ (last check September 11, 2020).

7 https://www.offenbach.de/leben-in-of/soziales-gesellschaft/integration_und_zusammenleben/integrationsfoerderung/modellregion-integration/index.php (last check September 11, 2020).

8 See https://www.offenbach.de//vv/oe/verwaltung/185010100000006809.php (last check September 11, 2020).

9 See https://www.offenbach.de/leben-in-of/soziales-gesellschaft/integration_und_zusammenleben/kompetenzteam-integration.php (last check September 11, 2020).

10 See Bundesinstitut für Bau-, Stadt- und Raumforschung 2015 and Hessisches Ministerium der Justiz, für Integration und Europa 2013.

11 Quotation from the article "Es geht darum, sich zugehörig zu fühlen" published in the Süddeutschen Zeitung, October 01, 2018.

12 Magistrat der Stadt Offenbach und "Offenbach offensiv" (2015: 11). For more details on these bailout agreements see Heinelt and Stolzenberg (2014) or Stolzenberg et al. (2016: 55ff).

13 See the article "Offenbach drives Innovation Campus forward" ("Offenbach treibt Innovationscampus voran") in the *FAZ*, April 8, 2020.

14 See https://www.offenbach.de/microsite/kreativwirtschaft/index.php and http://www.gruenderstadt-offenbach.de/highlights/highlights-details/article/foerder-programm-fuer-kultur-und-kreativwirtschaft-in-offenbach-wird-fortgesetzt.html (last check November 02, 2020).

15 See https://www.offenbach.de/microsite/kreativwirtschaft/aktuelles/berichte/Lokale-Oekonomie.php (last check September 11, 2020).

16 See https://wirtschaft.hessen.de/landesentwicklung/efre/eu-regionalfoerderung-2014-bis-2020 (last check September 11, 2020).

17 See https://www.evo-ag.de/evo-startwerk/ (last check September 11, 2020).

18 See the article "Ugliness is not even half the truth forward" ("Hässlichkeit ist nicht einmal die halbe Wahrheit") in the *FAZ*, June 26, 2018.

19 See https://www.hfg-offenbach.de/de/pages/stiftungsprofessur#ueber (last check September 11, 2019). One project which showcases different local creatives and small businesses is "OF Loves U" (https://www.oflovesu.com/about; last check September 11, 2020), where locals can present themselves and their work but can also connect and find rooms for exhibitions.

20 See also https://www.faz.net/aktuell/feuilleton/hochschule-fuer-gestaltung-kleine-offenbacher-weltgeschichte-15658831.html?printPagedArticle=true#pageIndex_0 (last check September 11, 2020).

21 Barbehöhn and Münch (2014) quoted an interviewee who states that Frankfurt's population changes completely every 15 years, which the interviewee sees as an indication of the dynamic nature of the city.

22 See the article "Rap differently" ("Anders rappen") in the *FAZ*, September 23, 2020. See also https://www.deutschlandfunkkultur.de/kulturszene-in-offenbach-am-main-ein-neues-eldorado-fuer.1001.de.html?dram:article_id=393087; https://www.zeit.de/2014/49/haftbefehl-csu-wahlkampf-plakat; https://www.faz.net/aktuell/feuilleton/hochschule-fuer-gestaltung-kleine-offenbacher-weltgeschichte-15658831.html?printPagedArticle=true#pageIndex_0; https://www.deutschlandfunkkultur.de/kulturszene-in-offenbach-am-main-ein-neues-eldorado-fuer.1001.de.html?dram:article_id=393087 (all checked September 11, 2020).

23 On the debate about the effects of New Public Management reforms in Germany, see Bogumil (et al. 2007).

24 On such a contextualized understanding of innovation, see Geißel (2009: 53) and Section 1.2 in this book.

25 https://www.offenbach.de/medien/bindata/of/Statistik_und_wahlen_/dir-18/dir-29/BEV3_-_Nationalitaeten_Zeitreihe_2004_-_2018.pdf (last check September 11, 2020).

26 "Offenbach offensiv e. V." is formed mainly by local businesses as members and is chaired by the local Chamber of Industry and Commerce. See the cooperation agreement under https://www.offenbach-offensiv.de/fileadmin/Daten_Micro-sites/Offensiv/PDF/Scan_Kooperationsvertrag_Unterzeichnet.pdf (last check September 11, 2020).

27 By "these placid cities around" the following cities are meant: Darmstadt, as the former residence city of the Grand Duchy of Darmstadt, Wiesbaden, as the today's capital of the Federal State of Hesse, and Frankfurt as a former imperial city and current global city.

28 See also https://www.deutschlandfunkkultur.de/kulturszene-in-offenbach-am-main-ein-neues-eldorado-fuer.1001.de.html?dram:article_id=393087 (last (last check September 11, 2020).

29 https://www.offenbach.de/stadtwerke/microsite/hafen/index.php (last check September 11, 2020).

12 Thessaloniki

Nikolaos-Komninos Hlepas

12.1 Introduction

The city of Thessaloniki is located on the Thermaic Gulf, at the northwest corner of the Aegean Sea and right next to the Chalkidiki peninsula. It is bounded on the west by the delta of the Axios River and on the southeast by the mountain range of Sivri and Chortiates.

This privileged geographic position and especially its huge natural harbor was the motive for the city's foundation back in 315 BC by King Kassandros of Macedon. He was one of the successors *(diadochi)* of Alexander the Great, whose half-sister Thessalonica he married. In Roman times, Thessaloniki grew to be a major trade hub located on the Via Egnatia, the road connecting Dyrrhachium on the Adria with the city of Byzantium, later called Constantinople.

By the Fall of Rome in 476, Thessaloniki was the second largest and wealthiest city of the Eastern Roman Empire and maintained this position for many centuries, therefore labeled as the *symvassilevoussa* (the "co-regent city" beside Constantinople), a place of traders, scholars, and churchmen (including Cyril and Methodius, known as "the apostles of the Slavs"). In the 14th century, the city's population exceeded 100,000, making it larger than London at the time.

In 1430, Sultan Murad II captured Thessaloniki, and the city was renamed *Selanik*. The decline of the city after its conquest was temporary because it soon regained its prestige as a major center of imperial administration and trading hub. In the early 16th century, the Sephardic community became the biggest one in the city, due to the massive influx of Spanish Jews. Being the only big city in Europe with a Jewish majority, Selanik was later on labeled as the *"new Jerusalem"* or the *"Mother of Israel"* where the Jewish Sabbath "was most vigorously observed" (Naar 2014; 2016).

In the late 19th century, the city acquired the status of a showcase for the modernization efforts of the declining Ottoman Empire with railways, trams, and street illumination. In 1908, Selanik was the place where officers of the Ottoman army (among them Kemal Atatürk, who was born in Thessaloniki in 1881) started the "Young Turk Revolution." In 1913, following

DOI: 10.4324/9781003084006-12

the defeat and surrender of the Ottoman Commander to the Greek army in 1912, the city was officially annexed to Greece. Most of the old center was destroyed by the Great Thessaloniki Fire, which started accidentally in August 1917. This was the start of new modernization efforts, including the redesign of the city according to the European-style urban plan, the foundation of the Aristotle University in 1925 (which is the biggest Greek university with 75,000 students), and of the international trade fair in 1926. Following the population exchange agreement between Greece and Turkey, the Muslim community left the city, while 160,000 ethnic Greek refugees arrived, establishing a new majoritarian community. Accordingly, the city was then labeled as the "capital of refugees." During the German occupation, the city lost nearly its entire Jewish population.

The Greek civil war (1944–1949) triggered a new influx of refugees, followed by internal migration that labeled the city as "the mother of the poor" (*Ftochomana*).

In the context of the Cold War, Thessaloniki lost its northern economic hinterland, while the East-West confrontation was a source of anxiety. Nevertheless, it became a very important industrial hub, also hosting important cultural events, such as the Thessaloniki International Film Festival (TIFF, since 1960), while the international airport boosted tourism toward Chalkidiki.

In 2011, the metropolitan area had 1,030,338 inhabitants, while the population of the core municipality had 325,182 (−16% compared to 1991). It is a major transportation hub for south-eastern Europe, notably through its harbor that was privatized in 2018 (rapidly expanding its container and other terminals) and its international airport (seven million passengers in 2019). The city lies at the crossroads of the E90, the "Egnatia" East/West autoroute (reaching from the Ionian/Adriatic coast to the Greek/Turkish border and then to Istanbul), with the E5 (Istanbul-Thessaloniki-Brussels) and the E75 (Athens-Thessaloniki-Helsinki) South/North autoroutes. Thessaloniki is also connected by high-speed train to Athens (since 2019).

Thessaloniki is the second most important media hub in Greece, as the seat of two national and eight regional television channels, and many radio stations, while the second oldest daily Greek newspaper still in circulation (*Makedonia*) is printed there. The city is also the seat of three public universities and several research and knowledge institutions.

12.2 Issues of Innovations

After the end of the East-West divide, Thessaloniki could not join the euphoria of other European cities that were close to the border. In 1991, the ten-years-long series of Yugoslav wars began. Yugoslavia was the main corridor toward Central Europe and the major land route for tourists. It was also an important market, especially for Northern Greece. These wars had a heavy impact on the economy of Northern Greece and especially on the industry that was already under pressure, due to the completion of the European single market (Kairidis and Kiesling 2020).

However, due to a new strategy (discussed in more detail in Section 12.3), the city has achieved impressive growth of tourism: from 1.3 million in 2010, the number of foreign tourists climbed up to nearly 3 million in 2019, offering an additional purchasing power of nearly €400 million to the city. An important part of this increase was due to Israeli tourists who occupy the first position among foreign visitors in recent years. There was also a considerable influx of Turkish tourists, while the "Ataturk house" (now the Turkish Consulate) became a trendy place for Turkish couples to get married. The city could also increase its attractiveness as a shopping hub for its northern neighbors: "We have this famous asset called Chalkidiki just around the corner, but very few tourists paid a visit to our lively and interesting city. This changed when we attracted Jews, Turks, and our northern neighbors" (Th7).

The boom in tourism could not, of course, fill the gap that was created by deindustrialization in the nineties and drastically increased since 2008 during the financial crisis. Leaning upon the existing industrial know-how (chemical and steel industries were using state-of-the-art technologies since the sixties) and human capital offered by local knowledge institutions, several attempts emerged to establish innovation zones and take advantage of the city's strategic position close to the markets of the neighboring transition countries.

The first attempt was the Thessaloniki Technology Park Management & Development Corporation S.A. (TTP) that was established in 1994. Its main stakeholder is the Centre for Research and Technology Hellas (CERTH), one of the biggest Greek research organizations. TTP actively participates in several regional and interregional initiatives enhancing innovative entrepreneurship.

Technopolis Thessaloniki ICT Business Park was an initiative of the Association of Information Technology Companies of Northern Greece (SEPVE) and was founded in 2001 with the participation of several companies as well as public entities. Technopolis established the first high-technology business park in Greece (an investment project of more than €12.5 million) and created a grid of modern infrastructure and investment opportunities. In the meantime, several companies settled in Technopolis, like Deloitte which launched its competence center employing 300 high-skilled scientists (Th11). The park is located on the eastern side of the city, which is the fastest-growing area and gradually evolved into a conglomerate of innovation and technology including within a short distance the CERTH, the Museum of Technology (NOISIS), and the European Centre for the Development of Vocational training (CEDEFOP). The latter is an EU institution based in Thessaloniki that helps the European Commission in developing and implementing EU vocational training policies.

In 2019, the Thessaloniki International Technology Center (THESS INTEC) was launched by TTP, several enterprises, and other private and public entities. THESS INTEC was endowed with 78 hectares by TAIPED (Hellenic Republic Asset Development Fund). The budget for the development of THESS INTEC (first phase) reached €70 million provided by the Greek government, the Stavros Niarchos Foundation, and the European Investment Bank.

THESS INTEC attracted 70 industrial companies who are establishing their research and development departments inside this new technology park in close cooperation with 17 research groups from local universities who are working on the following six innovation mega projects:

- advanced materials and manufacturing processes;
- flexible organic nanotechnology applications;
- artificial intelligence and simulation applications;
- clean energy innovative solutions;
- competence center for business and logistics challenges; and
- future mobility applications.

Within the framework of these megaprojects, THESS INTEC has already signed cooperation agreements with renowned international partners, such as the Texas A&M Transportation Institute, the Technology Parks of Karlsruhe (KTP), and Barcelona (La Salle), while negotiations have started with the Technology Authority of Israel. Two additional mega projects— biomedicine and nanotechnology—are already on track (Th7).

The exodus of young scientists and engineers, however, seems to be a major worry, among the initiators of such projects (Th7, Th4). Even before the financial crisis of 2008, the city was suffering from brain drain, since many highly skilled people tend to move to Athens. And this phenomenon drastically worsened after the crisis and the exodus of thousands of high-skilled young engineers seeking proper employment and carrier opportunities abroad.

Although many young engineers receive excellent academic education at the city's universities, research centers, and other knowledge institutions, they are hardly familiar with business skills. Moreover, in parts of the academic and research communities, there was, until recently, some resistance against cooperation with businesses. Therefore, the city of Thessaloniki started the "OK! Thess" initiative in 2016, based on a memorandum that included various stakeholders from knowledge institutions, businesses, chambers, and innovation-driven communities. It soon became Thessaloniki's leading start-up hub and a catalyst for the growth of a local innovation-friendly environment. "OK!Thess" helps entrepreneurs bring innovative ideas to market through a program that includes training, coaching, matchmaking with mentors, and access to capital. "OK!Thess" is also the place where open events allow like-minded peers to mix and connect. As a former member of local development company emphasized (Th6):

> Even if tomorrow, in a magical way, the crisis would end and the demand would increase again, we could not employ in our industries more than

20% of today's unemployed. We need a new social stratum of innovative young businessmen/women. This would take some time, of course until we have the necessary critical mass and a virtuous circle can start, just as it happened in previous times. We know that only a small percentage of our young entrepreneurs will finally succeed that will eventually employ the others. We also created an innovation network including similar initiatives and businesses in our neighboring countries, because we all know that we must bundle forces and we are all interested and involved in each other's market. And we did all that without a penny of public funding and this paralyzing bureaucracy, of course. Our partners invested no less than €14m in our work. We already have 80 people from start-uppers who absolved our courses and programs. [...] Their impact is already visible.

Another initiative supporting young people emerged through the cooperation of the municipality with the Culture Society of Businessmen from Northern Greece, whose president had been the later Mayor Boutaris. The basic idea was initially to create a platform of public discourse about arts and culture in Northern Greece, but it soon included activities for the promotion and support of young artists, poets, and writers.

> Supporting debutants was a strategy to keep them here, to prevent them from moving to Athens or from emigrating abroad. Moreover, we wanted to show these youngsters that they have an audience, a public here in their hometown, and also show to the local society that we have many talented people in this city and we must be alert to discover them and keep them in Thessaloniki.
>
> (Th5)

The Culture Society launched the "Mataroa" platform and awards for the benefit of young artists. "Mataroa" was the name of the ship that transported to France young scholarship holders in 1945, saving them from the civil war. Some of them became famous, like the composer Yannis Xenakis, the director Costas Gavras, and the philosopher Cornelius Castoriadis.

The city government also appointed a Chief Resilience Officer (CRO) and managed to be included in the network of 100 resilient cities (100RC) which is supported by the Rockefeller Foundation. This happened against the background that—from the point of view of local actors (Th1, Th14)—the city had not only proved its resilience after the great fire of 1917 and also after the great earthquake of 1977, but as a coastal city had to face the challenges of climate change and as a harbor city the challenges of globalization in order to develop an appropriate strategy for the future. Thessaloniki's resilience strategy is shaped by the City Resilience Index (CRI) which was adopted by 100RC and has been used as the basis to map and shape the city's resilience.

The resilience strategy is based on eight urban values (social cohesion, local identity and heritage, environmental management, health and wellbeing, youth empowerment, multi-stakeholder engagement, technology adaptation, economic prosperity), which represent Thessaloniki's identity and will guide how the city will plan for the future. These values cut across the city's four main goals that together form the basis of the strategy:

- shape a thriving and sustainable city;
- co-create an inclusive city;
- build a dynamic urban economy and responsive city;
- re-discover the city's relationship with the sea.

These goals are broken down into 30 objectives and more than 100 actions. The elaboration of this strategy followed a common methodology of 100RC, but in Thessaloniki particular attention was given to the inclusion of social categories who hardly voice their concerns and demands in public deliberation procedures, such as the elderly and children. Especially for the latter, experiential workshops were organized, which provided impressive creative and innovative ideas for the future of the city as a resilient and children-friendly place (Th14).

The resilience of Thessaloniki has, of course, been challenged by the long-lasting (2008–2017) financial crisis. Due to restricted competence in social affairs and limited resources, the city administration did not have the experience, skills, and personnel needed to cope with unprecedented, in the post-war period, levels of unemployment, impoverishment, and homelessness.

> The city did not have its own social policy, there was just some help offered in a fragmented and non-transparent way to people in need. We had to start from point zero in times where we were short of money but the social needs for assistance were immense. We had to be inventive and cooperative, trying to attract any kind of help we could get.
>
> (Th4)

> I am addressing most vulnerable groups of people and aim to support them to avoid becoming homeless, or in any event, we are trying to support them as well as possible. [...] These actions do not have a charity character. These actions adopt the philosophy of solidarity and support.
>
> (Th2)

The municipality launched the "Anti-Poverty Network," including actions such as "time banks" (which provides unpaid services and assistance on a mutual support basis), a dormitory for the homeless, a homeless center (primary health care, hygiene, psychosocial support), mobile kitchens, social mini-markets, social dispensaries, and social pharmacies,[1] a mobile school, a mediation center for the housing of refugees and homeless people, and more. Most of these actions addressed pressing needs that were due to the financial crisis after 2008. For instance, the city barely faced a problem of homelessness before, while also the "time banks" evolved within the context of the crisis: the latter are addressing needs that were previously covered by families, friends, and neighbors. The crisis dramatically increased the need for unpaid services and assistance, while the supply decreased, due to emigration or impoverishment of many helpers (Th9).

12.3 Actors, processes, and structuration through local discourses

Thessaloniki has traditionally been a stronghold of right-wing conservatism since the end of the civil war that broke out in Greece after the World War II. Particularly important was also the influence of the local Greek Orthodox Church, as this was the organization of the ethnic Greek community with which the ancestors of the current residents were particularly familiar until the first decades of the 20th century. Many citizens of Thessaloniki perceived the central state with distrust, as a distant power center dominated by Athenians as well as by people from the Peloponnese and Crete, although since the 1950s the Karamanlis family emerged as a national political dynasty originating from Greek Macedonia.

On the other hand, the dynamic liberal and/or left-wing minority of the local society was dominant in universities as well as among intellectuals and in the vivid cultural scene of the city. Some locals were leaders of language and legal reforms, of literature ("the city of poets") and artistic innovation, and protagonists of the national pop culture. Thessaloniki is also a historical place for trade unionism and the socialist-communist movement in Greece (Mazower 2004). More generally, the extermination of nearly the whole Jewish community through the Holocaust has been an irreparable disaster for the dynamics of social and cultural innovation in the city. In the local business community, however, rising businessmen of refugee origin (mostly Anatolian Greeks) soon filled most of the gap.

As many local interlocutors stressed, local politics and discourses are characterized by extreme polarization, usually following the lines of these two political-cultural groupings: on the one side the conservatives and on the other side the liberals and leftists (Th1, Th3, Th4, Th6). Emotionalized polarization is manifest even concerning choices about major infrastructure projects:

> One part of the city wanted a subway to be built since such a subway was going to be built in Athens. The other part preferred a light metro system. The first part prevailed and now that the subway is under construction there is a fierce dispute over some findings of ancient ruins in a metro station under construction. Our society loves to dichotomize every aspect of collective choices. Always an incredibly vehement

controversy arises that reminds me of conflicts between the "greens" and the "blues" in old Constantinople. It seems that we truly are "the last byzantine city", as some Athenians say.

(Th3)

The city government remained in the hands of the conservatives for 25 years, starting with Mayor Kouvelas, who "was also the one who set the main agenda of the city for the following three decades" (Th3). In times of state monopoly in radio/television Kouvelas (illegally) founded municipal radio and TV stations; he even launched some preparatory works for a sub-way line, while at the same time promoting the idea of an underwater ring autoroute. His successor Cosmopoulos (1990–1998) stood at the forefront of huge demonstrations at the peak of the name dispute with the former Yugo-slav Republic of Macedonia. He was supported by the eccentric prefect of Thessaloniki, Psomiadis (an exponent figure of the Pontic community—i.e., Greeks originating from the Black Sea), Bishop Anthimos, and the local MPs of nearly all parties. This advocacy coalition put enormous pressure on the central government and the Greek foreign policy. This kind of ideologi-cal "urban regime" including the deeply rooted religious-conservative "gray eminences" of the city did not simply dominate the local discourse arena, it even set standards of ethnic and local "appropriateness" and "correctness." In this way, these local leaders managed to discredit local opponents and dissident voices, while at the same time acting as an alliance efficiently se-curing the reproduction of local power.

This system was shaken by the financial crisis and the scandals that termi-nated the political career of the last conservative mayor, Vasilis Papageor-gopoulos, who was the most powerful figure in local politics for many years since he had been a local MP for 15 years before he became the mayor who governed the city for three successive terms.

In 2010, Papageorgopoulos lost his re-election for a fourth term by just 150 votes. The winner (who had lost the previous election in 2006) was a contrasting figure in local politics and discourse: Yannis Boutaris, a suc-cessful businessman and enfant terrible of the local bourgeoisie, an ecolog-ical activist, a left libertarian, and a non-partisan cosmopolitan who liked to provoke the local ideological establishment. With close ties to urban ac-tivists and civil society, he managed to forge an independent list supported by nearly all locals seeking a change in local politics. Finally, he gained the support of the Socialist Party in 2010:

> Boutaris didn't need to prove anything to others or himself, he didn't need to enrich himself, he was renowned for his integrity and his ruth-less frankness. He managed to bring together the alternative scene and the old bourgeoisie of the city. They both felt suffocated by the bigotry and the narrow-mindedness of the city rulers. Boutaris was the only one who could integrate this heterogeneous body of followers.

(Th6)

As a mayor, Boutaris pursued the strategy of an "open city." Like his Athenian peer Kaminis (see Chapter 3 in this book), he opened the formerly party-politicized and self-contained city hall to different urban groups and activists, as well as to private foundations and businesses. As per him, Thessaloniki should also open up for its Balkan and Eastern neighbors. He repeatedly emphasized that the city should overcome its inferiority complex to Athens and its underdog mindset, undertake its initiatives, and claim its international role.

A key factor was the naming dispute with the former Yugoslav Republic of Macedonia (that was finally settled in 2019), which revitalized old anxieties that were ruthlessly exploited by ambitious local politicians, who were at the same time accusing the "Athens-centric state" of having abandoned Thessaloniki. Central governments responded by promoting huge construction projects, such as the Egnatia autoroute, the metropolitan subway, and even an underwater ring road (that was soon abandoned). The financial crisis after 2008, however, and the following rigid austerity measures caused a sudden drop in income and demand that ruined many businesses and led to massive unemployment. The local political establishment, alongside its ethnocentric and localist-provincial narrative, was discredited, since it became obvious that it was not offering a way out of the crisis.

By contrast, the new municipal government under Boutaris that was elected in 2010 offered a new, alternative narrative that was quite the opposite to the previous one: Thessaloniki should overcome its phobic approach toward northern and eastern neighbors and its provincial underdog attitude toward Athens. Proximity to the border is nowadays not a risk; it is a chance of easier access to foreign markets and clients. The new city motto should be "extrovert Thessaloniki" (Th1; Th2). As a former local politician put it, "instead of accusing Athens of everything we should take our own initiatives" (Th4). After all, Thessaloniki has always been a big and important city, while Athens was an irrelevant town for many centuries. Finally, it has been emphasized:

> instead of feeling uncomfortable about the fact that our hometown was a predominantly Jewish city for four centuries, we should be proud of the fact that Thessaloniki was so important for Jewish history, perceive this legacy as a precious asset, and face the dark side of collaboration and antisemitism in our history.[2]
>
> (Th4)

This new, open, inclusive, and pragmatic narrative about the city should foster the self-confidence of the citizenry and mobilize creative forces:

> Boutaris instrumentalized the multi-cultural heritage of the city in order to change the mindset of the people, to help them overcome their "underdog" feelings towards Athens, their idea that they are condemned to provinciality, and the belief that their future is not shaped

by themselves but from some distant decision-makers in Athens or even in Brussels.

(Th1)

This new narrative opened up new perspectives in the contemporary globalized world, even though this was not the primary target at the very beginning. Being a former businessman, Boutaris realized that this new narrative could be monetized (Th1). It should not only mobilize the locals but also rebrand the city in a way that would boost tourism and attract investments in a time of crisis, where they were badly needed. As Boutaris emphasized in our interview:

> In the beginning, I approached the Jews. This was the easiest part because they were open and friendly. Then I visited Turkish Airlines and I asked them to launch direct flights since we are the native city of Ataturk. They were bewildered but they soon did it. I also traveled to Skopje [the capital city of Northern Macedonia] and told them that my mother was born in Krusevo, a city that now belongs to their country. Especially in the media of the Jewish diaspora, but also in Turkish media and the media of Northern Macedonia there was overwhelmingly positive feedback about our activities.

Therefore, the following was crucial for the development in Thessaloniki and the innovations achieved in this city—as stated by an interviewee:

> The personality of Boutaris brought an unprecedented amount of social capital and trust that could be used for the benefit of the city. There were many ideas in the universities and the business community for extrovert strategies and cooperation. Now they activated these plans because they trusted the mayor and gathered around the new city leadership who acted as a catalyst and mobilizer. Our northern and eastern neighbors also trusted him and opened themselves for cooperation. Private foundations trusted the Mayor and offered support and "know-how" to various local projects where the city was involved. And, of course, there was a stronger mobilization of civil society. We know that not everyone is eager to participate in civic activities. It is just a minority, around 10–15 percent of the inhabitants, and they are usually better educated, the ones who are not short of financial and time resources. Boutaris mobilized quite a few of the formerly mistrustful absentees, thanks to his own credibility.

(Th6)

Moreover, Boutaris took—at least from the point of view of one interview partner—

> advantage of the authority that the universities and scientific knowledge, in general, enjoy in order to create social capital. Involving universities

and other research institutions in several actions and discourses meant that these actions would start with a certain amount of trust that they would otherwise not enjoy. Moreover, as knowledge institutions, they are based on rationalism. They tend to rationalize the whole debate about a certain issue. Publicization and dissemination of their position on controversial issues can reveal the irrationality of populist agitators.

(Th2)

In the shadow of the economic crisis prevailing in Greece since 2008, the visibility of the new leadership increased, and public interest in the offensive, uneasy discourse initiated by Boutaris rapidly expanded. By initiating uncomfortable debates and not conforming to the stereotype of a Greek mayor, he increased his visibility abroad at a time when Greece was constantly in negative headlines. The mayor was interviewed by several leading foreign newspapers and other international media, and this was the first time that this happened to a mayor of this city (Katsinas 2019). This led to repercussions in the local discourse arena and made him and his statements more interesting and significant (Th3).

Boutaris was personally involved in public discourse about foreign policy, actively campaigning in favor of a compromise in the name dispute with the former Yugoslavian Republic of Macedonia: "since we are the strongest part, we should be more generous" (Th4, by referring to Thucydides).[3] He also stood for a new Greek-Turkish rapprochement that would gradually bring the two nations closer together. The local discourse was focusing on the economic benefits of tourism from Turkey, also highlighting wider possibilities for economic cooperation with a huge neighbor and his rapidly growing economy (Th3; Th4).

Economic aspects were also highlighted concerning the Jewish heritage of the city, but in reality, unlike the Ottoman history of Thessaloniki, this was not about the simple recognition and re-evaluation of a non-Greek local legacy: there was a forgotten record of collaboration during the Nazi occupation and the post-war exploitation of Jewish property (Saltiel 2020).[4] The latter coincided with the early stage of long-lasting persecution of leftist citizens during and after the civil war. While this dark history of political persecution became an integral part of the narrative of the Greek Republic after the end of the dictatorship in 1975, the fate of the Jewish community was forgotten. This was in the early 1990s when intellectuals and artists began to highlight the Jewish heritage and made, for instance, a revival of local Sephardic music quite popular. Taking the self-critical approach to one's history as a common European reference point, a wider local discourse about the lost multicultural heritage of the city began. And especially some parts of the economic and cultural elites of the city have tried to make good use of this heritage, promoting a strategy of openness and the vision of a new, extrovert, and, once more, cosmopolitan Thessaloniki. The pragmatic approach of Boutaris and visible results in city tourism seemed to persuade, step by step, a wider circle of the citizenry to embrace this vision.

In recent years, however, new powerful actors emerged that claim their position in local politics and the local discourse arena: one of them is Ivan Savvidis, a Russian businessman of Pontic origin, one of the wealthiest men in Russia and a close friend of President Putin. Savvidis has bought several enterprises (hotels, tobacco industries, TV and radio stations, newspapers) and taken over with his partners the biggest of the privatized harbors of the city. In 2015 he bought the sports club "PAOK" which is the most popular in Northern Greece, and paid all its debts. "Savvidis has become very important, he is the biggest private investor in Northern Greece now" (Th1). In the final phase of negotiations that led to the Prespes Agreement that settled the name dispute between Greece and Northern Macedonia, Savvidis was accused of supporting nationalists in both countries on behalf of Russia who would undermine this rapprochement but he denied it.[5]

In May 2018, Mayor Boutaris was attacked by right-wing demonstrators in the center of the city. A few months later he announced that he would not be running in the municipal elections of 2019.

Following the withdrawal of Boutaris from the local political scene, obvious disorientation prevailed among his followers.

In 2019, a former vice-mayor of Boutaris who had resigned in 2017 after a quarrel was elected as mayor. Although his list was the second strongest in the municipal council, he managed to forge a coalition that supported him. Initial fears that his term would launch the comeback of the old conservative establishment have not been confirmed, for the time being. The resilience strategy of the city, for instance, is still on track including the municipal resilience observatory (Th13, Th14). An obvious change, however, is the fact that the mayor of Thessaloniki is not at the epicenter of media attention anymore.

12.4 Key findings

It is a widely accepted opinion (Th1; Th3; Th12; Th15), that Thessaloniki has an ideal size: the city is not too big and ungovernable like Athens, and it is not too small to offer a critical mass for several activities, as is the case in all other provincial cities of Greece (none of them has more than 300,000 inhabitants). Thessaloniki offers a high quality of life, by Greek standards, and it is the home of a vivid and young (150,000 students) local society.

Following the end of the Cold War and the beginning of the Yugoslav wars, the city has become the place of a long-lasting controversy about its character and its orientation. Conservative predominance was shaken by the financial crisis after 2008 and a new, open, and innovative municipal leadership offered a new narrative. It used the forgotten multicultural heritage of the city as a passage to rebranding as an open and cosmopolitan city, a way to win the future in a globalized world. It challenged the formerly dominant, underdog mindset about the "fate" of the second biggest city that was condemned to provinciality and to living in the shadow of Athens. According to this new narrative, the true character of a city that has been at the crossroads of all historic changes in the region and a constantly important trade and culture hub for 24 centuries would not be a provincial one. On the contrary, Thessaloniki would be a cosmopolitan city by its nature and its geographic location. Therefore, the city should create bonds with its multi-ethnic diaspora and rebrand itself as a traditionally cosmopolitan city, attracting tourism, events, and businesses.

Due to the visible success in tourism and the attention of the international media, this new narrative seemed to have persuaded an important part of the local society. Apart from his charisma, Mayor Boutaris developed a "bridging" function among important stakeholders of the city, offering his social capital and triggering their cooperation. As an explicit anti-populist politician, he often engaged knowledge institutions, experts, and renowned personalities to "rationalize" public discourse on various matters. These discourses created the reference points for innovations, which are the visible positive effects of some of his policy choices.

The changing mindset mentioned above has led to an obvious re-framing. The new mindset is characterized by a stronger self-confidence in the future of the city and a spirit of cooperation and internationalization and is reflected in impressive progress achieved in the technology parks of the city and its enterprises.

The innovation dynamics that have been developed seem to be sustainable, especially because the city has already experienced and, to a great extent, realized the multiple positive effects of changes that were launched ten years ago, starting with a new city narrative.

Notes

1　For similar services in Chania and Elefsina see Sections 5.2 and 6.2.
2　Extracts by the author from speeches and texts of Mayor Boutaris.
3　According to Thucydides (History of the Peloponnesian War, chapters 84–116, Pantianos Classics 1914) the stronger polis should refrain from humiliating the weaker polis, even after a war. Being generous to the weaker polis would most likely become the base of a long-term cooperation. Being arrogant and humiliating to the weaker would ensure an enduring hostility and, by given opportunity, the revenge.
4　The story of the Jewish cemetery is the best documented case of expropriation that started long before the German occupation: the huge areal of 32 hectares right in front of the Eastern city wall was already a victim of the city's expansion in the 19th century. In 1886 an Ottoman gymnasium was established on the cemetery ground which was later taken on by the Aristotle University of Thessaloniki (1924). In the 1930s the city administration officially decreed that the Jewish cemetery would be expropriated and given to the expanding Aristotle University. The plan never came into effect, but fear of demolishment motivated the Jewish community to give the university a section of unused cemetery ground. During the German occupation (when 90% of the local Jews were killed) the

Jewish cemetery (the biggest one in Europe) was destroyed by the German army in close cooperation with its Greek collaborators in the city administration. The desecrated areal was used by the university after the war and it was not before 2014 that the university erected a memorial for the Jewish cemetery.

5 https://www.nytimes.com/2018/10/09/us/politics/russia-macedonia-greece.html (last check October 20, 2020).

13 A comparative analysis of communicative mechanisms and narratives supporting innovations

Björn Egner, Hubert Heinelt,
Nikolaos-Komninos Hlepas,
Panos Koliastasis, Melina Lehning
and Alexia Timotheou

13.1 Introductory remarks

In this concluding chapter, the results of a comparative analysis of the discourses on innovations in the cities of our enquiry will be presented. As outlined at the beginning of the book (in Chapter 2), local discourses address challenges faced by cities as well as the particular local constraints and opportunities for dealing with these challenges through innovation. As also mentioned in Chapter 2, these discourses are not confined to a particular local narrative reflecting a local self-image. Through these discourses, local narratives can also be changed. The communicative mechanisms explained in Chapter 2 play a crucial role in changing local narratives. Through these mechanisms—whether used by actors deliberately or not, narratives—or more precisely, the uniquely combined dimensions of narratives (also explained in Chapter 2) which result in a narrative pattern typical for a given city—can be altered.

As shown in Section 1.4, the documents on which our comparative analysis of innovation discourses in the selected cities is based cover only a portion of the overall period in which innovations were observed. In some cities, such as Frankfurt, the innovations under consideration were introduced as early as the late 1980s and early 1990s and have been maintained continuously since then. However, for practical reasons, the collection of documents focused on approximately four years between April 2016 and the end of 2019. Nonetheless, where possible we also collected documents before and after this period—particularly for those cities where there has been controversial public debate about innovation that still continues (see Section 1.4). In addition, interviews in particular, but also other types of documents, provided an insight into the discourses on innovation beyond these four years, including distinctive local narrative patterns and the communicative mechanisms used to influence the discourses.

For these reasons, this chapter is divided into two parts reflecting the difference in the data collection periods. Section 13.2 compares the discourses

DOI: 10.4324/9781003084006-13

on innovations in each of the selected cities for the entire period under consideration. The information made available by the collected documents for analysis of the total period allows well-founded statements to be made about the narrative patterns that dominate in the local discourses examined. This is because it becomes clear relatively quickly whether or not there is a dominant narrative pattern in debates about local innovation over many years. The situation with regard to the use of communicative mechanisms is different. Their usage changes over time, depending on the dynamics of the struggles over the introduction, continuation, and/or modification (if not termination) of innovations. Furthermore, the occurrence of certain communicative mechanisms for the entire period during which innovations were developed may be influenced by the fact that we occasionally included some material in the corpus of documents analyzed lying outside the four years mentioned above. In this context, it must also be taken into account that—as already explained in Section 1.4—depending on the type of document, certain communicative mechanisms can occur frequently, without this necessarily implying that they figured prominently in the local discourse at the time in question.

The situation is different in Section 13.3, in which the results of the analysis are based on a large number of documents of various types collected between April 2016 and the end of 2019. In this section, the appearance of individual communicative mechanisms and what this means for discursive struggles over innovations in the selected cities has been examined more closely. Narrative patterns identified for this period in the cities analyzed are also considered, but this has been done primarily in order to examine whether or not the particular narrative pattern identified for the respective city has been changed or challenged during this time.

The two sections are structured in the same way: each section starts with a subsection in which some general observations are presented referring to quantitative results of the documents analyzed with the help of the MaxQDA software tool. This subsection is followed by one with more detailed (qualitative) reflections related to selected passages quoted in the documents.

13.2 Comparison of local narratives of the cities studied

The main purpose of this section is a comparison of the structure of the local narratives in the cities analyzed. The focus of interest here relates to the particular dimensions of narration (introduced in Chapter 2), whose specific combination leads to a certain narrative pattern, which—according to our premise—influences debates about innovations and implementing such innovation.

13.2.1 A quantitatively oriented comparative view of local narratives

Figure 13.1 presents figures on the coding of the dimensions of narratives in the corpora of the individual cities.

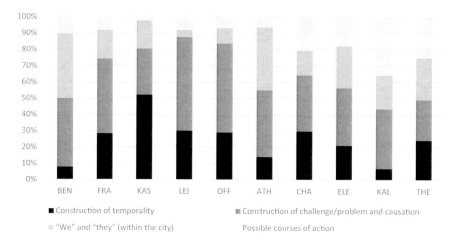

Figure 13.1 Proportion of the individual dimensions of narratives detected in the corpora across cities.

Source: Own compilation and calculation.

Percent figures indicate what proportion the individual dimensions of narratives had in the coded occurrence of all these dimensions in the respective city.

As these figures for *Bensheim* show, the narrative there exhibits a differ-ent pattern from the other cities studied, except for the dimension of the construction of challenges and opportunities for action: the construction of temporality, or more precisely reference to a (glorious) past with which cur-rent action is justified in order to achieve innovations in the future, which are also perceived as improvements, hardly plays a role in this. Moreover, possible courses of action are not discussed; they not only seem clear but are simply taken for granted. This has become clear in recent years in the he-gemonic assessment that for possible courses of action the limits of growth have been reached for the city—these limits involve the expansion of com-mercial space, the number of inhabitants (and thus building and housing ca-pacities), as well as traffic. Still, there are struggles over what the challenges are and what they result from. However, as shown in the case study of this city (see Chapter 4), these struggles are more about current decisions taken in city hall regarding specific issues (especially the issues of renovating or building the community center (*Bürgerhaus*) and redesigning the market place), but also in general about the upcoming issue of (re)developing the whole city center. Another striking feature of the narrative pattern in Ben-sheim is the distinction between "we" and "they" within the city. This refers to "locals" as opposed to "newcomers" but also to the distinction between decisive actors in city hall and the "alliance of doers" on the one hand, and those who feel ignored but still organize politically on a case-by-case basis on the other. The percentage of coded material in the corpus of documents collected for Bensheim is much higher than in the other German cities analyzed with regard to this dimension of narration. This phenomenon has already been addressed (in Chapter 4) and will be taken up again below (in Section 13.3).

The distinction between "we" and "they" within the city is much lower in *Offenbach* and *Leipzig*, where a stronger manifestation of this dimension of local narratives could have been expected due to the high number of immigrants or newcomers. The reference to the past, with which current action is justified in order to achieve novelties in the future which are also seen as an improvement, is clearly most pronounced in *Kassel*. However, such a construction of temporality is also a characteristic of the particular narrative pattern exhibited in *Leipzig*. For *Leipzig*, the construction of particular challenges, if not problems, on the one hand, but also of special areas of potential viewed as characteristic of the city on the other hand, plays a prominent role in local narratives. This is similarly true for *Frankfurt* and *Offenbach*. Frankfurt and Leipzig currently face challenges regarding the disputes over urban growth and related competition for the use of (still) available space and the lack of housing. In Offenbach, specific potential has been identified in discussion related to the development of the master plan and also the "arrival city" concept. In Leipzig, the emphasis on the city's special areas of potential, which appears again and again in the local discourse, is expressed in the metaphor of "sleeping beauty," the significance of which has already been addressed in Chapter 10. The prominent role played by debates about current challenges and how to address them effectively in local narratives in these three cities is probably also related to the finding that (obvious) possible courses of action are also more frequently a topic in public discourses in these cities than in Kassel and Bensheim.

Among Greek cities, Athens is the one in which public discourse seems least concerned with the construction of temporality as a dimension of the local narrative—in the sense of discursively linking a glorious past with present potentials for action in order to achieve a promising future. At first glance this finding seems surprising, but it seems that Athens' heritage is taken for granted as something that does not need to be mentioned. On the other hand, the public discourse is also the least concerned with possible courses of action for the future compared with the other Greek cities in this study. Apart from the lack of resources that preclude ambitious and costly plans, the vast number of innovations set in motion and in progress simply seems to tie up most of the energy in ongoing debates. Pressing current challenges are addressed in a pragmatic manner. The discussion focuses on explaining causes, and most of it is geared toward highlighting and supporting the need for innovative action. The distinction between "we" and "they" is the second most common dimension in Athens. In addition to a polarization that is common in Greek public debate, it also reflects a rhetoric that emphasizes the new inclusive politics that highlights overlooked potentials, in sharp contrast to earlier, exclusively practiced political patronage and in the face of rising populism during the crisis period.

Despite traditionally polarized local politics in *Thessaloniki*, the distinction between "we" and "they" appears less frequently than in the other Greek cities. The process of redefinition as a "cosmopolitan city" has focused on convincing people of upcoming benefits and thus circumvents recent cleavages in local politics and culture. The new image of the city is based on its multicultural urban heritage, and the construction of linkages between past, present, and future is an important dimension of the narrative that seeks to overcome underdog feelings and the provinciality of the postwar decades. Future ambitions are clarified by emphasizing possible courses of action through which local potential and relationships with the diaspora abroad could be utilized for economic growth.

In the case of *Elefsina*, the construction of challenges and problems has dominated the local narrative for two main reasons. First, in Elefsina, in line with all Greek cities, the implications resulting from the economic crisis were placed on the agenda. This exerted pressure on the municipal authority to develop various social services in order to secure social cohesion and protect the most vulnerable. Hence, the social innovations described in Chapter 6 were created. Second, the challenge for the city in successfully organizing the project of the European Capital of Culture and thus rebranding itself from an industrial and highly polluted area to a modern, clean, and dynamic city advancing cultural development has been a core topic of local debates. This second challenge is connected with a particular feature of the distinction between "we" and "they" within the city—namely, among those involved in the heated controversy regarding the organizational capacity of the municipality to run this project and meet the deadlines. The distinction between "we" and "they" within the city also became a notable part of the narrative pattern in Elefsina in the context of broad support for the social innovations, on the one hand, and criticism of their concrete organization (and funding) by parts of the local community, on the other. Reference to its past had played a limited role in Elefsina, but in the context of the application to become the European Cultural Capital efforts were made to develop a new narrative for linking the ancient cultural tradition of the city with the future of environmental protection, a service-based economy, and cultural advancement.

For *Chania*, the construction of challenges and problems plays a crucial role in the local narrative pattern. Dealing with the severe implications of the economic crisis has also been high on the public agenda in Chania. In response to this, the municipal authority developed several social services to protect those in need. In addition, the problem of traffic remained one of the most pressing issues facing the city despite promotion of relevant policy initiatives by the local authorities in recent years. Construction of temporality, i.e., referring to the past in looking to a better future by introducing innovations, appears to contribute to constructing challenges to some extent, since the ancient monuments in the old city of Chania remain the most prominent tourist sites in the area and attract thousands of tourists every year. Some disputes within the city concern the issue of how to deal with the traffic issue. In particular, it seems that there are differing views between local businesses and ordinary citizens, as the former are skeptical about the creation of wide pedestrian zones and bicycle lanes because of how this would limit space for cars. The thematization of possible courses of action does not play a particularly important role in the local narrative. This may be due to the fact that local options for action appear to have been clarified and related questions thus focus at most on the promotion of tourism and on using new technologies for communication between citizens and the municipal administration.

In *Kalamata*, the construction of challenges and problems emerges as the most influential feature of the local narrative pattern. This is underscored by the fact that, although the city has managed to develop remarkable cultural activities since the 1980s, it is not utilizing its full potential. The city's cultural strategy (2016–2025) did not convince the Selection Committee, which finally crowned Elefsina European Capital of Culture. On top of that, the dance hall does not have a viable business plan and is underused. Thus, it is evident that from the perspective of local people achievements of the past years have not received the attention they deserve, with the local population now taking innovations achieved in previous decades for granted. In the local narrative, possible courses of action appear to have almost equal importance with the construction of problems. Possible courses of action that have been recorded mostly refer to a new vision for the city, based on a coherent and consolidated strategy on tourism. A strategy that will revitalize and develop the city further, based on its comparative advantages, includes the natural environment, culture, local products, and digital achievements. The conflicts between "we" and "they" within the city also emerge as quite important, but are mainly related to the protection of the environment and technological solutions for transforming Kalamata into a smart city. As far as the construction of temporality is concerned, references to the past to outline possible innovations to be undertaken for achieving improvements for the future do not seem to be very relevant in the local narrative.

13.2.2 A closer look at the narrative patterns to be found in the cities analyzed

The narrative patterns just briefly sketched that can be identified for the cities studied will now be presented in more detail.

As is the case in Frankfurt and Leipzig, for *Bensheim*, too, challenges are seen regarding growth and prosperity and the side effects of these developments, as expressed in the following two quotations from articles in the local newspaper: "Bensheim has been growing and prospering for years, with all its advantages and disadvantages. This is nothing new [...]."[1] This is commented on more concretely as follows:

> Low unemployment, a strong economic context and an extraordinary structure of clubs and schools with a high level of voluntary work—are all good reasons [...] favoring [the city]. However, as is well known, popularity also has its downside. For years, rents and land prices have been so high.[2]

At the same time, in the local discourse there is a widespread perception and self-image that these challenges (and others) can be addressed effectively. Although the (re)development of the city center and particularly of the marketplace and the surrounding pedestrian area are currently the subject of heated local debate, the following example shows how this discursive feature is rooted in a historically rooted self-awareness:

> It is nothing new that Bensheim's city center is constantly undergoing change, too. In the seventies, the pedestrian zone was opened and cars were banned from the main street. The space gained was used for shopping... But today people often order online from home. The result is empty shops in the city center.[3]

What is crucial is the spirit underlying this statement that it will be possible to solve this problem too. Driven by this spirit, there is also no general talk about possible courses of action, but rather of concrete guiding principles for action that are actually followed in practice—as is illustrated by the following: "The real estate business with commercial premises is extremely important for urban development. It's not a plan that matters, but the position the municipality has as a real estate owner which it can use to achieve particular goals" (B6). Another person interviewed, a senior municipal official, added: "We don't sell commercial real estate to make money. We sell it to companies that fit in with our development goals" (B1).

What distinguishes the narrative pattern that can be identified in Bensheim from those of the other German as well as the Greek cities (as already mentioned in the previous section) is the emphasis on the distinction between "we" and "they" within the city—namely, between the "locals" and the "new arrivals." Although some interviewees stressed that this distinction is no longer as relevant as in the past, others argued that it still prevails—as stated in the following:

> Of course, there are the long-established [bonds among the locals]. The Kolping House [serves as] a classic example. I have been involved in the Kolping House for about 50 years. I was pushed in there in a pram, and these are networks that last a lifetime. Catholic Youth is also a network that lasts until today. Now I can pick up the phone and in ten

minutes I have eight people helping me with something. There are these old Bensheim networks, some of which you can't get into as an outsider, because you've been part of them [since] kindergarten, through First Communion, as an altar boy, and from the altar boys [you then went] into the Kolping family. You can join the Kolping family [as someone who moved to Bensheim recently], that's no problem at all, you are integrated, but you don't have this history.

(B14)

Nevertheless, it is usually also emphasized that, although there may be "two worlds, they are held together by a common basic understanding. Here we are at home!" (B5). And it is normally underlined: "Here the globalists feel at home. One acts globally. However, you have to [...]—especially if you have your family [...]—live somewhere. That's where the schools and the culture [to be found in Bensheim] play a role" (ibid.). Moreover, these "two worlds" do not merely coexist; they can also complement each other. This applies particularly to those "new arrivals" who occasionally but more or less continuously actively engage in urban life, and particularly local politics, and explains their involvement in a manner similar to the way one of the people interviewed did in the following quotation:

You get into some group of people you do not know and after half an hour you are engaged in a deep conversation with three out of 30. And you meet them again because they live in the same city, social contacts develop and so on. At the end of the day, it is a question [of] being active [...]. I have enough to do here [in a local company], I do not have to be chairman of the board of the business association as well. I would not have to be in *Bensheim aktiv*. On Sunday [...] I will be president of the Rotary Club. I could definitely do something else, but I do it because it interests me. It has to do with the family. My wife is also active [in a local association]. And then, whether you have lived here for a long time or not, you are suddenly on the same wavelength as the movers and shakers. [...] That happens quickly, and then you also know very quickly who is doing what and who is doing nothing, and who only had a big mouth at the wine festival, what they are going to do next week. And when you check, nothing has happened. You look at that three times and know that you do not need to rely on the promises [of such people] anymore. But then [such people are] no longer invited to play. *That is a doer culture.* And whether this is perceived afterwards in local politics, in business, or in clubs or associations, it doesn't really matter [...]. At the end of the day, it all comes down to the same thing. It is similar personalities who say: "We wanted to make a difference here and believe that we can make a difference."

(B3)

Based on such contacts and a proactive culture, an "alliance of doers" has emerged in Bensheim (as already mentioned in Chapter 4), in which "locals," who are traditionally anchored in local associations and local politics, interact with "new arrivals," who actively and permanently take care of social life in the city.

"Locals" and "new arrivals" also interact effectively in Bensheim in a form different from the "alliance of doers"—namely, rather occasionally. This has become particularly evident in recent years with the initiatives of citizens against tearing down the *Bürgerhaus* (community center) and the *Haus am Markt* (house on the market), both of which resulted in citizens' petitions. The statement of one participant in these initiatives is revealing for these cases and makes clear how they differ from the "alliance of doers." He strongly emphasized that these activities have "cost me a lot of time. [...] You cannot do that in the long run, and I do not really want to become politically active. I just want to bring this initiative to a clean end" (B19).

As already briefly mentioned in the previous section, a distinction between "locals" and "new arrivals" like that observed in Bensheim could not be found in the other German case study cities. This applies particularly to *Leipzig*, where an interview partner emphasized:

> That's the typical thing about Leipzig. You come to Leipzig, look at everything on the first day and are relatively enthusiastic. [...] And on the second day you are already a Leipziger [i.e., a "local"]. You are no longer [...] seen as a visitor by the people of Leipzig. On the second day you are a Leipziger. And then they [the Leipzigers] expect you to behave like one.
>
> (L4)

And, referring to Leipzig's past, the same person states at another point in the interview:

> Leipzig has been a commercial city with a trade fair for over 800 years. In order for traders to meet in Leipzig to exchange goods, the people of Leipzig had to be open to trade with others and to make houses and rooms available to other people who wanted to trade. The people of Leipzig have therefore become people who trade and are simply open to other people. *Leipziger Allerlei* (a regional German dish consisting of mixed vegetables) represents the characteristics of Leipzig. *Leipziger Allerlei* actually combines the differences. You leave what all the people have brought to eat as it is, you don't change it, but instead accept it and enjoy it yourself.
>
> (L4)

When a distinction is made in Leipzig between "we" and "they," it refers to Dresden, and by Dresden is meant not another major city in eastern

Germany and especially in the federal state of Saxony, but the seat of the government of that state. That the reference to Dresden does not express the communicative mechanism of comparison with others, but rather a very specific feature of a local narrative pattern that refers to the distinction between "we" and "they" becomes clear from the following quotation:

> [...] of course, Leipzig always has a certain special role. We have the largest cultural budget of any city of comparable size, and the city itself is shouldering it. With the Gewandhaus, the opera and the Schauspielhaus, I think €120 million go into it. [...] Dresden also has a lot of culture. But it's paid for by the State of Saxony. The Semperoper and the Staatsschauspiel, the State of Saxony pays for Dresden's culture, and of course that always causes a bit of resentment in Leipzig.
>
> (L8)

The reference to the history of the city as well as a specific identity—the "we" just outlined—is combined with the self-image of having potential and particularly the ability to adapt to change through innovations, as expressed in the following two quotations:

> Leipzig has always been an innovative city over the centuries. Whether that was industrialization [...], and also when it succeeded created privately such important infrastructures as the Leipzig canal network, or the Leipzig-Dresden railway, which then led to Nuremberg. [And last but not least] the trade fair business.
>
> (L7)

> [...] the city is actually a very large, gnarled, very strong oak. And then there are times of drought, times of floods, but the oak stands. And just now it blossoms again, or every four years it bears fruit, a particularly good harvest. Maybe that's how it is now. But I am pretty sure it will go down again a bit more. But that does not change anything at all about the construct as a whole. The roots are all these abilities that are there, and you cannot take them away from the city.
>
> (L13)

While building on such an understanding of the city's distinctiveness, at least in the first two decades after the reunification of Germany, challenges the city faced were, as a matter of course, also linked to opportunities and possible courses of action—as expressed in the following quote:

> When Hinrich Lehmann-Grube came to Leipzig [after reunification] and then became mayor, it was clear that we had a lot of catching up to do in terms of renovating housing [...]. The old buildings were simply worn out and it was not possible to catch up in a few years.

[We] needed a coordinated approach [...]. The warden houses [described in Section 10.2] were more of a by-product. It [...] simply happened along with it.

(L11)

In relation to the guardian houses (*Wächterhäuser*), this is also emphasized by this statement by another interviewee:

I think that in order to make something new, you need two things. [Firstly] somehow a need, a problem. Let's take the warden houses. There were streets where the things [houses] were ruined. [...] And if no one can take care of that, then you are happy if there are people who have an idea [...]. [Secondly, the] city had to say out of sheer necessity: Yes, we have to allow new ideas [...]. They [the municipality] had to let it happen. [At] the end of the day [...] the warden houses were not just normal houses where people lived, but always had to serve culture or a social component.

(L13)

Therefore, in "the decades of high vacancy rates, Leipzig built up an image as a city of opportunity."[4] However, due to the successful development of the city after 1989, challenges related to growth have arisen in Leipzig in recent years to which, from the point of view of various actors in the city, no satisfactory answers have yet been found (as outlined in Section 10.3).

Frankfurt has many similarities with Leipzig. This begins with the heated debates on how to deal with urban growth as just mentioned regarding Leipzig, which have also been going on in Frankfurt for several years and, as in Leipzig, have not yet been resolved. The similarities between Leipzig and Frankfurt also include the cities' openness to new residents and ultimately new citizens, which is emphasized by references to the past—as shown by the following extract from a minute of a council meeting:

The openness of our city to strangers is not only a high basic value. A basic value that has been upheld in Frankfurt am Main in particular for over 1,000 years, but it is also an important factor for the prosperity of our city, for jobs. That is also why we are purposely welcoming to refugees and open to all cultures and traditions. Frankfurt benefited from this in the 17th century, when the Huguenot refugees came to us; in the 18th century, when the Brentanos, for example, made decisive contributions to the development of industry and trade here; in the 19th century, when the Rothschilds and other dynamic Jewish families were finally freed from centuries of discrimination and made a decisive contribution to the city's prosperity; and in the 20th century, when, as a symbol of modern Germany, Frankfurt became the gateway to the world for American and other international investments.[5]

As in Leipzig, self-confidence prevails in Frankfurt in the form of the view that problems can be solved and that possible courses of action will arise and are expressed as if it were self-evident. This is not contradicted by the current debate on the housing issue, which—as already mentioned—has not yet concluded insofar as all those involved are convinced that this problem can also be solved by applying the options they advocate. This self-confidence is linked to a self-image that "Frankfurt seems gigantic,"[6] "is a city undergoing rapid changes,"[7] and "is unique in Germany, especially [as a] restless city that is constantly being transformed."[8] With the emphasis on restlessness and thus also on speediness, however, a first difference from the narrative pattern observed in Leipzig already emerges. The acceptance of remarkable speediness in Frankfurt is expressed in the following quotation from an interview: "So I think we are a very fast city. The speed is expressed, I think, even in the speed of the pedestrians" (F10). And it is not speed in general, but speed in political decisions that is emphasized as a feature unique to Frankfurt. This is also linked to the attitude that all political challenges facing the city are side effects of its dynamic development—and it is this dynamic development (especially its economic aspect) that would also provide the city with the resources to solve challenges quickly.

As already mentioned, the reference to the past, which is used to justify actions currently pursued in order to achieve innovations that are also seen as improvements in the future, is particularly pronounced in *Kassel*. This results from the special industrial and cultural traditions of the city, which are interrelated as "the industrial history that Kassel has with Bombardier, with Henschel, i.e., the mobility industry, which is also an industry rich in tradition, has been incorporated into the cultural self-image" (K2). Long-standing cultural traditions as an old residential city are an important and unique characteristic of the city. It is true that culture was once seen more as a "foreign body" because of Kassel's image as a working-class city. However, it is increasingly becoming an integral part (K7) or something "sacred" for Kassel (K6) and a new narrative has developed: Kassel, the city of variety and contrasts, which is often underestimated, has more to offer than people first think.

In contrast to Frankfurt, the self-confidence and the self-image associated with Kassel is more characteristic of an up-and-coming city and is oriented toward the changed role of the city, which came to the fore as a result of reunification. Although Kassel had long been a benchmark in northern Hesse, it was seen as a purely working-class city and lacked appeal, and so special challenges such as a high unemployment rate emerged in the "shadow of southern Hesse," as one interviewee explains: "Kassel was once really on the decline. It was a peripheral city that was pretty much cut off. There was hardly any positive momentum. On the contrary, the demographic forecasts were downward and there was this typical brain-drain problem" (K8). The city was "[...] at the butt end of the world until 1990 and was then pulled into the center with the decision in 1990" (K3). In order to fight their way out of this shadow and to actively use the new situation in the center of Germany, "in the last ten years, measures [...] that have to do with the region have resulted in cooperation between actors in the region and so on. This [has] contributed to a more powerful dynamic emerging here" (K8). While the unemployment rate is continuously falling, as in Bensheim, Frankfurt, and Leipzig, other challenges arise from these realignments as side effects of growth, globalization, prosperity, and an increasing attractiveness. An important aspect in facing these challenges was the creation of networks, both economic and cultural, as one interviewee pointed out:

> There are very many, very open networks here in Kassel. Each time we think about who else we can involve, who else can be invited, who perhaps does not yet have a connection to us but the know-how, the expertise, the perspectives that we can still integrate. If you think of specific areas, such as the creative industries, [then you come across] a very, very lively, very exchange-oriented scene, which [...] is developing its formats, networks and structures in order to build bridges between creativity and business and to develop future perspectives.
>
> (K2)

In connection with the economic sector, this statement is also supported by another interview partner:

> We have always said very early on what is possible in Kassel and how to do it. That naturally had a self-reinforcing effect. [...] We have created a positive climate of expectations, and to me this was also associated with some very painful statements, because the strategy for mastering this structural change was that the decisive companies, players, politics, research [...] in certain sectors had to be networked regionally within the framework of so-called cluster initiatives—by networking from within.
>
> (K6)

In combination with highly informal structures and processes, it becomes clear that certain processes unfold slowly. However, as shown in Chapter 9, these networks took on a key role and developed into a dominant narrative. They can be characterized as open and strongly consensus-based, because "it is not only the fact that Kassel hosts the most important world art exhibition every five years that is a unique selling point. The spirit of openness and innovation is also part of the city's DNA—even in earlier centuries."[9]

This openness also has limits, as not every change is accepted immediately. The reason for this is a special distinction between "we" and "they." This distinction can be found in Kassel in relation to Wiesbaden as the seat of government of Hesse, in the same way as it can be found in Leipzig in its relation to Dresden. However, the distinction becomes clearer with regard to particular challenges within the city that can lead to innovations, as is illustrated by the example of the university. As explained in Chapter 9, the *Gesamthochschule* was not initially accepted by the population, and many in Kassel were of the opinion that "there are many people around the university who don't really get involved with Kassel" (K5). However, through the commitment of the university president at the time, the city and the university "found their way back to each other," as an interview partner (K3) emphasized, who added:

> New deals, new projects and a close cooperation have actually been agreed upon, which then also opened the doors of the civil society for the university and makes a closer cooperation between university and city possible, even though it is not comparable with Göttingen, which is a city that is [...] even a bit larger than Kassel, but overall is strongly shaped by the university and here it was just like that: It's a city that also has a university, but actually this university is not really in keeping with the image of this city.
>
> (K3)

But as a result of the renaming of the university and the resulting demographic change, Kassel developed into a young, open city with an international orientation—or as one interviewee emphasized, became "a university city" (K9). At the same time, this change fostered the emergence in the networks just mentioned of pluralistic, active, and civil society participation in meeting the new challenges.

In the local narratives of *Offenbach*, strong emphasis, comparable to Leipzig and Frankfurt, is placed on potential that is seen as a characteristic feature of the city, as well as on the construction of challenges. This can be attributed to deindustrialization and the city's geographical location. As a direct neighbor of the city of Frankfurt am Main, Offenbach, like Kassel, is in the "shadow" of the banking metropolis. However, while Kassel has no comparable competitors around it in northern Hesse, Offenbach is dominated by a constant attempt to emphasize the differences "from the neighbor," as an interview partner pointed out:

> Offenbach has always acted under the constraint of having to react to developments. So, if you look back at history. Offenbach is also strongly influenced by the development in Frankfurt. [...] It goes back a long way. The Frankfurt guilds once decided that no factories were allowed to settle in Frankfurt. Which all came to Offenbach. So that was the cornerstone for Offenbach's rise as a workers' town, as an industrial town. It's been similar now since 2010/2011. The housing market in Frankfurt is overflowing and Offenbach is therefore benefiting from developments that actually started in Frankfurt. Although, it's a bit of folklore, both the people of Frankfurt and Offenbach still try to set their cities apart from each other. But they are pretty close to each other. One is simply interwoven in the development.
>
> (O2)

At the same time, this interconnectedness is expressed in a convergence of different dimensions of narratives, especially the construction of problems and challenges, and a distinction between "we" and "they," as an interview partner clarified:

> I come more from the perspective of the location and, I believe, the greatest challenge from this perspective [...] is [...] that Offenbach has, on the one hand, quite a serious budget problem and, on the other hand, very high potential that is not being utilized. On the one hand, there is a high level of debt, a difficult social structure, a high expenditure burden, a structural deficit, and on the other hand, there is potential for the use of real estate not found elsewhere in the Rhine-Main region in such a concentrated form or having such excellent connections. In other words, very large areas of potential that have somehow not developed as dynamically in the past, in recent years, as they have in the Rhine-Main region as a whole. That [...] is [...] on the one hand [the] potential and on the other hand [there is] the great challenge. Offenbach [...] is the poverty island in the Rhine-Main, so in terms of social structure, in terms of household structure [...] Offenbach is simply different from the rest of Frankfurt Rhine-Main.
>
> (O4)

This essentially influences the actions of the actors, since

> the city has always acted under duress. Under the constraint that it has been in debt for years and decades. This is due to a structural history, the social burdens are immense in Offenbach. These are social burdens imposed by the federal government, and out of this compulsion to make something out of this shortage and still create something, people try to get things done partly through voluntary work, partly also by rigorously cutting back on services.
>
> (O2)

The reference to the past still plays an important role today because Offenbach has always been an industrial city and the socioeconomic differences that developed there resulted in a very high unemployment rate and high fluctuation (see also Chapter 11). As a result, Offenbach developed into an "island of poverty" in an economically highly developed region, as the following passage from a budget speech makes clear:

> if we walk through the city with our eyes open, we all see that this function of the city of Offenbach also presents us with great challenges. Many of the people who come to us will not immediately be able to contribute to the city's tax revenue. There are many bitter fates among them, among destitute and exploited people. For these people, Offenbach is a

promise and sometimes a false promise; for many of these people, Offenbach is something like the promised city.[10]

But, instead of surrendering to fate, people used the references to the past to justify current actions intended to bring about innovation. The situation in which the city finds itself is understood as involving both challenges and advantages, which the city knows to use. On the one hand, this was reflected in the early modernization of the municipal administration in order to cope with an increased administrative workload due to a high fluctuation of people moving into and out of the city. In addition, the city changed the narrative of the "problem child." This can be illustrated most clearly by the topic of migration, as the proportion of citizens with a migration background is particularly high in Offenbach. Instead of perceiving this issue as a problem, a shift in perspective was taken and the issue used as a special feature of the city expressed in the concept of the "arrival city." This re-thematization of immigration implies that immigration is part of the "DNA of the city" (see also Chapter 11), which "may have grown historically, [since] migrants have always been here [and] that relatives, acquaintances move in" (O2). With the help of a plausible story, the negative image increasingly began to change into a positive one. As one interview partner pointed out:

> [In local politics] they realized very early on in Offenbach that the integration of immigrants is a major challenge for them. They noticed this earlier [...] than all other municipalities in Germany. [...] We have tried to turn what had a negative connotation [...] into something positive, but also into something that is credibly positive. [...] The concept of an "arrival city" has led to a change in image.
>
> (O3)

People in Offenbach are aware that the city is not perfect. Nevertheless, as an arrival city, it plays a crucial role in the fields of integration and labor market for the entire region, and especially for Frankfurt.

In *Athens*, one obstacle standing in the way of a new narrative was the lack of trust—as emphasized in the following passage from an interview:

> people do not trust politicians because they lied to them, they misled them, they convinced them that the municipality cannot offer solutions to their collective problems. A vicious circle emerged, A new kind of policy was made difficult because of this lack of trust.
>
> (A10)

This particular distinction between "we" (the people) and "they" (the politicians) was challenged by a new leadership, made up of renowned personalities who were not professional politicians, including a mayor whose integrity was unquestionable. This new leadership has managed to gain the trust of active citizens and private donors, especially after the consolidation of municipal finance and the implementation of transparency measures. Along with trust, a new approach to tackling problems and challenges was developed, as one interviewee said:

> The party-politicized municipality focused on reproductive clientelistic practices. The civil service of the city was introverted and hostile toward civic activists. We changed that. I tried to approach these people to receive an input of ideas from the civic field. We jointly elaborated different sorts of platforms and organizational schemes to bundle forces. The city had a dynamic strategic vision that was open enough to integrate a wide range of inputs. I was impressed by the richness and the originality of ideas and actions that were already existing in Athens but remained unrecognized and were sometimes flickering because they were deprived of any kind of institutionalized recognition and support.
>
> (A10)

Civic and, in general, human capacities of Athens that had been long overlooked were supported and coordinated in innovative ways that they could be deployed and flourish. Demanding challenges were tackled and, as emphasized in policy documents and statements by people interviewed—the city once more proved its adaptiveness to successive changes in different fields and on different scales, formulated by the Athens city government as follows: "During the last centennial, the social and urban structure of our city has been characterized by constant change and successive shocks" (City of Athens 2015) and with one interviewee expressing this view:

> Athens is characterized by incredible multiformity, and also by change. Look at what happened during the previous 30 years: The city had an important industrial component that nearly vanished. It used to be a Greek city and now it is a multicultural city.
>
> (A2)

Having the ambitious attitude of a capital city and building on its huge and multifaceted potential, Athens deployed a wide range of innovations affecting various sectors. While some of these innovations were mainly a response to crisis-driven challenges (e.g., in the fields of social and immigration/integration policy), other innovations were a response to middle- and long-term challenges of modernization, urban regeneration, economic competitiveness, and socio-environmental resilience (such as innovative entrepreneurship as well as a digital and resilience strategy). The visionary and at the same time pragmatic approach of innovative leaders in Athens was combined in self-critical, honest, and value-oriented rhetoric that directly confronted the rising populism of the crisis period. In Athens, "populists experienced probably the first episode of political defeat in the political sequel of the crisis era" (A10).

International recognition through being selected as a "European Capital of Innovation" demonstrates that the previous narrative about Athens as an "inhuman" metropolis, a barren "asphalt jungle" characterized by anonymity, social alienation, and selfish attitudes is slowly fading away. A new narrative seems to be emerging in its place, highlighting aspects such as resilience, tolerance, and open-mindedness in a vivid, inclusive, and innovative city.

Like Athens, although more deeply, *Thessaloniki* was seeking to redefine itself and establish a new, self-confident, and inclusive narrative. Just as in Athens, the new leadership had to gain the trust of the citizens to be able to plan and implement a bundle of innovative policies. In addition to the financial crisis that had radically shaken up the country's entire political system, an infamous legacy of clientelism—resulting in a distinction between "we" (the people) and "they" (the politicians)—and a series of scandals not only damaged the previous city leadership but also destroyed precious social capital, as formulated here by an interviewee:

> We all know that clientelism undermines trust in institutions. People anticipate and finally see that they can resolve their problems through informal clientelistic networks. At the same time, they feel frustrated because they face traumatic situations whenever rival clientelistic networks prevail to their disadvantage. They can be privileged in one situation and underdogs in another situation. Institutions are bypassed and arrangements are results of case-by-case power plays and bargaining. Within such a context there is scarcely any incentive for citizen participation and cooperation with the municipality. People feel excluded and the gatekeepers are the politicians and some organized interests. Local democracy is damaged.
>
> (Th2)

In times of mass unemployment and impoverishment, it was important to demonstrate that new courses of action are possible and innovative, open, and inclusive policies could succeed where exclusive clientelism had failed, or as stated by an interviewee in Thessaloniki:

> We could not lean upon a well-established mechanism of social assistance: The city did not have its own social policy, there was just some help offered in a fragmented and non-transparent way to people in need. We had to start from point zero in times where we were short of money but the needs for social assistance were immense. We had to be inventive and cooperative, trying to attract any kind of help we could get. We opened up to new ideas, new networks and new kinds of resources.
>
> (Th4)

The transformation of social services addressed the weakest part of the local society and drastically increased the acceptance of municipal leadership.

Another important factor on the way to a new narrative was the personality of the non-partisan Mayor Boutaris. It was the right moment to re-invent the city with this new, unconventional leader and launch a narrative that would be quite the opposite of the ethnocentric, xenophobic, and provincial narrative that had prevailed in previous decades. Boutaris personified an alternative, self-confident, open-minded, and cosmopolitan Thessaloniki. Reinforcing self-confidence and attracting tourism, events, and, especially, businesses would not only boost the economy but would also reduce the tremendous brain drain flowing to Athens and abroad.

Furthermore, an important topic in local discourses in the city concerning its challenges was that it had to face unfavorable conditions before the outbreak of the economic crisis in 2008:

> The city has suffered from its position close to the NATO-Warsaw Pact border during the Cold War. Impressive industrialization performance during the sixties and early seventies has been frustrated when de-industrialization started soon after European Economic Community (EEC) membership [...]. Changes in the early nineties favored geographical proximity to large markets accessible since the collapse of the Berlin Wall. [...] The Yugoslav wars have frustrated, however, the economic perspectives of the city.
>
> (City of Thessaloniki 2017: 445)

However, it was highlighted (as shown in Chapter 12) that in a globalized world a city like Thessaloniki should take advantage of its multicultural heritage, its precious Jewish legacy, its proximity to the Balkans, and its symbolic value in Ottoman and Turkish history. The city should also cultivate bonds to its non-Greek diaspora in order to attract tourism and investments. Boutaris tried to market the new image of Thessaloniki as an open, vivid, and cosmopolitan city from the very beginning, while developing transnational cooperation:

> Our "foreign" policy for the international relations of the city comes from our new, open-minded, European and non-provincial self-understanding, and this already has visible beneficial effects on our tourism and our attractiveness for foreign investment. IT investments from Israel as well as this spectacular increase of tourism from Israel, Turkey and the Balkans would have not happened without this municipal "foreign policy."
>
> (Th1)

Openness to diversity also helped the Greek communities of the city to acknowledge that in reality the multicultural character of their city had never been lost. Today, the majority of its citizens are descendants of refugees from different regions:

> Multi-culturalism has always been a core characteristic of our city: From the very beginning when the diadochs of Alexander brought settlers from Southern Greece and merchants from Asia. It was multicultural both in Byzantine and Ottoman times. And even after the population exchange between Greece and Turkey, the city remained multicultural: The refugees were Greek, but they were coming from so many different places: From East Rumelia, Eastern Thrace, and Istanbul; from Ukraine and Armenia; from Izmir, from Pontos at the Black Sea, and Cappadocia in the heart of Anatolia. The refugees brought from these places so many different cultures. This is reflected in our wonderful culinary scene: We have so many different kitchens and flavors, a diversity that you can hardly find in other cities and certainly not in any other Greek city, including Athens. The culinary scene of the capital is a joke, compared to ours.
>
> (Th10)

Thessaloniki is emerging, once more, as an ambitious, extroverted, and cosmopolitan city that is attracting people and resources across borders, taking advantage of its strategic location for tourism, shipping, and land transportation, of its symbolic value for different cultures and nations, of its knowledge institutions, and of its human capital.

The challenges perceived in *Elefsina*, which the city faced due to the impact of the economic crisis starting in 2008, are expressed in the following statement made in an interview by a senior official of the municipal social administration:

> After the outbreak of the economic crisis, we noticed that citizens, who were not in need of social services before, started seeking financial help from the municipality. So, we took action and planned and developed social structures in order to meet the social demands, since there was a lack of a relevant institutional framework allowing us to provide welfare to the most vulnerable citizens.
>
> (E1)

Organizing the European Capital of Culture project has confronted the city—according to a former local politician—with

> a great challenge. The title of the European Capital of Culture is "Euphoria: Transition to Euphoria." Alternatively, we call it "Coexistence". We cannot forget our sacred past, the rich, precious, irreplaceable, and unfortunately for many years marginalized [past], but we can neither

overturn, nor forget, nor marginalize our industrial image and heritage. It is both an image and a heritage.

(E6)

Apart from the fact that it is a great challenge for the city to organize the European Capital of Culture project, the project has also turned out to be politically controversial (as already mentioned in Section 13.2.1). This was expressed by an editor of a local newspaper as follows:

> The problems that emerged considering the implementation of the project "European Capital of Culture" resulted from the lack of consensus between the ruling majority in the city council and the opposition. Both failed to work together for the benefit of the city. They chose to criticize each other in a hardly constructive way undermining the promotion of the project.

(E17)

Similar disputes arose on other issues including the contribution of local industries to the social services of the municipality—as shown by the following quotation from an interview:

> There have been clear disputes about the sponsorships offered by local businesses to the social structures of the municipality. Many argued that in a city like Elefsina, which has suffered from the pollution generated by local industries, the municipality should reject such financial contributions since the latter may undermine our struggle to reduce the magnitude of the pollution and protect the environment of the city.

(E11)

With regard to the construction of temporality, references to the industrial past of the city along with its environmental repercussions were used by the municipality in order to formulate its vision for the rebranding of Elefsina in the context of the implementation of the project European Cultural Capital—as stated in one of the concept documents:

> In the 1960s and 1970s, the city's environment deteriorated significantly due to pollution caused by industrial activity. For the Greeks, the image of Elefsina is inextricably linked to industry and the destruction of the natural environment [...]. Although the city has changed radically since then, the stereotype of the Industrially devastated city remains strong in the public consciousness, discouraging most people from visiting Elefsina and experiencing its important cultural heritage. If the title of European Capital of Culture is given to Elefsina, the image of the city

will be permanently connected with art and culture, changing the stereotype of the industrial city.

(City of Elefsina 2019: 4)

Finally, a strong emphasis on possible courses of action has contributed to a particular local narrative, stemming from a widespread perception of the need to improve the provision of social services to citizens.

For *Chania*, the construction of challenges and problems within the local narrative concerns the need to deal with the pressing issue of traffic in the city. Nevertheless, one of the people interviewed emphasized:

> Traffic is probably the most serious problem that Chania has been facing for at least 15 years. No substantial interventions have been made. Neither from the current municipal authority nor from the previous ones. It was argued that there is a management system with smart traffic lights, which in practice are not so smart.
>
> (C4)

Chania's past, as reflected in the monuments in the old city, is used to promote the current identity and image of the city. As mentioned by an interview partner:

> The city of Chania retains all the characteristics of all the people who have passed the last four-five thousand years […]. Especially the old city retains elements from the pre-historic period of Chania as one can see in specific monuments until today.
>
> (C13)

Similarly, the recent political past, related to one of the most prominent prime ministers in the history of modern Greece, is reflected in the local narrative of Chania, as is identified in the following quote:

> In Chania, there is I would say a peculiar egoism which might be attributed to the fact that we were once the capital of Crete and Eleftherios Venizelos was from Chania. So there is a strong point of reference to the past […].
>
> (C15)

Considering the distinction between "we" and "they" within the city, a dividing line between local businessmen and ordinary citizens concerning the resolution of the traffic issue is apparent in the local debates (as already mentioned in Section 13.2.1). According to one person interviewed a

> solution to the traffic jam would be welcomed by residents, but not necessarily by local businesses. For instance, if you have a store and you

are suddenly told that the bike path will pass outside your store or that the street in front of your store will turn into a pedestrian area, you will probably react turning against the municipality's decision.

(C2)

With respect to possible courses of action, the municipal authority seems to have focused on the use of new technologies to improve its transparency and accountability. An interview participant noted:

> We want to create a five-digit number to which the citizens will be able to call for declaring the problems they face in everyday life in Chania. At the same time they have the opportunity to use an application to take photos of various damages in the city's infrastructure and send them directly to the municipality.

(C11)

In *Kalamata*, the distinction between "we" and "they" comes from the past, and more specifically the 1980s, when the former municipal leadership of Mayor Benos was trying to hold on to their initial master plan, following the disaster of the earthquake, while other groups with personal interests within the city were pushing for a change of priorities. As one person interviewed noted: "Very often, interests, big or small, were trying to penetrate and overturn our planning. That was our biggest challenge and a lot of effort was invested in not missing our target, not allowing changes in our initial planning" (Ka2).

The construction of challenges stems from the fact that the local leadership after the era of Mayor Benos clung to the past, neither trying to change the local narrative nor developing the city based on its assets.

> We have an administration far beyond our expectations [...] by all means, they declare that they support culture, but they won't make a consolidated evaluation of its value, and most importantly, they lack the willingness to formulate a coherent plan, so as to support and further develop our cultural capital.

(Ka3)

Nevertheless, emphasis is placed on courses of action that could benefit the development of the city, as indicated by the following quotation from the minutes of a meeting of the municipal council: "We came up with a Plan B, a plan for the cultural development of Kalamata, in case of not being awarded as the European Capital of Culture."[11] The emphasis given to courses of action is also expressed by the following statement made in an interview: "What Messinia really aims at, is to develop tourism, especially because of the Costa Navarino project and the business activities of Mr. Konstanta-kopoulos" (Ka6; see for the Costa Navarino project the details presented in Chapter 8).

Finally, as already mentioned, the construction of temporality is only a weak attribute of the local narrative, with only a few quotations in the Kalamata corpus relating to it: "To be honest, there are no new ideas in the city [...] there are only old successful recipes [...] for example, the International Dance Festival which started in 1995 and is now an established institution across Europe" (Ka6).

13.3 Communicative mechanisms in comparison

This section focuses on a cross-case comparison of the communicative mechanisms (presented in Chapter 2) and the question of the role they played in local discourses in the ten case studies (mainly) during the period from April 2016 to the end of 2019. The aim of the analysis is to work out

- what communication mechanisms occurred in public debate in the cities during this period;
- how often individual mechanisms occur and whether their frequency varies across cities;
- whether individual mechanisms are "typical" for certain cities or whether they shape certain perceived problems or challenges;
- whether individual mechanisms are more frequent in some types of document (e.g., in interviews or council meetings), since this could imply the strategic use of certain types of mechanisms depending on the audience/the participants in a particular communicative interaction process.[12]

13.3.1 A quantitatively oriented comparative view of communicative mechanisms

When looking at broad variations in the frequency of communicative mechanisms (see Figure 13.2), it is first of all striking that there are differences between the German and Greek cities involved in the analysis. This applies mainly to observation of others (frequent among the German cities, infrequent among the Greek ones) and framing (infrequent among the German cities, frequent among the Greek ones). This may be a result of the different institutional settings the cities are embedded in. Cities in Germany enjoy a considerable degree of autonomy (cf. Heinelt et al. 2018: 42–47 and Ladner et al. 2019), setting up and maintaining their administrative structure, deciding on their own policies, to a high degree raising their own income, and employing significant numbers of personnel. As a consequence, it is very common in Germany to compare cities with another; in some ways, German cities are frequently perceived as being in a highly competitive environment regarding population, resources, the attraction of industries/ employers, the well-being of the citizens, air quality, traffic management, and various other indicators. In some *Länder*, the performance of cities is

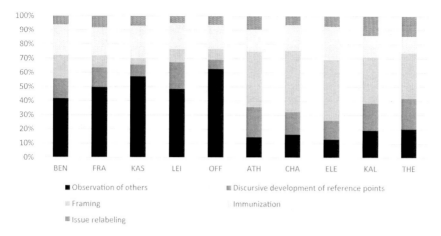

Figure 13.2 Proportion of communicative mechanisms detected in the corpora across cities.

Source: Own compilation and calculation.

Percent figures indicate what proportion individual communicative mechanisms had in the coded occurrence of all these mechanisms in the respective city.

virtually put to the test by using benchmarking processes, e.g., for the redistribution of public resources. Greek cities, on the other hand, are highly dependent on state budget transfers and their resources hardly depend on attracting large and medium-sized businesses. A local corporate or business tax such as found in other countries has not been introduced in Greece, and even local taxes on tourist businesses have been minimized in recent years. Consequently, Greek municipalities have no incentive to attract investment and businesses. They are more interested in small local businesses, mostly belonging to local voters, and providing a small but not negligible share of municipal resources, especially in tourist and shopping areas. Finally, it is also important to take into account that responsibility for physical planning, environmental protection, and development policies are allocated to regional and state administration, while the functions of municipalities are restricted to an advisory and/or complementary role in these policy fields.

Interestingly, when it comes to different document types in German as well as Greek cities notable emphasis is given to certain communicative mechanisms:

- Concept papers seem to be linked strongly to the *development of reference points for future argumentative debates*. This seems to be plausible since the aim of writing a concept paper is to present arguments for the case (i.e., the innovation) in order to persuade the readers and to define the objectives of the concept and the measures which will have to be implemented in order to achieve it. Consequently, concepts often cite public debate (e.g., in the case of participatory development of the "master plan" in Offenbach) and use traditions for communicating a case (e.g., the *Grüngürtel* report in Frankfurt). In Greek cities, the development of reference points for future debates is most frequently stressed in actor's positions. Given the fact that political parties are not permitted in municipal elections, short-lived municipal lists (usually active only for one or two terms) present their main policy choices in their programs and election brochures. Important local corporate or collective actors (chambers, unions, citizens' groups, etc.) publicize their views on relevant local challenges and on the appropriateness and feasibility of pertinent solutions and actions under discussion. The actors' positions address the general public and therefore preferably use self-evident truths (such as demographic change or the environmental crisis) or the authority of recognized expertise (e.g., of knowledge institutions or international institutions/networks).

- Interviews, both in German and in Greek cities, show a higher share of the communicative mechanism of *framing*, especially relating to the manner of dealing with challenges. This is obviously a consequence of the common interview guidelines, which includes questions about the city itself, what makes it special, how innovations were developed and are working, and how societal and political processes take place in the city. Moreover, interviewees, especially those directly involved in local politics, may show a tendency to highlight their own contribution to the framing and thus promote innovative policies.

- The same applies to the *observation of others*, a mechanism more common in interviews which include questions about comparisons with other cities, their contexts, and characteristics, pointing out similarities and, implicitly, differences. In German cities, *delineation from others* applies most frequently, probably reflecting both the self-confidence and the high degree of autonomy and self-awareness that characterizes German cities.

- In the case of the mechanism of *immunization*, in both German and Greek cities it refers most often to decisions of other authorities and higher levels of government. In Germany this mechanism is most often used in actors' position papers and in council minutes. It seems that this mechanism is well suited to fending off alternative knowledge claims under conditions of competing political rhetoric in the city council or when actors present political positions publicly. With regard to the council minutes, the same applies to Greece.

- *Issue relabeling* can be found quite frequently in concept documents, but also in media reports and actors' positions in the German cities. This coincides with the idea that issue relabeling is used as a supporting communicative mechanism in order to either feature the innovation by naming its positive side effects on other policies or cite the effects of other policies as positive for the innovation at hand. In Greek cities, *issue relabeling* is most frequently found in actors' positions and council minutes. Usually, it refers to the positive effects of the relevant policy choice on other policy objectives, in an attempt to gain the support of a broader spectrum of stakeholders.

Delving even more deeply into the quantitative analysis of communicative mechanisms, from April 2016 to the end of 2019 we counted the occurrence of mechanisms for the different German and Greek cities.

For *Frankfurt* and *Leipzig*, we found that the share of the different groups of mechanisms did not change over the four years of the analysis, meaning that use of the mechanisms remained relatively stable over this period. This is not surprising, since the innovations in both cities are described in positive terms and there is a broad consensus that their development was a success. Also—and this is the crucial point—innovations such as the *Grüngürtel* and the *Wächterhäuser* were implemented decades before and were never seriously challenged. Consequently, it seems reasonable to state that the proportion of different mechanisms has not changed significantly.

Offenbach is the prime example of the opposite: cities with an innovation which was introduced only recently. Since the master plan was formally enacted by the municipal council shortly after the beginning of the research project (June 2016), we can observe an interesting pattern in the share of mechanisms. It all begins with a large share of *comparisons* between Offenbach and other cities; in this phase actors are clearly trying to develop an orientation. Interestingly, the comparisons converge almost equally on two different consequences—there was about an equal share of calls for imitation and for delimitation. After some time, observation of others decreases significantly, with a high proportion of the comparisons emphasizing delimitation, or how it is distinct from other cities: Offenbach has found its position in comparison with others, has made a decision on its own strategy, and now emphasizes differences between itself and other cities to justify its innovation. This is accompanied by a decline in efforts to develop a reference point for further action. Once the master plan has been adopted, the mechanisms of framing, immunization, and issue relabeling are used more frequently—and at about the same level.

A similar development can be seen in *Kassel*, where the strategic plan for regional cooperation is a rather new phenomenon as well as the reorientation from being an industrial city to a city of culture. At the beginning of the time frame, the observation of others is clearly dominant and diminishes over the course of the four years. Other mechanisms clearly gain ground in Offenbach, where issue relabeling is the mechanism most commonly used by the end of the four-year time period.

The corpus of *Bensheim* is a special case, since there are very few observations for the years 2016, 2017, and 2018, and thus dividing the corpus into segments for years is not feasible. If the years are combined and compared with the year 2019, it becomes apparent that in Bensheim there is no clear picture like those evident in the other four German cities. The reason for this may be the overlapping of main topics in Bensheim during the time frame under consideration: (a) the continuation of innovations previously introduced (such as—among others [see Section 4.2]—the climate masterplan which was enacted in November 2016) and (b) the processes for dealing with the newly detected challenge of redeveloping the city center and particularly the market square, which culminated in 2019. Because both contexts overlap in Bensheim, the typical cyclical sequences of the use of communicative mechanisms also overlap: while the orientation phase regarding the redevelopment of the city center is ongoing, innovations established earlier worked in a "framed" way were subject to issue relabeling, or had to be immunized against being questioned—as in the case of the municipal marketing and development company (MEGB).

In *Athens*, over time the overlapping of different phases of different innovations seems to blur the lines of development by communicative mechanisms. While some very important innovations like the SynAthina platform and the InnovAthens hub started in 2013 and 2014, respectively, the "Open Schools" were launched in 2015, the digital strategy in 2016, the Athens Resilience Strategy and Athens Coordination Center for Migrant and Refugee issues (ACCMR) in 2017, and Polis[2] and ImpactHub in 2018. Thus, from 2016 to 2019 the share of different groups of mechanisms shifted without following any obvious pattern. Observation of others (especially competition with others), discursive development of reference points (especially by referring to external expertise), and issue relabeling (especially concerning the contribution of innovations to achieving other policy objectives) tended to increase their share, despite some fluctuations, from 2016 to 2019. Toward the end of a five-year term of office, the governing list (Mayor Kaminis declared in 2018 that he was not running for a third term) tended to highlight scientific evidence, competitive advantages, and beneficial side effects stemming from its innovative policies. On the other hand, the share of immunization (especially of agreed self-commitments) and framing mechanisms (especially the ongoing explanation of manners of dealing with challenges) decreased near the end of the period of observation.

Thessaloniki presents a similar picture: some important innovations such as the rebranding of the city and several social innovations had already started in 2011 and 2013, respectively. Four important innovations were launched in 2016: the Holocaust Museum, the new policy for refugees, the OK!Thess initiative for entrepreneurship, and the Thessaloniki Resilience Strategy. The city's digital strategy was launched in 2017, while the new ThessINTEC business and innovation park was inaugurated in 2018. Observation of others (especially competition with others), discursive development of reference points (especially by referring to tradition), and issue relabeling (especially concerning the contribution of innovations to achieving other policy objectives) tended to increase their share, despite some fluctuations from 2016 to 2019. Toward the end of a five-year term of office and only a few weeks after Kaminis in Athens, Mayor Boutaris declared in 2018 that he was not running for a third term. It was at that point that the governing list and its supporters tended to highlight in public debate scientific evidence of innovations and how Thessaloniki served other cities as a role model. By contrast, the share of immunization (especially of the decisions of upper-level authorities) and framing decreased as the term of office neared its end. It should be emphasized that the decrease in the observed use of immunization reveals a change in self-perception and increasing self-confidence—that is, on the basis of the new narrative of the cosmopolitan city Thessaloniki no longer perceiving itself as a provincial underdog vis-à-vis Athens and Brussels.

In *Elefsina*, the most important innovations took place from 2011 to 2015. This involved (as mentioned in Section 6.2) the protection of vulnerable citizens and the efforts to lend the city a new image by implementing the European Capital of Culture project. As was the case with Athens and Thessaloniki, the proportion of different mechanisms used changed without following a clear pattern. Framing (especially stabilization of how challenges were dealt with), immunization (especially by means of reference to decisions of other authorities/upper-level government), and issue relabeling (especially by emphasizing the contribution of innovations to achieving other policy objectives) emerge as the most significant communicative mechanisms from 2016 to 2018. The dominance of these communicative mechanisms fits in with the efforts of the city government at the time to promote and finance social innovation and to initiate the implementation of the European Capital of Culture project in order to improve Elefsina's image. However, the communicative mechanisms which dominated during the period from 2016 to 2018 lost relevance in 2019, to some extent due to the rise of observation of others (especially in comparison with and delineation from others, as well as competition with others) and discursive development of (new) reference points for future communicative interactions. This may have been due to the fact that 2019 was an election year and debate between competing candidates and competing local parties came to the fore.

In *Chania*, most innovations were introduced from 2011 to 2019. With regard to the communicative mechanisms, framing (especially justification of actions/decisions) emerged as the dominant mechanism from 2016 to 2018, while it seems to have been partially weakened in 2019. In addition, immunization (especially by referring to previously agreed upon self-commitments) and issue relabeling (particularly by emphasizing the contribution of innovative measures to achieving other policy objectives) and discursive development of reference points (especially by referring to recognized external experts) tended to increase their relevance throughout the 2016–2019 period, despite obvious fluctuations, while the mechanism of observing others (particularly in respect to the competition with others) emerged as the second most important mechanism in 2019. In line with Elefsina, it seems that since the local government elections in 2019, observation of others and the discursive development of (new) reference points became as significant as other mechanisms. The local parties and candidates involved in the electoral race probably used these mechanisms more frequently in the political debate in order either to defend their record (the local governing party) or to criticize (the local opposition parties) the record of the governing party.

Since the most important innovations in *Kalamata* were introduced several decades ago and are also relatively uncontroversial, the frequency of communicative mechanisms tends to follow the dynamics of the electoral cycle rather than the struggle over innovations. Most of the mechanisms coded in the document corpus appeared in 2019, which was an election year (at the European, the municipal, the regional, and, finally, the national level). Mayor Nikas had already announced that this would be his last term of office; thus, many candidates were engaged in a competitive campaign. Additionally, half of the interviews with actors from Kalamata were conducted during that year, providing another explanation for the frequency of codes. Concerning the frequency of each mechanism across the years, framing emerges as the dominant mechanism from 2016 to 2019. Observation of others ranks second, followed by the discursive development of reference points and immunization.

13.3.2 A closer look at the communicative mechanisms used in recent debates in the cities analyzed

In some of the cities, the connection between communicative mechanisms used and the development of narratives and innovations is obvious.

This is clearly the case for *Bensheim*. The innovations developed there, most of them more than ten years ago, contributed to the image of a dynamic city (Stadt Bensheim 2016) "as can be seen from the well-known companies that operate worldwide from the local business parks"[13]; but also from the perception of residents who, for example, emphasized that "Bensheim has it [in respect to urban life], and it is a Lilliput Frankfurt" (B5). At the same time, one of the interview partners compared the city metaphorically with a "plush sofa. In Bensheim it is cozy, it is homely, it is comfortable. Warm" (B8). However, this did not prevent public debate on the further development of the city. A prime example is the debate (if not controversy) about the development of the city center, which started (at the latest) with the decision of the municipal council to tear down the *Haus am Markt*. Although this debate took place not only in the municipal council but was embedded in a participatory approach through the *Bürgernetzwerk* and fueled by a citizens' initiative that launched a citizens' petition (see Section 4.4), it is striking that the communicative mechanism of comparison with other (cities) was hardly ever used publicly—except for one case (B17), where reference was made to the *Leerstandsretter* (rescuer of vacancies) model practiced in some German cities, in other words, the temporary use of vacant retail stores. The debate concentrated more on the city itself (who did what and how—or did nothing), and solution proposals were developed more from the inside (or through insights from the people involved) instead of through "importing" ideas. The reason for this might be the self-esteem because of the economic position of the city as well as the self-perception of being a relaxed place to live (see the "sofa metaphor" mentioned earlier). Consequently, the current narrative is more inwardly oriented and shows a pattern in which the inward-looking distinction between "we" and "they" remains dominant insofar as those who do not feel part of the "alliance of doers" and the local politicians associated with them emphasize that they are being ignored. Although this has made the style of political debates rougher (and hardly resembles an exchange of ideas on a cozy sofa)—the former coalition in the municipal council split up and the former mayor was voted out of office—it is highly unlikely that this situation will jeopardize the innovations achieved so far and the ability of the city to innovate in the future.

Frankfurt also exhibits some unique features. Although local politics can be characterized as a competitive democracy in which there is a defined governing coalition of parties in the city council as well as opposition parties, emphasis is placed on identifying possible courses of action. This means that the opposition parties are called upon to point out alternative ways of dealing with challenges and not just to express criticism, and the majority far more frequently refer to external experts than in other cities when defending innovations. There are innovations, such as the *Grüngürtel*, which are virtually uncontested within the city, but the way to enhance housing opportunities is vigorously debated within the city and the council. Although it may be self-evident that something has to be done about a given issue, there is no consensus across parties on *how* this challenge actually should be addressed. The high frequency with which decisions of upper levels of government are addressed is interesting. This is especially true for the housing problem, as local politicians frequently refer to the role of the federal and state governments in terms of regulation of the housing market as well as their role as owners of a significant amount of real estate within the city, which the council likes to develop into housing zones. Both the *Grüngürtel* and the housing issue are strongly connected to the city's self-perception as a vibrant, international, and highly attractive city fostering strong growth both economically and in terms of the city's population. Attractiveness is considered both a blessing and a curse: growth causes wealth and greater size, but also causes density and increased demands. The term "growing city" occurs frequently in council speeches, where nearly all parties acknowledge the trend as a positive sign, but also draw attention to different secondary effects. This is also a reason for deviations of local Frankfurt party groups from the platform endorsed by their parties at the state and federal level. For example, the local chapter of the Christian Democratic Union of Germany (CDU) actively advocates better public transportation and the expansion of bicycle traffic zones.

Kassel is on its way to developing self-esteem compared with decades where it was on the decline. Local actors are keeping an eye on other cities, often not only to compare themselves with them but also to compete with them. This becomes particularly clear with regard to Kassel's unique cultural offerings. The density of museums, which represents the "fourth largest museum landscape" (K2), as well as the particular relationship to the cultural scene take on special significance. What is interesting here is that despite the use of superlatives to describe Kassel's culture, not only the competitive edge over others, but also a clear delineation from others is recognizable, according to which Kassel can be perceived as larger than other cities with a comparable number of inhabitants. In this context, a discursive development of reference points can also be observed, as Kassel not only has more to offer in the cultural sector than might be assumed. Due to its history as an old residential city, the cultural sector also reflects a long tradition of the city. This is also expressed in the example of the major documenta art exhibit. It was viewed critically for a long time but now serves as a flagship for the city of Kassel, which has also referred to itself as the "documenta city" for a number of years. In addition, the city is proud of its network culture combined with its transformation from an industrial to a cultural city. Consequently, innovations are mostly seen in connection with the past and future in combination with comparison with other cities. As already explained, narratives are less focused on describing a problem and its causes, but more to linking current problems to the past and especially by pointing to differences between the past (a city on the margins of Germany) and the present (the city at the center of Germany). This development toward being an international city of culture not only shapes the city's self-image, but also has a positive impact on other policy areas, underpinning Kassel's ambition to be a model for others.

The outstanding feature of *Leipzig* is its frequent use of the communicative mechanism of development of reference points for further communicative interactions, which are used significantly more often in relation to its innovation. As the *Wächterhäuser* are a unique innovation developed in the city, there is less need for comparison with other cities, especially given that big cities such as Leipzig usually have not seen a sharp decline in population in the era under consideration. Since there are fewer external points of reference, communication focuses on arguing that the policy choices taken in the city were self-evident. This constitutes a tradition in local politics which favors local expertise as the basis of the development and implementation of innovations. The emphasis on local expertise in developing and implementing innovations is strikingly connected with a narrative pattern where a distinction between "we" and "they" is used only in a particular way—to point out differences between Leipzig and the state capital Dresden (see Chapter 10)—not to distinguish between different groups in the city itself. This became particularly obvious in the case of the *Wächterhäuser* and other kinds of use of vacant houses. Since these innovations have been strongly connected to the self-perception of a city to ensure freedom during the time of a declining population, there was no need for an internal struggle over power, influence, and resources as in other cities (such as Frankfurt).

Offenbach reveals interesting interrelations between communicative mechanisms, narratives, and the city's self-perception. Given that Offenbach is in a difficult economic and fiscal situation, the city stresses its own unique position in communicative interaction especially in comparisons that set it apart from Frankfurt. As an "island of poverty," its socioeconomic differences from other cities are often emphasized. Focusing its outlook on others in this way results in an infrequent use of communicative mechanisms only referring to itself. In particular, traditions are scarcely cited for developing a reference point for further actions. This observation demonstrates that the city is endeavoring to find new ways to solve problems. As in the case of Leipzig, this results in infrequent distinction between "we" and "they" to describe the city: Offenbach is searching for the way out of the perceived trap, where pointing a finger at somebody else would not solve a problem. Instead, as a major innovation the master plan is specifically designed to find a common way using participatory inputs as well as expert knowledge to pave the way forward. This "can do" mentality contributes to an ongoing (self-)explanation and stabilization of ways of dealing with challenges and becomes clearer with regard to the topic of integration and the resulting challenges, which, compared to other cities, were recognized earlier in Offenbach. As in Leipzig, the city is characterized above all by an openness to new residents, which is why its residents call it an "arrival city"—in this case also with reference to the past. Due to the strong fluctuations within the population, the city's inclusive character is notable, and not only with regard to ideas from the outside.

In *Athens*, observation of other cities and focusing on their innovative policies was a strategic approach for the promotion of a new narrative about the possible courses of action for tackling evolving challenges. Taking advantage of its diaspora, the city became involved in several international innovation networks ("resilient cities," "mayors for inclusive growth," "impact hubs," etc.) and adopted many new ideas that had already been tested elsewhere. The communicative mechanism of issue relabeling promoted the "open schools" and the protection of sculptures, which were innovations that contributed to the achievement of other policy objectives, such as the integration of migrants and the improvement of both learning and socialization methods in the public education system. The communicative mechanism of framing was the most frequently used, as in all Greek cities under investigation. Framing is mostly implemented in order to rationalize ways of dealing with challenges and, especially in the case of Athens, justifying priorities. Knowledge institutions and their staff were influential in including issues on or excluding them from the agenda. They also played a crucial role in developing reference points for further activities to which the mechanism of framing could refer in order to justify and to stabilize a particular policy choice and priorities regarding particular measures. For instance, the city's new digital strategy was supported by the communicative mechanism of framing insofar as actors referred to particular interpretations of relevant issues and acted accordingly. The recognized expertise of knowledge institutions provided a reference point for communicative interaction. Cooperation with these institutions was facilitated through flexible organizational schemes (such as InnovAthens) that permitted flexible responses. Bypassing bureaucratic blockades was a recurring reference point in public discourse and was widely accepted as "self-evident." The municipality used a plethora of schemes, such as special bureaus, non-profit companies, and contracting out, in order to facilitate external funding, donations, and several forms of volunteerism and mutual help, implying the "open city" narrative about possible courses of action that would follow a multilateral and inclusive manner of dealing with challenges. The "SynAthina" metaphor expressed the new approach to local politics through the discursive development of reference points for (further) innovative practices, for example, with the e-bridge for Migrants and Refugees (ACCMR), and the POLIS^2 initiative. Commitment to the public interest underpinned the breaking away from the discredited patronage politics that had prevailed in the pre-crisis period, while the status of Athens as a role model of innovation for other cities highlighted its new image as an open and inclusive, vivid, and resilient city.

In *Thessaloniki*, the observation of others was found to be more frequent than in any other Greek city. The city often imitates Athens, although competition with the capital is a permanent issue in local public discourse. In the previous decade, Thessaloniki had become more ambitious. It joined several international networks (such as the "resilient cities" network) and re-discovered its non-Greek diaspora and tried to re-establish strong bonds with it. Focusing on the multicultural heritage of the city and its value for cultural and economic networking was basic to the new narrative and the new image of Thessaloniki as a "cosmopolitan city." As a result of the emerging trend of internationalization, awareness of other cities and their innovations and successes increased dramatically. Another mechanism that was more important in Thessaloniki than in the other Greek cities under investigation was the discursive development of reference points for communicative interaction. The multicultural and cosmopolitan tradition is an example of a reference point that backed the new narrative of the city. Mayor Boutaris, as an explicit anti-populist politician, often involved knowledge institutions, experts, and renowned personalities in an attempt to "rationalize" public discourse on various matters. Especially in connection with the tragedy of the Jewish community and the forgotten dark side of the history of the city, the collaboration with the Nazis, and the widespread antisemitism (particularly among Christian refugees from Anatolia; as shown by Saltiel 2020), the expertise of such actors has been used to promote a self-critical approach to history and a shared frame of reference in local public debate. This approach sparked a wider discourse on the long overlooked multicultural heritage of the city. The mechanism of issue relabeling, which was connected with the new narrative of an open and cosmopolitan city, was also particularly important. Rebranding Thessaloniki had a wide range of positive side effects in the fields of tourism, the real estate market, knowledge and technology transfer, and especially in connection with foreign direct investment in innovative technologies that have considerably decreased the brain drain from the city.

In *Elefsina*, as the empirical evidence suggests, the immunization was a particularly frequent communicative mechanism compared with the other four Greek cities. This is evident in the funding of social innovations in the municipality's budget which highlighted the commitment of the municipal authority to the provision of social services to the most vulnerable citizens. Moreover, the mechanism of immunization through the role of upper-level government including the Attica region and the Ministry of Culture can be seen in the effort of Elefsina to promote and organize the European Capital of Culture project. Immunization also occurred through references to the status of Elefsina as a role model for other cities in respect to the local center for collecting recyclable materials; this is the first and only one in the country. Apart from immunization, framing emerged as the second most important communicative mechanism in Elefsina compared with the other four Greek cities. This mechanism justified the municipality's decision to establish social innovations in order to deal with the repercussions and after effects stemming from the economic crisis that had struck Greece in the previous decade. The development of social support during the decade of the economic crisis seems to have been the result of the mechanism of observation and imitation of the practices of other Greek cities. In the same context, the municipality made an effort to implement these social innovations more efficiently than other municipalities, especially neighboring cities, by employing the particular mechanisms of comparison with others and delineation from them. In terms of the development of reference points for the promotion of innovative policies, the choice of Elefsina to create a local recycling system is attributed to the epistemic authority of a local figure, namely, the former Mayor George Abatzoglou who was seen as an expert in recycling since he held a PhD in chemical engineering. In addition, another instance of this particular mechanism is the commissioning of the NGO Faros to run social services because of its expertise. Issue relabeling, and specifically reference to the point that an innovation also contributes to the achievement of other policy objectives, played a significant role in the implementation of the European Capital of Culture project, which is seen as an opportunity for Elefsina not only to accomplish cultural improvements but also to rebrand itself as a clean, modern, and dynamic city.

In *Chania*, the communicative mechanism of framing played a crucial role for the promotion of innovative policies in the local debate. There, framing was related to the justification of actions of the municipality as well as the stabilization of ways of dealing with the social consequences of the economic crisis. Another communicative mechanism contributing to local innovations is the development of reference points—particularly through external experts in the application of social services. However, local NGOs and activists play a crucial role in running these services. Finally, the mechanism of observation of others and either orientation toward them or competing with them is evident in Chania. This applies to social services, but also to the promotion of a certain type of tourism (outlined in Chapter 5.2) and to innovations in waste management and traffic management related to tourism.

In *Kalamata*, framing emerges as the most important communicative mechanism in the promotion of local innovations. Priorities regarding particular measures and the stabilization of ways of dealing with challenges are the most frequent effects of the framing mechanisms highlighting the long history of innovations in Kalamata that have to be continued. Kalamata was actually an early starter in innovation, taking advantage of the window of opportunity that emerged with the disastrous earthquake of 1986. Consequently, the mechanism of developing a reference point for further debates by applying expertise and the mechanism of immunization could often be observed in the collected corpora of documents for the city. The latter is made clear by the fact that Kalamata is very often referred to as a role model for others and a source of expertise and know-how. As far as the observation of others is concerned, comparison and competition with others is by far the most frequent mechanism, since Kalamata is prone to defend its role, not as an imitator of others, but rather by actively leading the way as a pioneer. Finally, the city's innovations in the cultural sector had a cross-sectoral impact, positively affecting tourism, social cohesion, and economic development; thus, the communicative mechanism of issue relabeling could also be observed frequently.

13.4 What have we learned?

The core question addressed by this book, posed at the beginning of Chapter 1, was, *What conditions favor the development of local innovations?* Our basic hypothesis was also outlined there—namely, that conditions favoring local innovations should not be sought primarily in economic, social, or institutional circumstances. Instead, what is crucial are the communicative interactions by means of which local actors develop a locally embedded understanding of or knowledge about these circumstances and the constraints and opportunities deriving from them. We assumed that this knowledge is expressed through communicative interactions in local narratives explaining why particular innovations are seen as necessary to solve problems or to improve existing conditions.

Returning to this question and the hypothesis just outlined we conclude that the empirical study of five German and five Greek cities has shown that a "science of stories" is needed to explain why particular innovations were possible in certain local contexts. We confirmed that humans have to be conceived of as "storytelling animals"—as noted by Jones et al. (2014)—although we do not fully agree with the narrative policy framework introduced and advocated by them (see Chapter 2): people have to convince each other by means of communicative exchange that political changes are necessary and in certain ways also possible. In the case of the study on which this book is based, it was not through storytelling that political change was generally agreed upon, but through something being perceived as new and an improvement. This storytelling leads to narratives, each of which has a particular local-specific pattern that is formed from a distinctive mixture of four dimensions. First, problems or challenges must be addressed in a narrative in such a way that they also appear to be solvable. If this is not the case, no narrative pattern can emerge by means of which actors in communicative interaction can feel certain that innovations are possible. Second, the idea must be woven into a narrative that innovations are possible by means of a particular course of action. It is crucial that this course of action is both based on causality assumptions that are considered correct and regarded as normatively appropriate. If such a course of action cannot be agreed upon in a given (local) context, there will be no innovations because disputes about an adequate choice of action will block them—and this even though the actors may agree that there are problems or challenges that need to be and can be addressed (as has been shown in Frankfurt and Leipzig with regard to dealing with urban growth or in Bensheim with regard to the development of the city center). These two dimensions of narratives and their specific expression in a local narrative pattern have proven to be the key for innovations in the cities studied. These two dimensions of narratives are complemented by two others, each in a specific form—namely, how and to what extent in narratives, on the one hand, past, present, and future are related to each other and, on the other hand, a distinction is made between "we" and "they" (the others). Unlike the construction of problems or challenges and the outline of a course of action, these two dimensions take on different salience in the narratives of the cities studied about why innovations are needed and in what ways it is useful and appropriate to achieve them: The construction of temporality—or the construction of a relation between past, present, and future—has a clearly different degree of importance in the cities studied—as shown in Figure 13.1. This might even suggest that a narrative about the necessity and possibility of innovation could function without this dimension. In the case of the distinction between "we" and "they," on the basis of our empirical study we can see that the distinction is expressed quite differently in local narrative patterns. While the distinction between "we" and "they" in the Greek case study cities is predominantly expressed in a split between supporters and critics of the innovations, the picture for the German cities is quite different. Whereas in Frankfurt, Kassel, Leipzig, and Offenbach this dimension of the narrative has only a comparatively low degree of importance concerning the innovations identified and, moreover, is not related to distinctions in the local community but to the state government or other cities or urban centers of the state, in Bensheim it refers to distinctions within its urban society. However, in Bensheim this distinction is not, or not only, related to internal rivalries, but primarily involves complementarity between the "locals" and the newcomers, who count themselves as part of an alliance of movers and shakers. Only those who feel they do not belong to these groups or feel ignored by them occasionally organize political protest.

A lesson that can and, above all, should also be drawn from the study and is deserving of emphasis is that local *narratives are changeable.* They can be challenged and must be protected, that is, they cannot be taken for granted. The communicative mechanisms described and examined in terms of their effects on the narratives play a decisive role in this regard: by means of *comparison with others (other cities),* a dominant narrative can be questioned by drawing attention to opportunities for innovations not considered in a given context so far. This can lead to a change in the narrative. However, observation and comparison with others can also have a totally different effect—namely, rejecting what could be observed according to the motto: "We will never, ever do it like that!" This effect stemming from the same mechanism can lead to a stabilization of the way things are understood and handled. In order to actually change a narrative and thus open up perspectives for (other) innovations *a reference point for future activities* has to be found. The cities in our case studies demonstrate how this can and has been achieved (such as by referring to recognized experts, but also through broadly based argumentative exchange in the city). Nevertheless, it has also been shown (see in particular the debates in Frankfurt and Leipzig on how to deal with the housing issue) that it is not a matter of course that a certain idea of what is feasible and desirable becomes dominant. As has been shown, once such a reference point for future activities or a certain idea of what is feasible and desirable has been established it can be referred to in communicative interactions. This results in communicative *framing* of (inter)actions. The case studies demonstrated that this communicative mechanism is often very effective in dealing with contradictions that arise in specific situations—for example, by pointing out that this has long since been clarified and that it is unclear why debates about what has been clarified should be reopened. This becomes even clearer when it comes to the communicative mechanism of *immunization.* By using this mechanism, the prevailing understanding of what can meaningfully be achieved and carried out is protected (immunized) from other ideas. And, finally, we empirically underlined the relevance of *issue relabeling.* This mechanism can play a role in fostering new ideas before a narrative is changed by pointing out that a novelty that has little or nothing to do with already widely accepted innovations contributes to these innovations. In this way, issue relabeling can contribute to a rethinking not only of these innovations but also of the narratives behind them, particularly through the perception or construction of problems and challenges and the course of action necessary to address them effectively and appropriately.

Although the effectiveness of these communicative mechanisms depends on adapting them to a particular local narrative pattern, skillful use of the communicative mechanisms can break open established narratives that express a certain fixed understanding of what can be achieved and how—in order to recognize, mobilize, and stabilize potential for innovation.

Notes

1 Cf. the article "Das völlige Verkehrschaos abwenden" ("Avoid the complete traffic chaos") in the Bergsträßer Anzeiger, July 11, 2019.
2 Cf. the article "755 Wohnungen bis 2024" ("755 Apartments by 2024") in the Bergsträßer Anzeiger, January 26, 2019.
3 https://gruene-bensheim.de/2019/11/zukunft-der-innenstadt-thema-bei-den-gruenen-2/; translation by the authors (last check March 11, 2021).
4 Cf. the article "Amtsleiter Gerkens geht heute in Ruhestand" ("Head of Department Gerkens is retiring today") in the Leipziger Volkszeitung, August 29, 2018.
5 Minutes of the meeting of Frankfurt's municipal council, February 23, 2017: 54.
6 Cf. the article "Sexy auch ohne Main-Philharmonie" ("Sexy even without the Main-Philharmonie symphony hall") in the Frankfurter Allgemeine Zeitung, October 27, 2017.
7 Minutes of the meeting of Frankfurt's municipal council, September 15, 2016: 35.
8 Minutes of the meeting of Frankfurt's municipal council, October 13, 2016: 96.
9 Cf. the article "Documenta liefert Motivation" ("Documenta brings motivation") in the Hessisch-Niedersächsische Allgemeine, November 29, 2018.
10 Speech of the chairman of the Free Democratic Party (FDP, liberal party) in the municipal council, December 24, 2016 (https://fdp-of.de/meldung/haushaltsrede/; last accessed April 14, 2021).
11 Minutes of the meeting of Kalamata's municipal council, Decision 411/2016, September 20, 2016: 28.
12 Before going into the questions, it should be noted that although the communicative mechanisms are theoretically distinguishable from each other, in the empirical work problems arose in distinguishing them. In particular, the mechanisms of "comparison and imitation of others" and "comparison and delimitation from others" were difficult to distinguish in a number of cases. This often occurred when someone compared their city with the actions of another city while using negative terms. For example, the statement "Look at city X, they solve the problem with innovation Y, but we do not" is definitely a comparison, but it is unclear whether it is meant as an invitation to imitate or as a delimitation.
13 Cf. the article "Erfolgreiche Entwicklung führt zu Zuzug" ("Successful development brings new residents") in the Bergsträßer Anzeiger, August 31, 2018.

Bibliography

Aring, J./Reuther, I. 2008: 'Die Regiopole. Vom Arbeitsbegriff zur konzeptionellen Idee.' In: Aring, J./Reuther, I. (Eds.): *Regiopolen. Die kleinen Großstädte in Zeiten der Globalisierung.* Berlin: Jovis-Verlag, 8–33.

Arundel, A./Bloch, C./Ferguson, B. 2019: 'Advancing innovation in the public sector: Aligning innovation measurement with policy goals.' *Research Policy* 48 (3): 789–798.

Asheim, B.T./Isaksen A./Trippl M. 2019: *Advanced Introduction to Regional Innovation Systems.* Cheltenham und Northampton: Edward Elgar.

Banta, B. 2012: 'Analysing discourse as a causal mechanism.' *European Journal of International Relations* 19 (2): 379–402.

Barbehön, M./Münch, S. 2014: 'Die Stadt als Sinnhorizont. Zur Kontextgebundenheit politischer Narrative.' In: Gadinger, F./Jarzebski, S./Yildiz, T. (Eds.): *Politische Narrative. Konzepte – Analysen – Forschungspraxis.* Wiesbaden: Springer VS, 149–171.

Barbehön, M./Münch, S./Gehring, P./Großmann, A./Haus, M./Heinelt H. 2016: 'Urban problem discourses. Understanding the distinctiveness of cities.' *Journal of Urban Affairs* 38 (2): 236–251.

Barbehön, M./Münch, S./Haus, M./Heinelt, H. 2015: *Städtische Problemdiskurse und die Bedeutung lokaler Sinnhorizonte.* Baden-Baden: Nomos.

Bartetzky, A. 2015: *Die gerettete Stadt. Architektur und Stadterneuerung in Leipzig seit 1989: Erfolge – Risiken – Verluste.* Leipzig: Lehmstedt.

Barthel, Ch./Spiegel, C. 2008: 'Qualitätsmanagement in der Stadt Offenbach.' In: Loring, W.H. (Ed.): *Moderne Verwaltung in der Bürgergesellschaft. Entwicklungslinien der Verwaltungsmodernisierung in Deutschland.* Baden-Baden: Nomos, 280–287.

Bartlett, D. 2017: 'Champions of local authority innovation revisited.' *Local Government Studies* 43 (2): 142–149.

Bennett, A. 2013: 'The mother of all isms. Causal mechanisms and structured pluralism in International Relations theory.' *European Journal of International Relation* 19 (3): 459–481.

Benz, A./Dose, N. 2010: 'Von der Governance-Analyse zur Policytheorie.' In: Benz, A./Dose, N. (Eds.): *Governance – Regieren in komplexen Regelsystemen.* Wiesbaden: VS-Verlag, 251–276.

Benz, A./Kemmerzell, J./Knodt, M./Tews, A. 2015: 'The trans-local dimension of local climate policy. Sustaining and transforming local knowledge orders through trans-local action.' *Urban Research & Practice* 8 (3): 319–335.

Berry, F.S./Berry, W.D. 2007: 'Innovation and diffusion models in policy research.' In: Sabatier, P. (Ed.): *Theories of the Policy Process.* Boulder: Westview Press, 223–260.

Bevir, M./Phillips, R. 2017: 'Genealogies of European governance.' *Comparative European Politics* 15 (5): 685–704.

Bianchi, A./Marin, G./Zanfei, A. 2018: 'New perspectives in public service innovation.' In: Gallouj, F./Djellal, F. (Eds.): *A Research Agenda for Service Innovation.* Cheltenham and Northampton: Edward Elgar, 166–186.

Bieber, H.-J. 2016: 'Universität Kassel. Vom ungeliebten Kind zum Motor der Modernisierung.' In: Schroeder, W. (Ed.): *Kassel 4.0. Stadt der Transformationen.* Marburg: Schüren Verlag, 145–163.

Bogumil, J./Grohs, S./Kuhlmann, S./Ohm, A. 2007: *Zehn Jahre Neues Steuerungsmodell. Eine Bilanz kommunaler Verwaltungsmodernisierung.* Berlin: edition sigma.

Braun, K. 2015: 'Between representation and narration. Analysing policy frames.' In: Fischer, F./Torgerson, D./Durnová, A./Orsini, M. (Eds.): *Handbook of Critical Policy Studies.* Cheltenham und Northampton: Edward Elgar, 441–446.

Braun-Thürmann, H. 2005: *Innovation.* Bielefeld: transcript Verlag.

Brieler, U./Rink, D. 2019: 'Das politische feld.' In: von Hehl, U. (Ed.): *Geschichte der Stadt Leipzig, Vol. 4: Vom Ersten Weltkrieg bis zur Gegenwart.* Leipzig: Leipziger Universitätsverlag, 819–842.

Bundesagentur für Arbeit. 2017: *Arbeitsmarkt 2016. Amtliche Nachrichten der Bundesagentur für Arbeit.* Nürnberg. https://statistik.arbeitsagentur.de/Statistikdaten/Detail/201612/ama/heft-arbeitsmarkt/arbeitsmarkt-d-0-201612-pdf.pdf?__blob=publicationFile (last check October 20, 2020).

Bundesinstitut für Bau-, Stadt- und Raumforschung. 2015: *Orte der Integration im Quartier: vernetzt – gebündelt – erfolgreich.* Bonn: BBSR.

Bunge, M. 1997: 'Mechanisms and explanation.' *Philosophy of the Social Sciences* 27 (4): 410–465.

Büttner, L./Rink, D. 2019: 'The heat transition as part of an Urban transformation to a post-fossil city: The case of Leipzig.' *Sustainability* 11 (21). doi:10.3390/su11216065.

Carstensen, M.B. 2011: 'Paradigm man vs the bricoleur. Bricolage as an alternative vision of agency in ideational change.' *European Political Science Review* 3 (1): 147–167.

Carstensen, M.B./Schmidt, V.A. 2016: 'Power through, over and in ideas. Conceptualizing ideational power in discursive institutionalism.' *Journal of European Public Policy* 23 (3): 318–337.

Chen, J./Walker, R.M./Sawhney, M. 2019: 'Public service innovation: a typology.' *Public Management Review* 22 (11): 1674–1695.

City of Athens. 2015: *Strategic Operational Plan of Athens 2015–2019.* Athens (in Greek; https://www.cityofathens.gr/sites/default/files/603-15.pdf; last check: 2021, April 17).

City of Elefsina. 2019: *Transition to Euphoria.* Elefsina, Final Application (in Greek; https://www.2023elevsis.eu/wp-content/uploads/2019/03/ELEUSIS21_BID_BOOK_ 2016_GR_outline-1.pdf; last check April 2, 2021).

City of Thessaloniki. 2017: *Strategic Operational Plan of Thessaloniki 2014–2019*. Thessaloniki (in Greek; https://diavgeia.gov.gr/luminapi/api/decisions/70%CE%91%CE%9D%CE%A9%CE%A15-3%CE%9F%CE%9A/document?inline=true; last check: 2021, April 17).

Cooke, P. 1992: 'Regional innovation systems: Competitive regulation in the New Europe.' *Geoforum* 23 (3): 365–382.

Cooke, P. 2001: 'Regional innovation systems, clusters, and the knowledge economy.' *Industrial and Corporate Change* 10 (4): 945–974.

Czarniawska, B. 2002: *A Tale of Three Cities. Or the Glocalization of City Management*. Oxford: Oxford University Press.

Dandulaki, M. 2018: 'Aspects of resilience in the reconstruction of Kalamata (Greece) after the earthquake disaster of 1986.' In: Othengrafen, F./Serraos, K. (Eds.): *Urban Resilience, Climate Change and Adaptation. Coping with Heat Islands in the Dense Urban Area of Athens, Greece*. Hannover: Leibniz Universität Hannover, Institut für Umweltplanung, 67–84.

D'Antonio, O. 2015: *Zwischen Rathaus, Milieu und Netzwerk. Über die lokale Verankerung politischer Parteien*. Wiesbaden: Springer VS.

Daston, L.J./Galison, P. 1992: 'The image of objectivity.' *Representations* 40: 81–128.

Davies, J.S. 2002: 'Urban regime theory: A normative-empirical critique.' *Journal of Urban Affairs* 24 (1): 1–17.

Davies, J.S. 2003: 'Partnerships versus regimes. Why regime theory cannot explain Urban coalitions in the UK.' *Journal of Urban Affairs* 25 (3): 253–269.

Davies, J.S. 2004: 'Can't hedgehogs be foxes too? Reply to Clarence N. Stone.' *Journal of Urban Affairs* 26 (1): 27–33.

Dente, B./Coletti, P. 2011: 'Measuring governance in Urban innovation.' *Local Government Studies* 37 (1): 43–56.

Doehler-Behzadi, M./Schiffers, B. 2004: 'Eine Dichte-Geschichte.' In: Lütke Daldrup, E./Doehler-Behzadi, M. (Eds.): *Plusminus Leipzig 2030: Stadt in Transformation*. Wuppertal: Müller + Busmann, 32–48.

Dunlop, C.A./Radaelli, C.M. 2020: 'Policy learning.' In: Morlino, L./Berg-Schlosser, D./Badie, B. (Eds.): *Sage Handbook of Political Science: A Global Perspective*. London, Thousand Oaks, New Delhi and Singapore: SAGE, 1121–1133.

Eckardt, F. 2014: *Stadtforschung. Gegenstand und Methoden*. Wiesbaden: Springer VS.

Edler, J./Fagerberg, J. 2017: 'Innovation policy: What, why, and how.' *Oxford Review of Economic Policy* 33 (1): 2–23.

Egner, B./Grabietz, K. 2018: 'In search of determinants for quoted housing rents. Empirical evidence from major German cities.' *Urban Research and Practice*, 11 (4): 460–477.

Elkin, S.L. 1987: *City and Regime in the American Republic*. Chicago: University of Chicago Press.

Elster, J. 1991: *'Arguing and Bargaining in Two Constituent Assemblies.'* The Storrs Lectures, Yale Law School, unpublished manuscript.

Escobar, O./Elstub, S. (Eds.) 2019: *Handbook of Democratic Innovation and Governance*. Cheltenham and Northampton: Edward Elgar.

Falleti, T.G./Lynch, J.F. 2009: 'Context and causal mechanisms in political analysis.' *Comparative Political Studies* 42 (9): 1143–1166.

Fay, B. 1996: *Contemporary Philosophy of Social Science. Reframing Public Policy. Discursive Politics and Deliberative Practices*. Oxford: Oxford University Press.

Featherstone, K. 2005: 'Introduction: "Modernisation" and the structural constraints of Greek politics.' *West European Politics* 28 (2): 223–241.

Fischer, F. 2003: *Reframing Public Policy. Discursive Politics and Deliberative Practices.* Oxford: Oxford University Press.

Fischer, F. 2007: 'Deliberative policy analysis as practical reason.' In: Fischer, F./ Miller, G.J./Sydney, M. (Eds.): *Handbook of Public Policy Analysis. Theory, Politics, and Methods.* Boca Raton, London and New York: CRC Press, 223–236.

Fischer, F./Gottweis, H. 2012: 'Introduction.' In: Fischer, F./Gottweis, H. (Eds.): *The Argumentative Turn Revisited. Public Policy as Communicative Practice.* Durham and London: Duke University Press, 1–27.

Flemming, J. 2016: 'Kassel im Spiegel der Zeit. Geschichtspolitik und historische Zäsuren.' In: Schroeder, W. (Ed.): *Kassel 4.0. Stadt der Transformationen.* Marburg: Schüren Verlag, 31–44.

Florida, R. 2002: *The Rise of the Creative Class.* New York: Basic Books.

Freeman, C. 1987: *Technology Policy and Economic Performance: Lessons from Japan.* London: Pinter.

Geissel, B. 2009: 'How to improve the quality of democracy? Experiences with participatory innovations at the local level in Germany.' *German Politics and Society* 27 (4): 51–71.

George, A.L./Bennett, A. 2005: *Case Studies and Theory Development in the Social Sciences.* Cambridge and London: MIT Press.

Getimis, P./Hlepas, N. 2005: 'The emergence of metropolitan governance in Athens.' In: Heinelt, H./Kübler, D. (Eds.): *Metropolitan Governance. Capacity, Democracy and the Dynamics of Place.* New York: Routledge, 63–80.

Getimis, P./Hlepas, N. 2006: 'Aspects of leadership styles: An interaction of context and personalities.' In: Bäck, H./Heinelt, H./Magnier, A. (Eds.): *The European Mayor: Political Leaders in the Changing Context of Local Democracy.* Wiesbaden: VS-Verlag, 177–199.

Gewandhausorchester 2019: *Das Gewandhausorchester. Von der Kapelle zur Weltmarke.* https://www.gewandhausorchester.de/orchester/geschichte/ (last check May 04, 2021).

Giddens, A. 1984: *The Constitution of Society. Outline of the Theory of Structuration.* Berkeley and Los Angeles: University of California Press.

Gottweis, H. 2006: 'Argumentative policy analysis.' In: Peters, B.G./Pierre, J. (Eds.): *Handbook on Public Policy.* London, Thousand Oaks and New Delhi: Sage, 461–479.

Haas, P.M. 1992: 'Introduction. Epistemic communities and international policy coordination.' *International Organization* 46 (1): 1–37.

Habermas, J. 1996: *Between Facts and Norms. Contributions to a Discourse Theory of Law and Democracy.* Cambridge: Blackwell Publishers.

Hajer, M.A. 1993: 'Discourse coalitions and the institutionalization of practice: The case of acid rain in Britain.' In: Fischer, F./Forester, J. (Eds.): *The Argumentative Turn in Policy-Analysis and Planning.* Durham and London: Duke University Press, 43–76.

Hajer, M.A. 1995: *The Politics of Environmental Discourse. Ecological Modernization and the Policy Process.* Oxford: Oxford University Press.

Hall, P. 1998: *Cities in Civilization: Culture, Innovation, and Urban Order.* London: Weidenfeld & Nicolson.

Hall, P.A. 2013: 'Tracing the process of process tracing.' *European Political Science* 12 (1): 20–30.

Hedström, P./Swedberg, R. 1998: 'Social mechanisms. An introductory essay.' In: Hedström, P./Swedberg, R. (Eds.): *Social Mechanisms. An Analytical Approach to Social Theory.* Cambridge: Cambridge University Press, 1–31.

Hedström, P./Ylikoski, P. 2010: 'Causal mechanisms in the social sciences.' *Annual Review of Sociology* 36: 49–67.

Heinelt, H. 2006: 'Do Policies Determine Politics?' In: Fischer, F./Miller, G.J. (Eds.): *Handbook of Public Policy Analysis: Theory, Politics, and Methods.* New York: CRC Press, 109–119.

Heinelt, H. 2016: *Governance und politisches Entscheiden. Zur intersubjektiven Erschließung der Grundlagen politischer Entscheidungen.* Baden-Baden: Nomos.

Heinelt, H. 2019: *Challenges to Political Decision-making. Dealing with Information Overload, Ignorance and Contested Knowledge.* London and New York: Routledge.

Heinelt, H./Hlepas, N.-K. 2006: 'Typologies of Local Government Systems.' In: Bäck, H./Heinelt, H./Magnier, A. (Eds.): *The European Mayor. Political Leaders in the Changing Context of Local Democracy.* Wiesbaden: VS-Verlag, 21–33.

Heinelt, H./Hlepas, N./Kuhlmann, S./Swianiewicz, P. 2018: 'Local government systems: grasping the institutional environment of mayors.' In: Heinelt, H./Magnier, A./Cabria, M./Reynaert, H. (Eds.): *Political Leaders and Changing Local Democracy: The European Mayor.* Houndmills Basingstoke: Palgrave Macmillan, 19–78.

Heinelt, H./Lamping, W. 2015a: *Wissen und Entscheiden. Lokale Strategien gegen den Klimawandel in Frankfurt a.M., München und Stuttgart.* Frankfurt and New York: Campus.

Heinelt, H./Lamping, W. 2015b: 'The development of local knowledge orders. A conceptional framework to explain differences in climate policy at the local level.' *Urban Research & Practice* 8 (3): 283–302.

Heinelt, H./Razin, E./Zimmermann, K. (Eds.) 2011: *Metropolitan Governance: Different Paths in Contrating Contexts – Germany and Israel.* Frankfurt and New York: Campus.

Heinelt, H./Stolzenberg, P. 2014: 'The "Rhinish Greeks". Bailout funds for local government in German federal states.' *Urban Research & Practice* 7 (2): 228–240.

Heinelt, H./Zimmermann, K. 2012: *Metropolitan Governance in Deutschland. Regieren in Ballungsräumen und neue Formen politischer Steuerung.* Wiesbaden: Springer VS.

Hessisches Ministerium der Justiz, für Integration und Europa. 2012: *Vielfalt ist Hessens Zukunft. Halbzeitbilanz.* Wiesbaden. http://www.efms.uni-bamberg. de/pdf/Bro sch%C3%BCre_Halbzeitbilanz_MRI_endg__WEB.pdf (last check March 18, 2020).

Hessisches Ministerium der Justiz, für Integration und Europa. 2013: *Landesprogramm Modellregion Integration.* Wiesbaden. https://soziales.hessen.de/sites/ default/fi les/media/hsm/handlungsempfehlungen_landesprogramm_modellregionen_web.pdf (last check October 8, 2020).

Hessisches Ministerium für Wirtschaft, Energie, Verkehr und Wohnen. 2012: *Leitbild Nordhessen. Entwicklungsstand & Perspektiven.* Wiesbaden. https://www. regionnordhessen.de/fileadmin/redaktion/regionnordhessen.de/dokumente/ Downloads /Leitbild_Nordhessen_2022Druckkorrigiert.pdf (last check October 20, 2020).

Hlepas, N./Chantzaras, T./Getimis, P. 2018: 'Leadership styles of European mayors: How much have they changed over the past 12 years?' In: Heinelt, H./Magnier, A./Cabria, M./Reynaert, H. (Eds.): *Political Leaders and Changing Local Democracy: The European Mayor*. Houndmills Basingstoke: Palgrave Macmillan, 209–241.

Imbroscio, D.L. 2003: 'Overcoming the neglect of economics in Urban regime theory.' *Journal of Urban Affairs* 25 (3): 271–284.

Imbroscio, D.L. 2004: 'The imperative of economics in Urban political analysis: A reply to Clarence N. Stone.' *Journal of Urban Affairs* 26 (1): 21–26.

Jacobs, K./J. Kemeny, J./Manzi, T. 2004: "Introduction." In: Keith, J./Kemeny, J./Manzi, T. (Eds.): *Social Constructionism in Housing Research*, Aldershot: Ashgate, 1–11.

Jones, M.D./McBeth, M.K./Shanahan E.A. (Eds.) 2014a: *The Science of Stories. Applications of the Narrative Policy Framework in Public Policy Analysis*. New York: Palgrave Macmillan.

Jones, M. D./McBeth, M.K/ Shanahan, E.A. 2014b: 'Introducing the narrative policy framework.' In: Jones, M.D./Shanahan, E.A./McBeth, M.K. (Eds.): *The Science of Stories. Applications of the Narrative Policy Framework in Public Policy Analysis*. New York: Palgrave Macmillan, 1–26.

Jones, M.D./Radaelli, C.M. 2015: 'The narrative policy framework. Child or monster?' *Critical Policy Studies* 9 (3): 339–355.

Kairidis, D./Kiesling, G.B. 2020: *Thessaloniki: A City in Transition – 1912–2012*. New York and London: Routledge.

Katsinas, P. 2019: 'The international face of Thessaloniki: The "Greek crisis", the entrepreneurial mayor, and mainstream media discourses.' *Area* 51 (4): 788–796.

Kern, K./Bulkeley H. 2009: 'Cities, Europeanization and multi-level governance: Governing climate change through transnational municipal networks.' *Journal of Common Market Studies* 47 (2): 309–332.

Klaube, F.-R. 2013: 'Auszug aus der Stadtgeschichte 1800–2000.' In: Flemming, J./Krause-Vilmar, D. (Eds.): *Kassel in der Moderne. Studien und Forschungen zur Stadtgeschichte*. Marburg: Schüren Verlag, 793–811.

Krehl, R./Steets, S./Wenzel, J. 2005: *Leipziger Protestatlas. Text, Bild, Karte*. Leipzig: General Panel für Experimentale e.V.

Kruska, C./Pröbstle, Y. 2017: *Kulturkonzeption Kassel. Auswertung der Experten-interviews*. https://www.kassel.de/buerger/kunst_und_kultur/kuko-dokumente.php. media/25243/koko_kassel_auswertung_experteninterviews_final.pdf (last check October 20, 2020).

Lackowska, M. 2011: 'Frankfurt/Rhine-Main: Governance without coordination?' In: Heinelt H./Razin, E./Zimmermann, K. (Eds.): *Metropolitan Governance. Different Paths in Contrasting Contexts – Germany and Israel*. Frankfurt and New York: Campus, 79–114.

Laclau, E./Mouffe, Ch. 1985: *Hegemony and Socialist Strategy. Towards a Radical Democratic Politics*. London: Verso.

Ladner, A./Keuffer, N./Baldersheim, H./Hlepas, N./Swianiewicz, P./Steyvers, K./Navarro, C. 2019: *Patterns of Local Autonomy in Europe*. Basingstoke: Palgrave Macmillan.

Lefebvre, H. 1968: *Le Droit à la ville*. Paris: Éditions Anthropos.

Lindner, R. 2003: "'Der Habitus der Stadt – ein kulturgeographischer Versuch." Petermanns Geographische Mitteilungen.' *Zeitschrift für Geo- und Umweltwissenschaften* 147: 46–53.

Logan, J.R./Molotch, H.L. 1987: *Urban Fortunes: The Political Economy of Place.* Berkley, Los Angeles, London: University of California Press.

Lowi, T.J. 1972: 'Four Systems of Policy, Politics and Choice.' *Public Administration Review* 32 (4): 298–310.

Luhmann, N. 1992: *Die Wissenschaft der Gesellschaft.* Frankfurt a.M.: Suhrkamp.

Lukes, S. 2005: *Power – A Radical View*, 2nd edition. Houndmills Basingstoke: Palgrave Macmillan.

Lütke Daldrup, E. 2003: 'Die "perforierte Stadt" – neue Räume im Leipziger Osten.' *Informationen zur Raumentwicklung* 1 (2): 55–67.

Lütke Daldrup, E./Doehler-Behzadi, M. (Hrsg.) 2004. *Plusminus Leipzig 2030. Stadt in Transformation.* Wuppertal: Müller + Busmann.

Machamer, P./Darden, L./Craver, C.F. 2000: 'Thinking about Mechanisms.' *Philosophy of Science* 67: 1–15.

Magistrat der Stadt Frankfurt. 2017: *Frankfurter Integrations- und Diversitätsmonitoring.* Frankfurt: Magistrat der Stadt Frankfurt. https://www.vielfalt-bewegt-frankfurt.de/sites/default/files/medien/downloads/amka-monitoring15-final-02.pdf (last check October 8, 2020).

Magistrat der Stadt Offenbach. 2015: *Kreativwirtschaft Report 2015: Bericht zur Entwicklung der Kreativwirtschaft in Offenbach am Main. Analyse des Gewerberegisters der Stadt Offenbach am Main 2007–2013.* Offenbach: Magistrat der Stadt Offenbach. https://www.offenbach.de/medien/bindata/of/Wirtschaft_/Kreativwirtschaft_Offenbach_Report_2015. pdf (last check March 18, 2020).

Magistrat der Stadt Offenbach. 2017: *Sozialbericht 2017.* Offenbach: Magistrat der Stadt Offenbach.

Magistrat der Stadt Offenbach und 'Offenbach offensiv.' 2015: *Masterplan Offenbach am Main: 2030.* Offenbach: Magistrat der Stadt Offenbach. https://www.offenbach.de/medien/bindata/of/dir-19/masterplan_/160303_Broschuere_Masterplan_Offenbach.pdf (last check March 18, 2020).

Magre, J./Vallbé, J.-J./Tomàs M. 2016: 'Moving to Suburbia? Effects of Residential Mobility on Community Engagement.' *Urban Studies* 53 (1): 17–39.

Maier, M.L./Hurrelmann, A./Nullmeier, F./Pritzlaff T./Wiesner, A. 2003: 'Einleitung. Kann Politik lernen?' In: Maier, M.L./Nullmeier, F./Pritzlaff, T./Wiesner, A. (Eds.): *Politik als Lernprozess.* Opladen: Leske & Budrich, 7–22.

Makaris, E.-L. 2017: *Proposal for Sustainable Urban Development of Kalamata.* MA thesis, Corinth: University of Peloponnese (in Greek; https://amitos.library.uop.gr/xmlui/bitstream/handle/123456789/3286/3812017%20%CE%9C%CE%91%CE%9A%CE%91%CE%A1%CE%97%CE%A3%20%CE%95%CE%9C%CE%9C%CE%91%CE%9D%CE%9F%CE%A5%CE%97%CE%9B%20%CE%9B%CE%95%CE%9F%CE%9D%CE%91%CE%A1%CE%94%CE%9F%CE%A3.pdf?sequence=1&isAllowed=y; last check November 17, 2020).

Maloutas, T. 2018: *Athens' Social Geography.* Athens: Alexandria [in Greek].

Manzi, T. 2004: 'Introduction.' In: Keith, J./Manzi, T. (Eds.): *Tony Social Constructionism in Housing Research.* Aldershot: Ashgate, 1–11.

Markusen, A. 1996: 'Sticky places in slippery space: A Typology of Industrial Districts.' *Economic Geography* 72 (3): 293–313.

Mayntz, R. 2002: 'Zur Theoriefähigkeit makro-sozialer Analysen.' In: Maynatz, R. (Ed.): *Akteure – Mechanismen – Modelle. Zur Theoriefähigkeit makro-sozialer Analysen*, Frankfurt a.M.: Campus, 7–43.

Mazower, M. 2004: *Salonica, City of Ghosts: Christians, Muslims and Jews 1430–1950.* New York: Alfred A. Knopf.

McBeth, M.K./Jones, M.D./Shanahan E.A. 2014: 'The narrative policy framework.' In: Weible C./Sabatier P. (Eds.): *Theories of the Policy Process*, 3rd ed., Boulder: Westview Press, 225–338.

Molotch, H.L. 1976: 'The city as a growth machine: Toward a political economy of place.' *The American Journal of Sociology* 82 (2): 309–332.

Moulaert, F./MacCallum, D. 2019: *Advanced Introduction to Social Innovation.* Cheltenham/Northampton: Edward Elgar.

Moulaert, F./Martinelli, F./Swyngedouw, E./González, S. 2005: 'Towards alternative model(s) of local innovation.' *Urban Studies* 42 (11): 1969–1990.

Mulgan, G./Tucker, S./Rushanara, A./Sanders B. 2007: *Social Innovation: What It Is, Why It Matters and How It Can Be Accelerated.* Oxford: Oxford Said Business School.

Münch, S. 2016: *Interpretative Policy-Analyse. Eine Einführung.* Wiesbaden: Springer VS.

Naar, D.E. 2014: 'Fashioning the "Mother of Israel": The Ottoman Jewish historical narrative and the image of Jewish Salonica.' *Jewish History* 28 (3–4): 337–372.

Newton, K./Geissel, B. 2012: *Evaluating Democratic Innovations – Curing the Democratic Malaise?* New York und London: Routledge.

Norck, S. 2014: 'Systemische und räumliche Aspekte im Innovationsgeschehen – Der Ansatz des regionalen Innovationsystems und seine Weiterentwicklung.' In: Hafner, S./Miosga, M. (Eds.): *Regionalentwicklung im Zeichen der Großen Transformation.* München: oekum Verlag, 121–156.

Nullmeier, F. 1993: 'Wissen und Policy-Forschung. Wissenspolitologie und rhetorisch-dialektisches Handlungsmodell.' In: Héritier, A. (Ed.): *Policy-Analyse. Kritik und Neuorientierung.* Opladen: Westdeutscher Verlag, 175–196.

Nullmeier, F. 2012: 'Interpretative Policy-Forschung und das Erklärungsproblem. Oder: Wie kann man diskursiven Wandel erklären?' In: Egner, B./Haus, M./Terizakis, G. (Eds.): *Regieren. Festschrift für Hubert Heinelt.* Wiesbaden: Springer VS, 37–56.

Nullmeier, F. 2013: 'Wissenspolitologie und interpretative Politikanalyse.' In: Kropp, S./Kuhlmann, S. (Eds.): *Wissen und Expertise in Politik und Verwaltung.* Opladen and Toronto: Verlag Barbara Budrich, 21–43.

Nullmeier, F. 2018: 'How to explain discursive change? An actor-centered approach to interpretive explanation.' In: Heinelt, H./Münch, S. (Eds.): *Handbook of European Policies.* Cheltenham and Northampton: Edward Elgar, 72–90.

Nullmeier, F. 2019: 'Interpretative Politikforschung und kausale Mechanismen.' *Zeitschrift für Politikwissenschaft* 29 (2): 153–171.

Ostrom, E. 1999: 'Institutional rational choice: An assessment of the institutional analysis and development framework.' In: Sabatier, P. (Ed.): *Theories of the Policy Process.* Boulder: Westview Press, 35–71.

Ostrom, E./Gardner, R./Walker, J. 1994: *Rules, Games and Common-Pool Resources.* Ann Arbor: University of Michigan Press.

Paul, K.T./Haddad, Ch. 2019: 'Beyond evidence versus truthiness: towards a symmetrical approach to knowledge and ignorance in policy studies.' *Policy Sciences* 52: 299–314.

Petraki, M. 2016: *Armut und soziale Exklusion in der lokalen Politik.* Dissertation, National and Kapodistrian University of Athens [in Greek].

Pierre, J. 2005: 'Comparative urban governance. Uncovering complex causalities.' *Urban Affairs Review* 40 (4): 446–462.

Prigge, W./Lieser, P. 1992: 'Metropole Frankfurt – Keine Metro. Aber Polarisierung: Lokale Politik zwischen Stadt und Land.' In: Heinelt, H./Mayer, M. (Eds.): *Politik in europäischen Städten: Fallstudien zur Bedeutung lokaler Politik.* Basel, Bosten und Berlin: Birkhäuser Verlag, 49–69.

Putra, Z.D./van der Knaap, W. 2018: 'Urban innovation system and the role of an open web based platform: The case of Amsterdam smart city.' *Journal of Regional and City Planning* 29 (3): 234–249.

Rink, D. 1996a: 'Leipzig. Gewinnerin unter den Verlierern?' In: Vester, M./ Hofmann, M./Zierke, I. (Eds.): *Soziale Milieus in Ostdeutschland. Gesellschaftliche Strukturen zwischen Zerfall und Neubildung.* Köln: Bund-Verlag, 51–90.

Rink, D. 1996b: 'Das Leipziger Alternativmilieu. Zwischen alten und neuen Eliten.' In: Vester, M./Hofmann, M./Zierke, I. (Eds.): *Soziale Milieus in Ostdeutschland. Gesellschaftliche Strukturen zwischen Zerfall und Neubildung.* Köln: Bund-Verlag, 193–229.

Rink, D. 2020: 'Leipzig. Wohnungspolitik in einem Wohnungsmarkt mit Extremen.' In: Rink, D./Egner, B. (Eds.): *Lokale Wohnungspolitik. Beispiele aus deutschen Städten.* Baden-Baden: Nomos, 177–195.

Rink, D./Egner, B. (Eds.) 2020: *Lokale Wohnungspolitik. Beispiele aus deutschen Städten.* Baden-Baden: Nomos.

Rink, D./Görbing, M. 2019a: 'Zwischennutzung in unterschiedlichen urbanen Kontexten. Die Beispiele Leipzig und Dessau-Roßlau.' *Raumforschung und Raumordnung* 77 (4): 1–15.

Rink, D./Kabisch, S. 2019: 'Von der Schrumpfung zum Wachstum – Demographische und ökonomisch-soziale Entwicklungen.' In: von Hehl, U. (Ed.): *Geschichte der Stadt Leipzig, Vol. 4: Vom Ersten Weltkrieg bis zur Gegenwart.* Leipzig: Leipziger Universitätsverlag, 842–881.

Rink, D./Siemund, S. 2016: 'Perforation als Leitbild für die schrumpfende Stadt? Erfahrungen aus Leipzig.' *disP. The Planning Review* 52 (3): 50–60.

Saltiel, L. 2020: *The Holocaust in Thessaloniki: Reactions to the Anti-Jewish Persecution, 1942–1943.* London: Routledge.

Saretzki, T. 1996: 'Wie unterscheiden sich Argumentieren und Verhandeln? Definitionsprobleme, funktionale Bezüge und strukturelle Differenzen von zwei verschiedenen Kommunikationsmodi.' In: Prittwitz, V. (Ed.): *Verhandeln und Argumentieren: Dialog, Interessen und Macht in der Umweltpolitik.* Opladen: Leske & Budrich, 19–39.

Saunders, D. 2011: *Arrival City. How the Largest Migration in History is Reshaping Our World.* Toronto: Knopf.

Schäfer, F. 2008: 'Die räumliche Kulisse der Regiopole Kassel. Plädoyer für variable Geometrie.' In: Aring, J./Reuther, J. (Eds.): *Regiopolen. Die kleinen Großstädte in Zeiten der Globalisierung.* Berlin: Jovis-Verlag, 129–140.

Schipper, S./Heeg, S. 2020: 'Wohnungspolitik in Frankfurt. Widerstreitende Positionen und gegensätzliche Entwicklungen.' In: Rink, D./Egner, B. (Eds.): *Lokale Wohnungspolitik. Beispiele aus deutschen Städten.* Baden-Baden: Nomos, 121–137.

Schmidt, V.A. 2008: 'Discursive institutionalism. The explanatory power of ideas and discourse.' *Annual Review of Political Science* 11 (1): 303–326.

Schmidt, V.A. 2010: 'Taking ideas and discourse seriously. Explaining change through discursive institutionalism as the fourth "New Institutionalism".' *European Political Science Review* 2 (1):1–25.

Schroeder, W. 2016: 'Die Neuentdeckung Kassels als Stadt der transformation.' In: Schroeder, W. (Ed.): *Kassel 4.0. Stadt der Transformationen.* Marburg: Schüren Verlag, 13–30.

Schulze-Böing, M. 2018: 'Man muss sich Sisyphos als glücklichen Menschen vorstellen. Ein Konzept für kommunale Integrationspolitik.' Stadtforschung und Statistik. *Zeitschrift des Verbandes Deutscher Städtestatistiker* 31 (2): 51–60.

Schwartz-Shea, P./Yanow, D. 2012: *Interpretive Research Design. Concepts and Processes.* New York and London: Routledge.

Semperoper. 2019: *Die Semperoper Dresden damals und heute.* https://www.semperoper.de/ihr-besuch/geschichte-des-hauses.html (last check November 28, 2019).

Serrano-Velarde, K. 2015: 'Words into deeds. The use of framing strategy in EU higher education policy.' *Critical Policy Studies* 9 (1): 41–57.

Shanahan, E.A./Jones, M.D./McBeth, M.K./Radaelli, C.M. 2017: 'The narrative policy framework.' In: Sabatier, P. (Ed.): *Theories of the Policy Process*, 4th ed., London and New York: Routledge, 175–213.

Smith, G. 2009: *Democratic Innovations: Designing Institutions for Citizen Participation.* Cambridge: Cambridge University Press.

Sorensen, A.B. 1990: 'Chapter 17.' In: Swedberg, R. (Ed.): *Economics and Sociology. Redefining their Boundaries: Conversations with Economists and Sociologist.* Princeton: Princeton University Press, 303–315.

Sorensen, E./Torfing, J. 2011: 'Enhancing collaborative innovation in the public sector.' *Administration & Society* 43 (8): 842–868.

Sotiropoulos, D. 2004: *Formal Weakness and Informal Strength: Civil Society in Contemporary Greece.* London: London School of Economics and Political Science. http://eprints.lse.ac.uk/5683/1/sotiropoulos16.pdf (last check November 2, 2020).

Sotiropoulos, D. 2017: *Greek Civil Society and the Economic Crisis.* Athens: Potamos [in Greek].

Sotiropoulos, D./Bourikos, D. 2014: 'Economic Crisis, Social Solidarity and the Voluntary Sector in Greece Journal of Power.' *Politics & Governance* 2 (2): 33–53.

Staatsministerium für Wirtschaft, Arbeit und Verkehr. 2019: *Europa fördert Sachsen.* Ausgabe Leipzig Stadt. https://publikationen.sachsen.de/bdb/artikel/33741 (last check May 4, 2021).

Stadt Frankfurt. 1991: *Klimaoffensive 1991* (*Council Decision B 6953 from 23 May 1991*). Frankfurt a.M.: Stadt Frankfurt.

Stadt Frankfurt. 1993: *Informationen zur Frankfurter Klimaoffensive – Blockheizkraftwerke für Frankfurt am Main* (*Report B 530 of the Magistrat from 23 August 1993 to the Council*). Frankfurt a.M.: Stadt Frankfurt.

Stadt Frankfurt. 1996: *Klimaoffensive Frankfurt am Main. Energie- und CO2-Bilanz 1987, 1992, 1995 und Energiekonzept für Frankfurt am Main.* Frankfurt a.M.: Stadt Frankfurt.

Stadt Frankfurt. 2008: *Klimaschutz in Frankfurt am Main. Bericht 1990–2008.* Frankfurt a.M.: Stadt Frankfurt.

Stadt Frankfurt. 2009: *20 Jahre AmkA: 1989–2009 Amt für Multikulturelle Angelegenheiten.* Frankfurt a.M.: Stadt Frankfurt. https://amka.de/sites/default/files/2018-05/20%20Jahre%20AmkA_2009.pdf (last check October 7, 2020).

Stadt Frankfurt. 2010: *Jahresbericht des Hochbauamtes 2008–2009.* Frankfurt a.M.: Stadt Frankfurt.

Stadt Frankfurt. 2011: *20 Jahre GrünGürtel: Frankfurt – Menschen, Daten und Projekte. 1991–2011.* Frankfurt a.M.: Stadt Frankfurt.

Stadt Frankfurt. 2017: *Frankfurter Integrations- und Diversitätsmonitoring*. Frankfurt a.M.: Stadt Frankfurt. https://www.vielfalt-bewegt-frankfurt.de/sites/default/files/medien/downloads/amka-monitoring15-final-02.pdf (last check July 15, 2020).

Stadt Frankfurt. 2018: *Stadtporträt. Globales Dorf*. Frankfurt a.m.: Stadt Frankfurt. https://frankfurt.de/sixcms/detail.php?id=3795&_ffmpar[_id_inhalt]=17169 (last check December 31, 2018).

Stadt Kassel. 2019: *Statistische Informationen Jahresbericht 2018*. Kassel: Stadt Kassel. https://www.kassel.de/statistik/berichte/Jahresbericht_2018.pdf (last check September 11, 2020).

Stadt Leipzig. 2015: *Wohnungspolitisches Konzept. Fortschreibung 2015*. Leipzig: Stadt Leipzig.

Stadt Offenbach. 2004: *Viele Kulturen. Alles Offenbacher. Zusammenleben in Offenbach. Integrationskonzept*. Offenbach. https://www.offenbach.de/medien/bindata/of/integration-und-zuwanderung/KonzeptOFweb.pdf (last check September 11, 2020).

Steets, S. 2008: *'Wir sind die Stadt.' Kulturelle Netzwerke und die Konstitution städtischer Räume in Leipzig*. Frankfurt a.M.: Campus.

Stolzenberg, P./Terizakis, G./Hlepas, N./Getimis, P. 2016: *Cities in Times of Crisis. Fiscal Consolidation in Germany and Greece*. Baden-Baden: Nomos.

Stone, C.N. 1989: *Regime Politics: Governing Atlanta: 1946–1988*. Lawrence: University Press of Kansas.

Stone, C.N. 2004a: 'It's more than the economy after all. Continuing the debate about urban regimes.' *Journal of Urban Affairs* 26 (1): 1–19.

Stone, C.N. 2004b: 'Rejoinder: Multiple imperatives, or some thoughts about governance in a loosely coupled but stratified society.' *Journal of Urban Affairs* 26 (1): 35–42.

Stone, D.A. 1989: 'Causal stories and the formation of policy agendas.' *Political Science Quarterly* 104 (2): 281–300.

Stone, D.A. 2012: *Policy paradox: The Art of Political Decision Making*, 3rd ed. New York: Norton & Company.

Sum, N.-L./Jessop, B. 2015: 'Cultural political economy and critical policy studies: Developing a critique of domination.' In: Fischer, F./Torgerson, D./Durnová, A./Orsini, M. (Eds.): *Handbook of Critical Policy Studies*. Cheltenham and Northampton: Edward Elgar, 128–150.

Teperoglou, E./Tsatsanis, E. 2014: 'Dealignment, de-legitimation and the implosion of the two-party system in Greece: The earthquake election of 6 May 2012.' *Journal of Elections, Public Opinion and Parties* 24 (2): 222–242.

Tilly, C. 2001: 'Mechanisms in political processes.' *Annual Review of Political Science* 4: 21–41.

Tolika, M. 2015: *Participatory Institutions, Checks, and Balances in Local Governance*. Thessaloniki: Aristoteles University of Thessaloniki (Unpubl. paper) [in Greek].

Vallbé, J.-J./Magre, J. 2017: 'The road not taken. Effects of residential mobility on local electoral turnout.' *Political Geography* 60: 86–99.

Vamvakas, V. 2019: 'Athens, an alternative city. Graffiti and Radical Tourism.' In: Panayis, P./Sotiropoulos, P.D. (Eds.): *Political and Cultural Aspects of Greek Exoticism*. Basingstoke, Palgrave Macmillan, 153–165.

van der Heijden, J./Kuhlmann, J./Lindquiest, E./Wellstead, A. 2019: 'Have policy process scholars embraced causal mechanisms? A review of five popular frameworks.' *Public Policy and Administration* 36 (2): 163–186.

van Winden, W./Braun, E./Otgaar, A./Witte, J.J. 2014: *Urban Innovation Systems*. London and New York: Routledge.

Vöckler, K. 2017: *Offenbach ist anders. Über die kleine globale Stadt, das Fremdsein und die Kunst*. Berlin: Vice Versa Verlag.

Wagenaar, H. 2011: *Meaning in Action. Interpretation and Dialogue in Policy Analysis*. Armonk und London: M.E. Sharpe.

Wirth, L. 1956: 'Urbanism as a way of life.' In: Marvick, W./Reiss, E./Albert, J. (Eds.): *Community Life and Social Policy. Selected Papers*. Chicago: University of Chicago Press, (first published in: American Journal of Sociology, Vol. XLIV: 1–24), 110–132.

Yanow, D. 1995: 'Practises of policy interpretation.' *Policy Sciences* 28 (2): 111–126.

Zürn, M. 2012: 'Autorität und Legitimität in der postnationalen Konstellation.' In: Geis, A./Nullmeier, F./Daase, C. (Eds.): *Der Aufstieg der Legitimitätspolitik. Rechtfertigung und Kritik politisch-ökonomischer Ordnungen*. Baden-Baden: Nomos, 41–62.

List of interviewees and interview dates

Athens

A1: Municipal councilor and representative of an event location (November 06, 2018),

A2: Senior employee of an innovation hub (November 06, 2018),

A3: Local politician involved in the resilience strategy of the city (November 16, 2018),

A4: Municipal civil servant at the Technical Directory (November 25, 2018),

A5: Civil servant responsible for digitalization (November 26, 2018),

A6: Local politician involved in the organization of child and youth services (November 18, 2018),

A7: Active member of a citizens' group (November 04, 2018),

A8: Local politician responsible in the area of civil society and innovation (April 22, 2019),

A9: Manager of cultural projects (July 01, 2019),

A10: Local politician (September 16, 2019),

A11: Local politician responsible in the area of social policy (September 27, 2019),

A12: Coordinator of a network of civil society (October 02, 2019),

A13: Local politician responsible in the area of immigrants and refugees (October 02, 2019),

A14: Member of an investment and tourism development company (February 26, 2020),

A15: Journalist (March 16, 2020),

A16: Journalist (March 23, 2020),

A17: Member of an institution studying the social geography of Athens (March 23, 2020),

A18: Member of the municipal administration (April 13, 2020),

A19: Member of the municipal administration (April 25, 2020),

A20: Member of a tourism company (April 30, 2020).

Bensheim

B1: Local civil servant (January 11, 2018, August 16, 2018, and August 29, 2019),

B2: Senior municipal employee for cultural affairs (January 11, 2018, and April 10, 2018),

B3: Manager of a global company with a site in Bensheim (June 25, 2018),

B4: Member of an upper-level parliament and former member of the municipal council (August 03, 2018),

B5: Former journalist (August 14, 2018),

B6: Former local politician (August 30, 2018),

B7: Local politician (September 27, 2018),

B8: Active member of a non-profit association (November 20, 2018),

B9: Former local politician (January 15, 2019),

B10: Member of a local association and local politician (January 23, 2019),

B11: Manager of a global company with a site in Bensheim (January 25, 2019),

B12: Local politician (January 31, 2019),

B13: Local politician (January 31, 2019),

B14: Local politician (February 13, 2019),

B15: Senior employees of the MEGB (February 20, 2019),

B16: Senior employees of the local energy supplier (February 28, 2019),

B17: Member of a local association (March 15, 2019),

B18: Member of a local civil society network (March 19, 2019),

B19: Person engaged in citizen participation (January 22, 2021),

B20: Person engaged in citizen participation (January 26, 2021).

Chania

C1: Former member of the Tourism Board and owner of a touristic facility (May 15, 2018),

C2: Former local politician (May 16, 2018, and December 28, 2019),

C3: Local businessman (May 06, 2019),

C4: Journalist (May 06, 2019, and December 05, 2019),

C5: Local politician responsible in the area of Tourism and e-Government (May 07, 2019),

C6: Member of the municipal council (May 07, 2019),

C7: Member of a professional association (May 08, 2019),

C8: Associate professor at the Technical University of Crete (May 08, 2019),

C9: Assistant professor at the Technical University of Crete (June 29, 2019),

C10: Journalist (October 06, 2020),

C11: Local politician (November 16, 2019),

C12: Member of the Regional Council of Crete (June 19, 2020),

C13: Former government official of the Region of Crete (April 07, 2020),

C14: Former local politician (April 08, 2020, and September 12, 2020, temporarily together with C1),

C15: Member of a local association (June 19, 2020),

C16: Member of a local association (October 13, 2020),

C17: Member of a supermarket responsible for sponsorships (September 25, 2020),

C18: Member of a local association (September 26, 2020),

C19: Member of a local association (September 26, 2020),

C20: Member of a local association (October 12, 2020),

C21: Senior employee of a bank (October 19, 2020).

Elefsina

E1: Senior employee of the municipal administration (March 04, 2019),

E2: Senior employee of the municipal administration (March 04, 2019),

E3: Senior employee of the municipal administration (March 04, 2019),

E4: Senior employee of the municipal administration (March 04, 2019),

E5: Senior employee of the municipal administration (March 04, 2019, and June 24, 2019),

E6: Local politician responsible for social services (March 27, 2019, and April 12, 2019),

E7: Senior employee of the municipal administration (May 21, 2019),

E8: Senior employee of the municipal administration (May 21, 2019),

E9: Former local politician (April 15, 2019),

E10: Person engaged in "Eleusis 2021: European Capital of Culture" (April 15, 2019),

E11: Manager of a national company with a site in the city (December 10, 2019),

E12: Journalist (October 29, 2019),

E13: Member of an association against violence to women. (March 24, 2020),

E14: Employee of a medical center (October 13, 2019),

E15: Member of a local association (July 16, 2019),

E16: Member of the popular university (March 08, 2019),

E17: Employee of the local employment service (March 27, 2019),

E18: Participant of "Eleusis 2021": European Capital of Culture (February 03, 2020),

E19: Civil servant (March 26, 2019),

E20: Journalist (January 29, 2020),

E21: Member of a local association (February 27, 2020),

E22: Member of a local association (February 27, 2020),

E23: Member of a local association (February 27, 2020),

E24: Member of a local association (February 27, 2020).

Frankfurt

F1: Professor at Frankfurt University of Applied Sciences (November 22, 2018),

F2: Partner of a planning office (December 04, 2018),

F3: Participant of a project group responsible for the *GrünGürtel* project (February 22, 2019),

F4: Local politician (March 05, 2019),

F5: Member of the municipal executive board/"Magistrat" (March 07, 2019),

F6: Local politician (March 11, 2019),

F7: Local politician (March 11, 2019),

F8: Employee of the municipal administration (April 10, 2019, and March 26, 2020),

F9: Member of the "Magistrat" (January 24, 2012, in the context of a research project on urban problem discourses),

F10: Former member of the "Magistrat" (September 05, 2011, in the context of a research project on urban problem discourses),

F11: Journalist (October 20, 2011, in the context of a research project on urban problem discourses),

F12: Journalist (November 08, 2011, in the context of a research project on urban problem discourses),

F13: Former member of the "Magistrat" (April 12, 2013, in the context of a research project on local climate policy),

F14: Employee of the municipal administration (June 25, 2013, in the context of a research project on local climate policy),

F15: Member of the "Magistrat" (January 11, 2013, in the context of a research project on local climate policy),

F16: Former employee of the municipal administration (December 20, 2012, in the context of a research project on local climate policy),

F17: Former member of the "Magistrat" (July 15, 2013, in the context of a research project on local climate policy),

F18: Former member of the "Magistrat" (June 07, 2013, in the context of a research project on local climate policy),

F19: Former member of the "Magistrat") (April 10, 2013, in the context of a research project on local climate policy),

F20: Member of a local variety theater (December 12, 2019),

F21: Member of a drug help organization (January 07, 2020).

Kalamata

Ka1: Former local politician (May 25, 2019),

Ka2: Member of the municipal council (May 10, 2020),

Ka3: Member of a local association (April 28, 2020),

Ka4: Member of a local network; former member of the Messinian Chamber of Commerce (May 7, 2020),

Ka5: Advisor of a local politician (April 1, 2020),

Ka6: Journalist (April 28, 2020),

Ka7: Municipal councilor (April 29, 2020),

Ka8: Journalist (September 11, 2020),

Ka9: President of a local company (September 15, 2020),

Ka10: Local businessman (December 20, 2020),

Ka11: Municipal councilor (December 21, 2020).

Kassel

K1: Regional representative of the German Trade Unions Federation (Deutscher Gewerkschaftsbund/DGB) (October 19, 2018),

K2: Member of the municipal executive board/"Magistrat" (October 19, 2018),

K3: Professor at the University of Kassel (November 13, 2018),

K4: Employee of a business network (November 13, 2018),

K5: Professor at the University of Kassel (December 03, 2018),

K6: Former member of a public-private partnership company (December 17, 2018),

K7: Member of a local association (18 January 2019),

K8: Employee in a forum for exchange between science and business (January 22, 2019),

K9: Member of the "Magistrat"—together with three employees (March 06, 2019),

K10: Local politician (April 09, 2019),

K11: Local politician (April 09, 2019),

K12: Former local politician in a municipality near Kassel (December 03, 2019),

K13: Former member of an energy network and employee of a local transfer organization (December 03, 2019),

K14: Former local politician (September 11, 2014, in the context of a research project on municipal debt).

Leipzig

L1: Researcher at the University of Leipzig (January 15, 2018),

L2: Member of a research institute located in Leipzig (January 16, 2018, and October 02, 2018),

L3: Researcher at a research institute located in Leipzig (January 17, 2018, September 02, 2019, and March 27, 2020),

L4: Local gallerist (September 19, 2018),

L5: Member of a local private planning office (November 29, 2018),

L6: Member of the municipal administration (November 29, 2018),

L7: Member of the municipal administration (November 30, 2018),

L8: Local politician (November 30, 2018),

L9: Local politician (November 30, 2018),
L10: Local politician (November 30, 2018),
L11: Local politician (January 08, 2019),
L12: Member of a local association (January 18, 2019),
L13: Member of a local planning office (March 13, 2019),
L14: Local politician (March 14, 2019, and August 26, 2019),
L15: Representative of a local network (March 14, 2019).

Offenbach

O1: Employee of the municipal administration (July 13, 2018, and August 20, 2019),
O2: Journalist (August 21, 2018),
O3: Professor at the Hochschule für Gestaltung/HfG Offenbach (August 28, 2018, and August 20, 2019),
O4: Employee of a business network (September 12, 2018, and June 21, 2016, in the context of a research project on municipal debt),
O5: Member of a local association (September 12, 2018),
O6: Representative of a local welfare organization (September 26, 2016, in the context of a research project on municipal debt),
O7: Member of the municipal executive board/"Magistrat" (June 07, 2016, in the context of a research project on municipal debt),
O8: Member of the "Magistrat" (June 10, 2016, in the context of a research project on municipal debt, conducted together with O9),
O9: Local politician (June 10, 2016, in the context of a research project on municipal debt, conducted together with O8).

Thessaloniki

Th1: Advisor to a former local politician (September 12, 2019),
Th2: Professor at the Aristotle University of Thessaloniki (April 09, 2020),
Th3: Local politician, responsible in the area of culture and tourism (April 22, 2020),
Th4: Former local politician (April 24, 2020),
Th5: Businessman engaged in the Culture Company of Northern Greece Businesses (April 27, 2020),
Th6: Former member of the municipal council (April 30, 2020),
Th7: Member of the municipal council and former member of a business network (April 27, 2020),
Th8: Member of a business network (April 28, 2020),
Th9: Local politician, engaged in civil society and municipal reform (April 28, 2020),
Th10: Urban activist (April 27, 2020),
Th11: Private consultant for municipal project (May 05, 2020),
Th12: Journalist (May 12, 2020),

Th13: Journalist (May 14, 2020),

Th14: Former local politician and member of a network for urban resilience (May 15, 2020),

Th15: Member of the city council of Thermes, a municipality near Thessaloniki (May 25, 2020),

Th16: Professor at the Aristotle University of Thessaloniki (May 25, 2020),

Th17: Senior staff member of the municipal administration (May 28, 2020),

Th18: Former municipal councilor (June 11, 2020).

Index

Manufactured by Amazon.ca
Acheson, AB

13131285R00131